Spiro N. Pollalis

Computer-Aided Project Management

A Visual Scheduling and Management System

Spiro N. Pollalis

Computer-Aided Project Management

A Visual Scheduling and Management System

Spiro N. Pollalis, born in 1954, is Associate Professor of Architecture at the Graduate School of Design, Harvard University, Visiting Professor of Architecture at the TU-Delft in 1991–93, and has been associated with the architectural-engineering firm Calatrava Valls SA for several years. He was awarded his PhD from MIT and an MBA in High Technology. His area is architectural and information technology, and his research and teaching focuses on technology, design process and product delivery. Currently, he heads the Committee on strategic planing for computing at the Graduate School of Design, Harvard University. He is the author of the book *A Visual Representation System for the Scheduling and Management of Projects* (1992), the editor of *Architecture: Design Implementation* (1991) and co-inventor of the patented *Task Management* (1991).

Key words: visual scheduling / visual representation / project management / construction management

Verlag Vieweg, P. O. Box 58 29, D-65048 Wiesbaden

Printed and bound by: Lengericher Handelsdruckerei, Lengerich
Printed on acid-free paper
ISBN 978-3-663-19853-6   ISBN 978-3-663-20191-5 (eBook)
DOI 10.1007/978-3-663-20191-5

This work presents a new efficient and effective method for the control and allocation of resources employed in the creation of a product. While most of the examples in the text refer to manufacturing of buildings, the method is general, applicable to the generation of even non-physical products such as research projects.

The superiority of the Pollalis system over traditional analytical Operations Research and Program Scheduling, in offering an easier comprehensive view of the process and in coping flexibly with qualitative data, results from the choice of representation for the specific problem of reasoning about actions. Visual descriptions of the system require less prerequisites to be comprehended and "cost" less effort to be used.

Prof. Alexander Tzonis
TU-Delft

to Tatiana

CONTENTS

PART II
THE VISUAL SCHEDULING AND MANAGEMENT SYSTEM
AND THE STATE-OF-PRACTICE REPRESENTATIONS

PART II
THE VISUAL SCHEDULING AND MANAGEMENT SYSTEM
AND THE STATE-OF-PRACTICE REPRESENTATIONS

LIST OF FIGURES

LIST OF TABLES

ACKNOWLEDGMENTS

The work presented in this book is the product of my research on *Task Management* at Harvard University. During the 1987-88 academic year, Mr. Yasuo Ueda, co-inventor of the patent, project manager of Shimizu Corporation of Japan and graduate student at Harvard University, worked extensively on this system. The following years, Mr. Masaji Kominato and Mr. Hiroshi Mimura worked to advance the system further. Mr. Mimura, in collaboration with Mr. David Shrestinian of Beacon Construction, prepared the data for the last two chapters of this book. Since the origination of this project in 1987, Prof. Daniel L. Schodek, of Harvard University, has been instrumental in the development of the system.

In 1991-92, during my Visiting Professorship at Bouwkunde, Technische Universiteit Delft, I had many interesting and challenging discussions with Prof. S. Menheere and Prof. A. Tzonis, and I prepared the first book on this system, entitled *A Visual Representation System for the Scheduling and Management of Projects*, published by TU-Delft.

Furthermore, over a number of years, I had fruitful discussions on the concepts contained in this book with many colleagues, among them Dr. D. Angelides, Prof. J. Bakos, Mr. F. Basius, Prof. D. Halpin, Dr. H. Irwig, Mr. J. Macomber, and Mr. J. Yagi.

Spiro N. Pollalis
Cambridge, Massachusetts
May 1993

ACKNOWLEDGMENTS

PREFACE

This book proposes a new system for the visual representation of projects that displays the quantities of work, resources and cost. The new system, entitled *Visual Scheduling and Management System (VSMS)*, has a built-in hierarchical system to provide different levels of schedules, and visually superimposes planned and actual data to become a control device. It is also designed to schedule and manage projects with repeating tasks at various locations. The system's visual identity makes it powerful for communication.

The first part of the book, consisting of Chapters 2, 3, 4, 5 and 6, presents the new system. The building block of the Visual Scheduling and Management System is the quantified bar that represents a single task of a project. The quantified bar is defined in Chapter 2 as an object that displays a task with an associated quantity in time. This quantity can be the work of the task, a resource for the task, the cost associated to that resource or the total cost of the task. These alternative displays allow the user to see the task from different points of view. The actual execution of a task is monitored by superimposing two quantified bars: the quantified bar for the original scheduling of the task and its mate quantified bar that depicts the actual data from the field. Based on the actual data, the schedule for the still non-executed part of the task is updated, using the properties of the quantified bar.

The quantified bar chart is introduced in Chapter 3 as the first quantified chart of the Visual Scheduling and Management System. A quantified bar chart displays a group of tasks, where each task is represented by a quantified bar. The permissible types of precedences are defined and the time interdependency of tasks is explicitly defined by their relative position on the chart. The quantified bar chart schedules tasks with well-defined precedences as well as projects composed of tasks with loose time interdependencies. The allowable operations on the quantified bars are described as shift, expansion or compression, addition of continuous tasks and addition of parallel tasks. Finally, the introduction of constraints through specific operations is explained.

The template is introduced in Chapter 4 as the next representation level of the Visual Scheduling and Management System. A template embodies a dual presentation of the information, both in graphic and alphanumeric forms. So, the input and output of information are interchangeable, either through text or through graphics. A template is employed to level the resources visually, using constraints on the summation of the intensities of the group of displayed tasks. Finally, a control template is designed to monitor the actual execution of the tasks by superimposing scheduled and actual data with mate quantified bars.

The matrix-balanced chart, the higher level of representation in the Visual Scheduling and Management System, is introduced in Chapter 5. The matrix-balanced chart includes the additional dimension of location in a project, necessary for the scheduling of repeating tasks. It can also display the effect of the learning curve from location to location. A re-arrangement of the tasks along the vertical axis allows the user to study the scheduling according to the constituency of the tasks rather than their location. Finally, a suppression of the intensity of the quantified bars, transforming them to connoting bars, produces a Gantt chart from this re-arranged matrix-balanced chart.

Chapter 6 concludes the presentation of the new system. The components, presented in the previous chapters, are linked to assemble the Visual Scheduling and Management System for the scheduling and management of entire projects. Folding-up provides the link of the different charts by aggregating visually a group of tasks to a folded-up task. So, microtemplate schedules, template schedules, matrix-balanced schedules and the master schedule are linked together with folded-up tasks to make a rigorous hierarchical structure. Changes are permitted at the different levels of this hierarchical structure. These changes can be introduced both upwards and downwards in the hierarchy. The entire system is used for monitoring the execution of projects by coordinating the display of the filed data on the various charts.

The second part of the book consists of Chapters 7 and 8. Chapter 7 presents the state-of-practice representation techniques for project scheduling and project management: the *Milestone chart*, the simplest and most widely used form of project scheduling; the *Gantt chart*, acknowledged as the most easily understood representation of project scheduling, and the *network diagrams* incorporating the concept of the critical path. The line of balance method is also presented for scheduling repeating tasks at different locations. Finally, the state-of-art computer graphics are briefly evaluated, to observe that no major advancement has occurred in the representation of project scheduling, despite the proliferation of personal computers.

In Chapter 8, the V sual Scheduling and Management System is compared to the state-of-practice representations. First, the comparison focuses on the preparation of the initial schedule and addresses the advantages of the proposed system. At this level the comparison refers to the visual display of the work, the visual display of the resources, the visual display of the repeating tasks, the hierarchical structure, the visual identification of the critical path, and finally the interactive feasibility studies during scheduling. Then, the comparison shifts to the fields of control and management. At this level the comparison focuses on the visual monitoring and forecasting capabilities of each system and their potential as a communication device. While the proposed system provides excellent quantitative displays and has built-in monitoring and forecasting capabilities, the Gantt chart, the network diagrams and the line-of-balance chart have a deficiency to juxtapose graphically the planned and the actual data.

The third part of the book, consisting of Chapters 9 and 10, presents in detail two examples of employing the system to actual construction projects. Chapter 9 presents the planning of the construction of a hotel building with repetitive floor layouts. The construction of the structural frame is discussed first, accompanied by a detailed assignment of the workers on the floor. Then, the hierarchical structure of the Visual Scheduling and Management System is employed, using a microtemplate for the structural floor, the template resulting from folding-up the tasks in the microtemplate, and the matrix-balanced chart constructed from the template. The matrix-balanced chart displays the moving of formwork from floor to floor as well. The new system is also applied to schedule the finishing of the building, presenting the construction of the bathrooms and the guest rooms.

Finally, a control matrix-balanced chart displays a delay in finishing and the corrective actions to bring the schedule back to order.

Chapter 10 presents the renovation of a building interior in an occupied building. The renovation should be scheduled in different phases, allowing the renovation of a single floor to serve as a pilot model for the project. The initial focus of the chapter lies on preparing a detailed construction template from the data contained in the construction drawings, under the constraint of a short deadline imposed by the owner. Then, the focus shifts on handling change and stop orders during the construction process, where control templates provide documentation for the flow of the execution. Finally, the next segment of the renovation is scheduled based on the information on productivity obtained from the pilot floor. The new system was actually applied during the execution of this project and the comments of the construction manager are included at the end of the chapter.

The concepts of the Visual Scheduling and Management System have been patented to Professor Spiro N. Pollalis and Mr. Yasuo Ueda with the U.S. Patent No. 5,016,170 of May 14, 1991. This is the first patent granted to research carried at the Graduate School of Design, Harvard University, as well as the first patent awarded at Harvard University on a computer software related subject.

CHAPTER 1

INTRODUCTION*

1.1   PROJECT MANAGEMENT

Project management is a highly behavioral field. The tasks are planned by people and executed by other people. Usually the tasks require a team effort and scheduling assumes a team harmony during the execution of the project. The tasks are also highly interdependent. They are progressing as long as other tasks are either completed or progressing at a certain rate. Different objectives within a project are common and it is hard to have a congruence of all the parties involved in what they expect from the execution (or not) of a project. In addition, external relations affect the planning and execution of projects, as a result of power dynamics and conflicts of interests.

Thus, the project planner and the project executer need handle human resources with the greatest care and they have to anticipate external interferences during the execution of the project. These aspects often lead to calculated inefficiencies in the planning or the execution of the projects, while managerial decisions may seem contradictory or even wrong.

---

* The concepts of the described system and its features have been patented by the U.S. Patent No. 5,016,170 of May 14, 1991, to Prof. Spiro N. Pollalis and Mr. Yasuo Ueda. The awarded patent is entitled *Task Management*.

So, what is the scope of a new system for the representation of projects? Certainly, it is not going to solve the behavioral problems of project management and it will not make projects start on time, finish on time, cost as planned, with the desirable quality and with the required safety. Such expectations would be unfounded and unreal since deterministic tools do not address and cannot resolve behavioral issues.

However, a new system for the representation of projects provides the planner with the means to plan better under the circumstances using prior data, to communicate better with the parties involved, and to monitor the execution of the project with less effort.

Scheduling and management systems are necessary tools for the scheduling and management of well-executed projects but their use is not sufficient by itself to make well-executed projects. The experience of the project planner and executer with their domain knowledge cannot be substituted. So, this system is handed out as a decision support system to facilitate the scheduling and execution of projects and improve communication.

1.2   SCHEDULING

A *task* is a set of actions toward imposing meaningful order. An individual, an organization or a machine capable of performing a certain task is a *processor* and constitutes a *resource* of the task. A task carried out by a single independent processor is a *pure task*. Since a pure task involves a single processor, it inherits a sequential nature. A task decomposed into several constituent pure tasks, each carried out by a single processor, is a *composite task*.[1] Time dependencies and precedence relationships are central to nontrivial composite tasks. Projects are

---

[1]   Frequently the distinction between pure and composite tasks depends on the employed level of abstraction, since what may appear as a pure task at a certain level of analysis, can often be decomposed into a number of subordinate pure tasks at a finer level of detail.

composite tasks and project scheduling deals with the timing constraints of projects and processors or resources.

Projects from the construction industry have been the pioneers in the field of project scheduling, and most project scheduling computer packages were developed with construction in mind. The size, complexity and uniqueness of most projects in the construction industry provide a challenge to project scheduling. The manufacturing, the aerospace and the shipbuilding industries have also been prime users of project scheduling and the *Critical Path Method* was invented to be applied for the building of the *Polaris* nuclear submarines in the late 1950s.

The proliferation of personal computers and the development of easy to use inexpensive software has augmented the users of project scheduling and changed their profile. There is a shift towards the services industry, where the projects are smaller, scheduled by non-experts and communication among professionals is a central part to the project. The use of scheduling is also expanding in the field of facilities management.

Projects are scheduled with the aid of computers. Computers handle a large number of tasks and their resources, calculate the critical path of a project fast and interact with the user with informative graphics. Any project that requires more than a simple milestone chart should be analyzed and scheduled with the aid of computers. However, the state-of-practice computer applications are bounded to those operations of scheduling that are well-understood and could have been executed manually, if time allowed. Only those operations are well-programmed and give reliable results. Current research focuses on developing the intelligence in the computer applications to supplement the planner's expertise during the process of scheduling. The final goal is to develop closed loop applications that schedule automatically without the intervention of the user.

1.3   DESIGN CONSIDERATIONS

The invention and the development of the Visual Scheduling and Management System originated from the need to use better scheduling and management tools at the construction sites. It is commonly accepted that the existing methods are not sufficient and thus underutilized. A critical review unveils that their weak representations is a central reason for their under-utilization.

The goal was set to create a decision support system to aid the project planner and the project executer to schedule and manage their projects. The system should augment the creativity of the user, rather than substitute the user's experience. So, a language was needed for the experienced user to employ as a tool for modeling the scheduling operations. Such a language, with its own concepts, symbols and rules for the manipulation of those symbols to simulate scheduling, should be visual for a better interaction between the user and the computer and for a better communication among the project participants.

The consistence and completeness of the symbols and the rules, in the domain of the foreseen applications, were the targets during the development process. First, these symbols and rules were designed to describe real situations and the actual conditions at a construction project site. Then, they were enhanced to handle the particularities of projects in other fields. The flexibility of the new visual language to represent both small and large projects with a profound easiness was a must.

Compatibility with existing systems was also desirable. At the request of the user, the scheduling should be able to start from existing systems, be converted to existing systems or employ the way of thinking of other systems, while keeping its identity and originality.

The visual language as a computer implementation was an underlying issue from the very early stages. Tasks were treated as objects with properties, and a computer display was always in mind when a chart was drawn. Procedures like the folding-up are conceived to function with a pointing device. However, the design for the computer implementation is not included in this book. There is a conscious decision to separate the description of the language and the presentation of the new system from its computer implementation.

1.4   ORGANIZATION OF CHAPTERS

The basic concepts, symbols and the associated rules for the manipulation of these symbols that make the Visual Scheduling and Management System are introduced gradually with illustrative examples in the *First Part* of the book, consisting of Chapters 2, 3, 4, 5 and 6.

- Chapter 2 introduces the quantified bar object, its properties and the rules that govern its alternative displays. The concept of the mate quantified bars is also presented for monitoring and updating the scheduling of tasks.

- Chapter 3 introduces the quantified bar chart as an individual schedule for a group of tasks, establishes the rules for the precedence relationships among tasks and introduces the rules that govern the operations on the assembly of the quantified bars.

- Chapter 4 introduces the template and its properties, including the input and output of data, the visual resource leveling and the built-in monitoring and forecasting capabilities.

- Chapter 5 introduces the dimension of the location in a project and proposes the matrix-balance chart, as the appropriate quantified chart for the scheduling of repeating tasks. Transformations of the matrix-balanced chart are also discussed.

- Chapter 6 links the quantified charts to assemble the hierarchical system for the scheduling and management of entire projects. Folding-up is presented as the link among the different quantified charts. The use of the system to monitor the execution of a project is also discussed.

The *Second Part* of the book, consisting of Chapters 7 and 8, relates the new system to the existing systems.

- Chapter 7 reviews briefly the state-of-practice representation methods and the state-of-art computer graphics for project scheduling and project management.

- Chapter 8 compares the existing representations with the proposed system. This comparison focuses first on the scheduling of projects and then it continues on the management of projects, during their execution.

The *Third Part* of the book, consisting of Chapters 9 and 10, presents two detailed examples of applying the new system in the construction of buildings.

- Chapter 9 demonstrates the use of the Visual Scheduling and Management System in the construction of a hotel building with a repetitive layout.

- Chapter 10 presents the application of the system in the renovation of a pilot floor in an occupied building, and uses the data that were collected during construction to plan the renovation of the remaining floors.

PART I

The Visual Scheduling and Management System

CHAPTER 2

QUANTIFIED BARS

The building block of the Visual Scheduling and Management System is the quantified bar that represents a single task of a project.

This Chapter introduces the quantified bar and discusses in length its properties and its proposed uses. In Section 2.1, the quantified bar is defined in a more abstract form as an indicator of quantity. The next Section 2.2 explains the alternative displays of the quantified bar that represent work, resources and cost. These displays are interchangeable transformations and allow the user to see the task from different points of view. Section 2.3 presents the monitoring of the execution of a task by quantified bars. Monitoring is achieved by superimposing two quantified bars: the quantified bar for the original scheduling of the task and the quantified bar that depicts the actual data from the field. Section 2.4 presents the updating of the schedule for the non-executed part of the task. Updating is achieved by extrapolating graphically the information from the field, using the properties of the quantified bar. Finally, Section 2.5 presents the independent variables that define the various transformations of a quantified bar that represents a single task. Examples throughout this chapter demonstrate the visual presentation of the quantified bar, its properties and its uses.

2.1 THE QUANTIFIED BAR

Each task of a project is represented by a *quantified bar*, an object displayed in two dimensions. The length of the object along the horizontal axis indicates the *duration* of the task and the height or width of the object along the vertical axis indicates *intensity*. The geometric area of the object indicates *quantity*, as the product of intensity and time (Fig. 2.1).

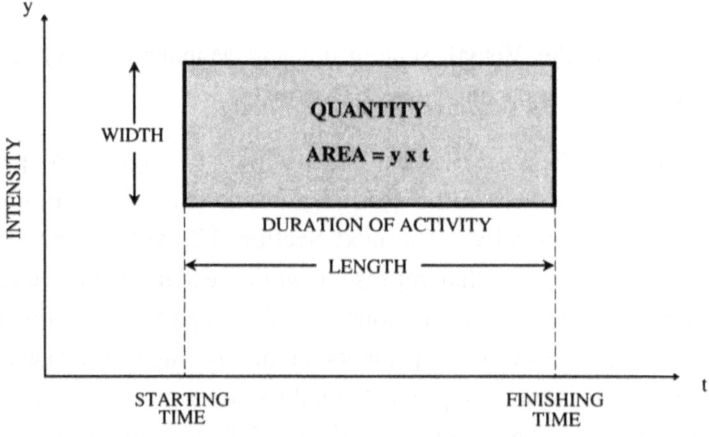

Fig. 2.1. The quantified bar, displayed in two dimensions.

If the quantity is constant, then there is a specific relation between the intensity and the duration of a task. Thus, as shown in Fig. 2.2, the same task could be planned in several intensities and durations, three of which are shown among the much larger selection. So, the areas of objects S1, S2 and S3 that represent alternative planning for the same task are equal, as they depict the same quantity of the task.

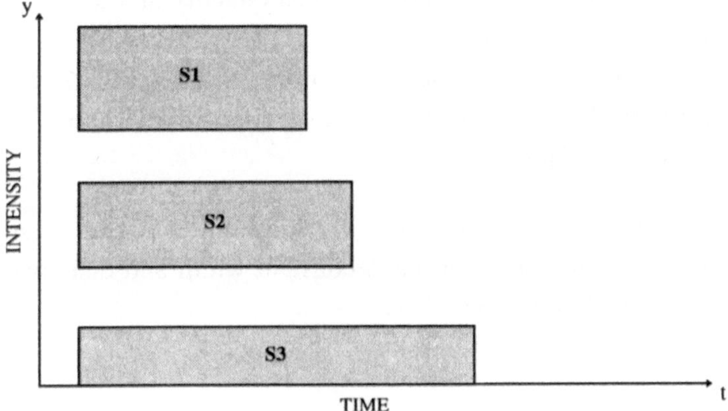

Fig. 2.2. Alternative scheduling of a task with quantified bars.

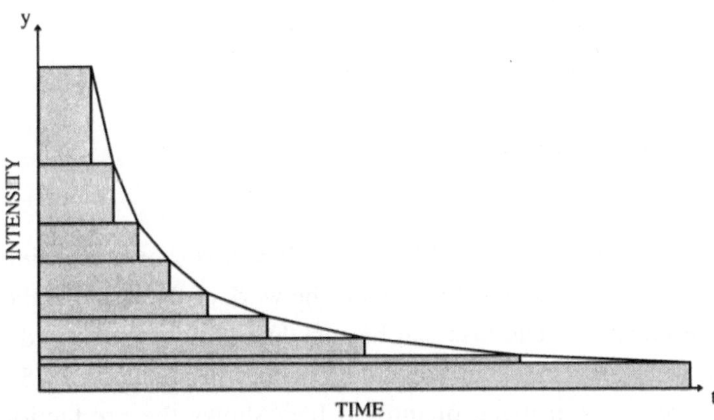

Fig. 2.3. Relationship between duration and intensity.

Sometimes, the quantity of a task depends on its duration. Both a very short duration and a very long duration may be inefficient and could lead to an increased quantity for the same task. Thus, the quantified bars that correspond to alternative planning scenaria of the same task may not have the same area. In such a case, the minimum duration and the maximum duration that maintain the same quantity must be specified. Information on the relation between quantity and duration must be provided for any duration beyond these limits. This relationship is either in a closed form expression or is described with discreet data. Fig. 2.3 shows the hyperbolic relationship between intensity and duration that assumes a constant quantity, regardless of the duration.

If the intensity is suppressed from the display of a quantified bar, the resulting bar is a *connoting bar*. A connoting bar has a constant width and displays only the identity of a task and its duration (Fig. 2.4).

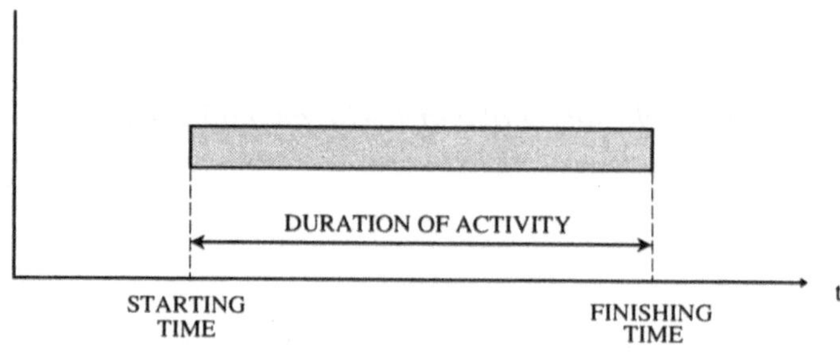

Fig. 2.4. The connoting bar.

Example: The building of a 300 ft^2 (28 m^2) brick wall is shown as a single task in Fig. 2.5. In this example, the quantity depicts the work of the task and the intensity depicts daily production. The task can be scheduled either to last 6 days with a production of 50 ft^2 (4.6 m^2) daily or 4 days with a production of 75 ft^2 (7 m^2) daily. The representation using quantified bars shows the production of each alternative planning together with its estimated duration. Both quantified bars have the same area since they represent the same quantity of work: 300 ft^2 (28 m^2).

If the intensity is constant throughout the duration of a specific task, as it has been in the examples that have been presented, then the corresponding shape of the quantified bar is rectangular. Often the intensity during the task varies and the corresponding quantified bar has a polygonal shape composed of a series of rectangles, with each rectangle corresponding to each intensity. So, the brick laying task that was represented in Fig. 2.5 could be scheduled with a variable intensity, as shown in Fig. 2.6. According to that schedule the production the first day is 25 ft², the second day and third days is 50 ft² (4.6 m²), the fourth day is 75 ft² (7 m²) and 33 ft² (3 m²) each following day until the completion of the task. According to this planning, the task will last 7 days.

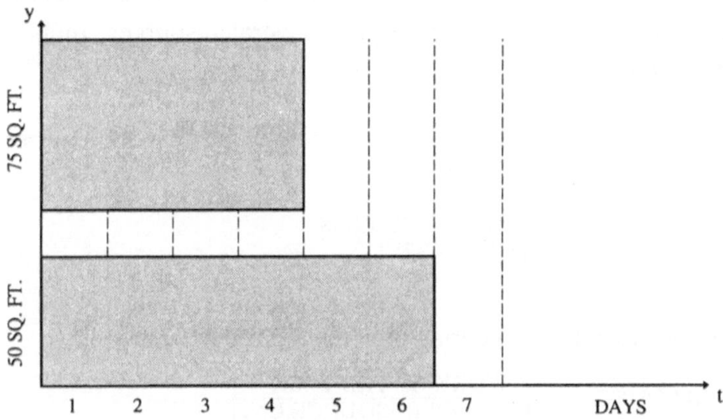

Fig. 2.5. Planning the brick laying task, either for 4 or for 6 days.

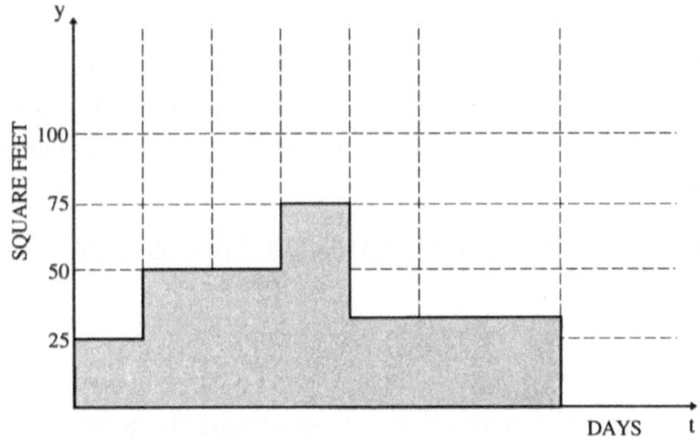

Fig. 2.6. Scheduling a task with a variable intensity.

2.2 ALTERNATIVE DISPLAYS

The area of a quantified bar depicts quantity. That quantity can be the *work of the task*, each of the *required resources* for executing the task, or the associated *cost* of each of those resources. A task can require several resources, including labor, materials and equipment.

If a resource produces work (such as labor or equipment) then the required resource is calculated as:

$$\text{REQUIRED RESOURCE} = \frac{\text{WORK OF THE TASK}}{\text{PRODUCTIVITY}} \tag{2.1}$$

If a resource is an expandable material, then the required resource is:

$$\text{REQUIRED RESOURCE} = \frac{\text{WORK OF THE TASK}}{\text{WORK PER RESOURCE UNIT}} \tag{2.2}$$

The cost of a resource is derived from the expression:

$$\text{COST OF A RESOURCE} = \text{REQUIRED RESOURCE} \times \text{UNIT COST OF RESOURCE} \tag{2.3}$$

Often, when a task is represented at a higher level of abstraction (less information), the total cost of a task is quite useful to be presented by a quantified bar. In such a case the total cost of the task is the summation of the costs of the various resources dedicated for the task.

$$\text{TOTAL COST OF THE TASK} = \text{SUMMATION OF THE COSTS OF ALL RESOURCES} \tag{2.4}$$

However, there are cases that the total cost may be entered approximately without a specific breakdown into the costs of the resources and the total cost of the task is derived from:

$$\text{TOTAL COST OF THE TASK} = \text{WORK OF THE TASK} \times \text{UNIT COST OF THE WORK} \tag{2.5}$$

The alternative displays of quantity indicate:
- the work of the task,
- each resource,
- the cost of each resource, or
- the total cost of the task.

These alternative displays provide multiple interchangeable views of the same task during the planning or execution of the project, depending on the needs of the user. The linear relationships of the alternative displays of a task are shown in Fig. 2.7.

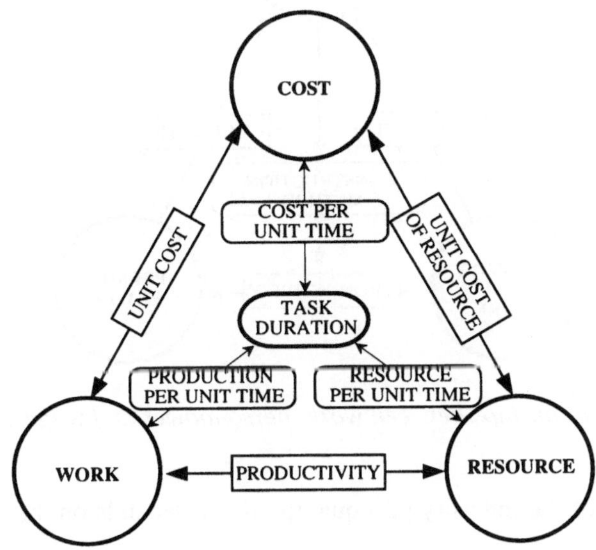

Fig. 2.7. Relationships between work, a resource and the corresponding cost, as related to the duration of the task.

Labor is the most common resource to be associated with a task, and it is the most challenging resource to plan and control. Fig. 2.8 shows the linear relationships of the alternative displays of a task, when labor is the resource on focus.

The resources and the cost are almost always measurable in units of persons, materials, equipment, machinery and money. In most cases, the quantity of work is also measurable in units of volume, surface, numbers of products, lines of code, *etc*. However, a quantity of work can be measured in the units of a dominant resource, if that measure is more meaningful. In the services industry, the quantity of work is usually measured by the person-time dedicated to execute the task. This is part of the features of the proposed visual system and it does not introduce any undue complexities, as it will be explained in Chapter 6.

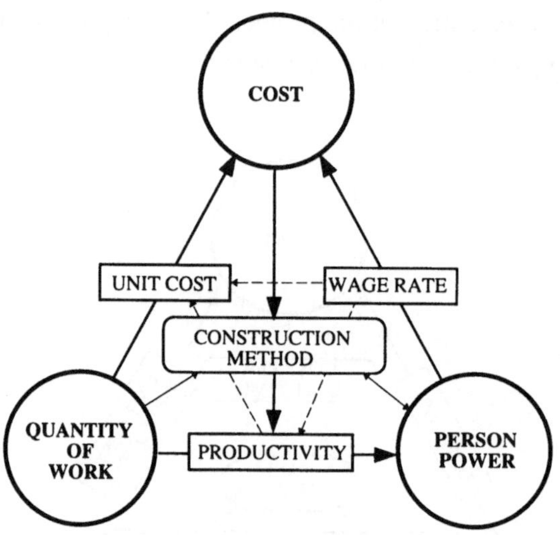

Fig. 2.8. Relationships between work, personpower and wages.

The significance of the intensity of a quantified bar depends on the significance of the quantity:

QUANTITY	INTENSITY
• work	• production or work per time unit
• resource	• required resource per time unit
• cost of a resource	• cost of a resource per time unit
• total cost	• cost per time unit.

Example: The scheduling of a single task and the alternative representations of the quantified bar are shown in Fig. 2.9. The task of placing tiles on a 2,800 ft^2 area (260 m^2) is planned based on an estimated productivity of 50 ft^2 (4.6 m^2) per person-day. Thus, $2800 \div 50 = 56$ person-days is the initial estimate for the labor requirements. The available crew of 4 workers would need $56 \div 4 = 14$ days to complete the task, finishing a 200 ft^2 (18.6 m^2) area per day. The second display of the quantified bar in Fig. 2.9 shows the quantity of persons-time. The third display shows $1,000 labor cost per day, based on a $250 daily compensation for each worker. Finally, the daily use of tiles is equal to the area that is covered and the cost of the tiles is $12.5 per ft^2 ($135 per m^2) or $2,500 per day, as shown on the last display in Fig. 2.9. The total cost of the task is $49,000, including materials and labor.

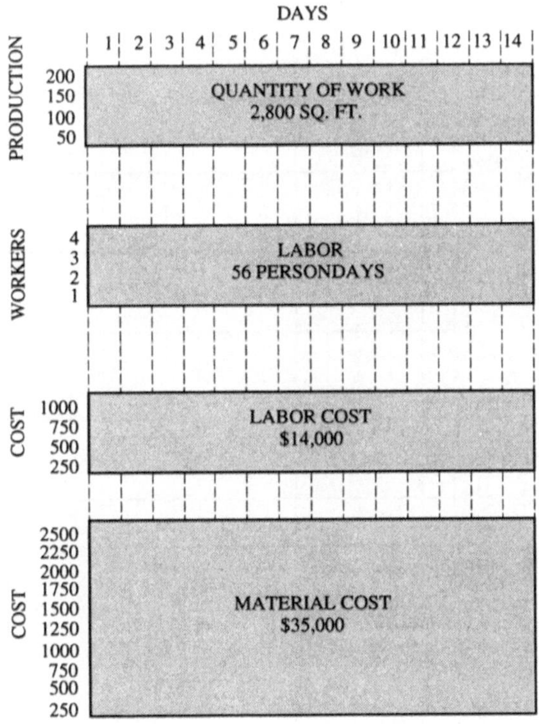

Fig. 2.9. Planning a task, shown in alternative displays of the quantified bar with quantities work, person-time, wages and cost of materials.

2.3 MONITORING A TASK

A superposition of two quantified bars for the same task, the first corresponding to the planning of the task and the second corresponding to the actual execution of the task, provides a visual comparison between the two. The quantified bar that corresponds to the actual execution of the task is the *mate quantified bar* of the bar that corresponds to the planning of the task.

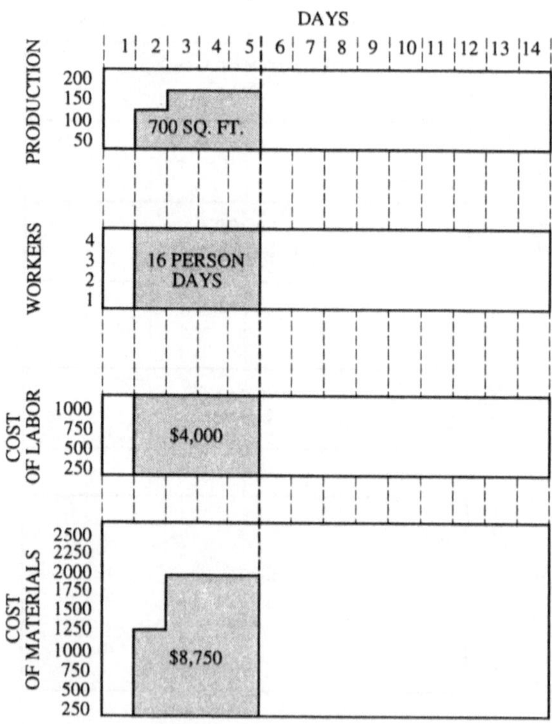

Fig. 2.10. *Monitoring the task of Fig. 2.9 at the completion of the 5th day with quantities work, person-time, wages and cost of materials.*

In an ideal case, the two quantified bars should be identical: the task should be executed as it was planned. However, if the execution of the task is different than the way it was planned, the two quantified bars will have a different shape. By superimposing the two quantified bars with different colors or hatching, the information is visually presented. Monitoring will confirm that the assumptions of the original planning were accurate, or it will detect the wrong assumptions early in the process.

Example: The example that was presented to introduce the concept of the quantified bar chart, will be further used to demonstrate the monitoring of the execution of that task. A superposition of the planning and the execution of the work, as it has occurred until the 5th day, is shown in Fig. 2.10. The quantified bar at the top of the figure shows that the work started on the second scheduled day. The quantified bar that displays production shows that the first working day 100 ft^2 (9.3 m^2) were completed, instead of 200 ft^2 (18.6 m^2). The following days 150 ft^2 (14 m^2) were completed. Thus the actual productivity is $150 \div 4 = 37.5$ ft^2 (3.5 m^2) per person-day instead of the planned productivity of 50 ft^2 (4.6 m^2) per person-day. By superposition, the differences between the planned versus the actual events are represented graphically. As a result of the reduced production, the quantified bars that show use of materials and cost paid for labor and materials are not as initially planned. The superposition of the planned versus the actual displays of the quantified bar are shown in the same figure.

2.4 UPDATING A TASK

If the project executer monitors the execution of the tasks and detects that the original assumptions were not accurate, he/she should correct them in order to avoid scheduling problems in the future execution of the project. In such a case, the part of the task that has been executed (*i.e.*, prior to the time of updating) is represented by the two objects as described in the monitoring section above. An *extrapolation of the intensity* of the mate quantified bar will serve to correct the planning for the remainder of the task, to the right of the vertical line that defines the time of monitoring and the time of the corrective action.

If the quantity of the work had been estimated correctly, the emphasis should be based on the daily productivity of the available resources. Updating the productivity will determine the required modification of the resources and the duration of the task and thus, the ending date. If a deadline exists, a modification of the work crew could allow the planner to meet that deadline.

Example: Following the example of monitoring, this example demonstrates how to update a schedule using quantified bars to represent different alternative scenaria. Based on the remaining work to be completed ($2,100$ ft^2, 195 m^2) and the remaining time (8 days) it is calculated that 233 ft^2 (21.5 m^2) need be completed each following day. This is represented by the quantified bar in Fig. 2.11, superimposed to the original quantified bar. Based on the actual productivity of 37.5 ft^2 (3.5 m^2) per person-day, the remaining work requires $2,100 \div 37.5 = 56$ persondays. So, a crew of 6 workers will complete the remaining part of the task in 8.5 days while a crew of 7 workers will need 7.5 days, which will be ahead of time. The representations of the updated planning of the work force, of the use of materials and of the cost are superimposed to the original planning for the same quantities and they are shown in Fig. 2.11. The wrong estimate of the worker's productivity resulted to an additional labor cost of $4,000, which is also depicted with the quantified bars.

The monitoring of execution and the updating of schedules can be accomplished as often as there are data available and it is meaningful for the project executer to update the project.

The above updating of the task was based on the assumption that the total quantity of work of the task had been correctly estimated at the beginning. Variations of the quantity of work are often in projects and they can be treated in a similar manner. However, the best way to deal with changes of quantity of work during the execution of a task is to add a new task that is parallel to the remaining of the task, if a certain deadline must be kept. If the deadline is flexible, then the change of the quantity of the work can be represented as a continuous task to the task being executed. In such a case, the size of the crew stays the same. Parallel tasks and continuous tasks are defined in Section 3.2.

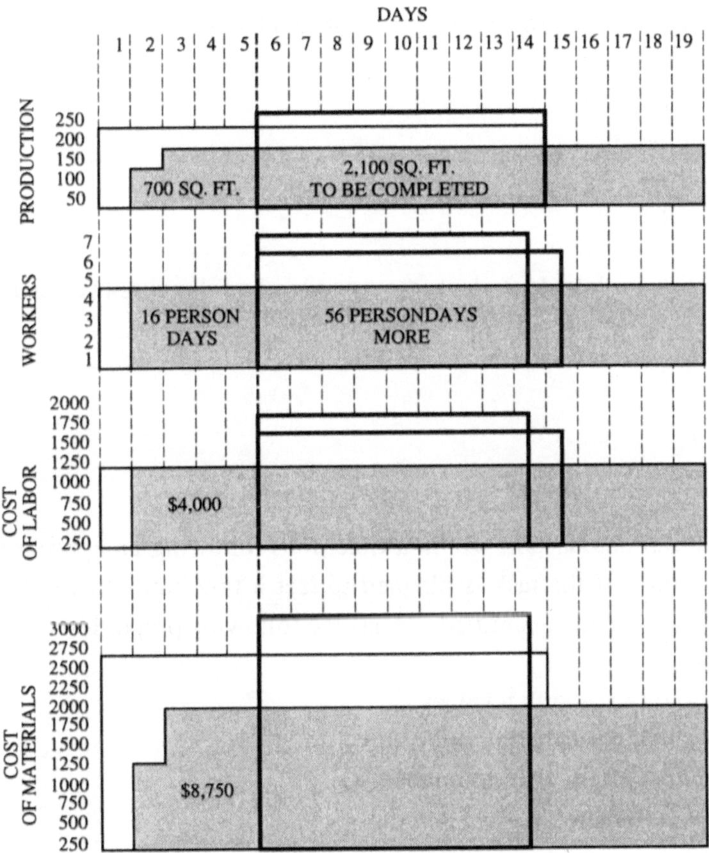

Fig. 2.11. Updating the planning of the task of Fig. 2.9 with areas representing work, personpower, wages and materials.

2.5 VARIABLES OF THE QUANTIFIED BAR

As described before, the properties of a quantified bar are:
- quantity, Q
- intensity, $I(t)$
- starting time, T_s
- ending time, T_e
- duration, T.

These properties are interdependent, governed by the following two relationships:

$$T = T_e - T_s \tag{2.6}$$

$$Q = \int_{T_s}^{T_e} I(t)\, dt \tag{2.7}$$

The intensity can be constant within a time unit, following an appropriate choice for that time unit. If the task is planned to last n time units t (*i.e.*, hours, days, weeks, months), then the quantified bar has the following properties:
- quantity, Q
- intensity, I_i (array with n values)
- starting time, k (integer, in time units)
- ending time, m (integer, in time units)
- duration, n (integer, in time units)
- time unit, t.

These properties are governed by the following relationships:

$$n = m - k \tag{2.8}$$

$$Q = \sum_{i=k}^{k+n} I_i \times t \tag{2.9}$$

A task must be extended a fraction of a time unit, when it cannot be interrupted. An example of such a task is the placing of concrete on a slab. The additional fraction of the time unit is added at the end of the quantified bar and it is treated separately, as follows:

- intensity, I_f (at the fraction of the time)
- additional fraction of the time f (in time units)

So, the properties of the corresponding quantified bar are governed by the following relationships:

$$n + f = (m + f) - k \tag{2.10}$$

$$Q = \sum_{i=k}^{k+n} I_i \times t + I_f \times t \times f \tag{2.11}$$

Since there are two governing equations, only two variables can be dependent. The additional fraction of the time introduces one more variable so, there are 3+n independent variables and 2 dependent variables to describe a single quantified bar for a single quantity, that represents a task that lasts n+1 time units.

time units

1 2 3 ...   n n+1

$$
\begin{array}{ll}
\text{intensity of quantity} & 1 \\
 & 1 \\
\text{intensity of resources} & 2 \\
 & \cdots \\
 & j \\
 & 1 \\
\text{cost of resources} & 2 \\
 & \cdots \\
 & j \\
\end{array}
\left[
\begin{array}{ccc}
x\ x\ x\ \dots & & x \\
x\ x\ x\ \dots & & x \\
x\ x\ x\ \dots & & x \\
 & & \\
x\ x\ x\ \dots & & x \\
x\ x\ x\ \dots & & x \\
x\ x\ x\ \dots & & x \\
 & & \\
x\ x\ x\ \dots & & x \\
\end{array}
\right]
\tag{2.12}
$$

However, as it was presented in Section 2.2, a quantified bar is transformed to display resources and the corresponding costs. In general, each transformation will introduce n+1 additional independent variables. So, a task with properties its size, j resources, and j costs will have $2 + (2 \times j + 1) \times (n + 1)$ independent variables. An array of 2 values (starting time, ending time) and a matrix of $2 \times j + 1$ rows and $n + 1$ columns contain these variables (equation 2.12). Each column of the matrix refers to a time unit and the corresponding row contains the intensities of that time unit.

In most cases the size of the matrix can be greatly reduced if the intensity of a resource, or the unit cost for a resource, are constant throughout the duration of the task. In such a case, the transformed quantified bar is the product of the original quantified bar multiplied by conversion factors, as shown in Fig. 2.9. Thus, there is only 1 more independent variable for each additional resource and 1 more independent variable for each additional cost of resource. So, a task with properties its size, j resources, and j costs for these resources will have $2 + (n + 1) + 2 \times j$ independent variables. An array of 2 values contains the starting time and the ending time, and array of $n + 1$ values contain the work for each time unit and an array of $2 \times j$ contains the conversion factors.

CHAPTER 3

QUANTIFIED BAR CHARTS

Following the definition of the quantified bar, the quantified bar chart is introduced as the first chart of the Visual Scheduling and Management System. A quantified bar chart represents a segment of a project that is composed of a group of tasks.

The definition of the quantified bar chart is presented in Section 3.1. Section 3.2 discusses the time, resource and location interdependencies of tasks, leading to the specification of the different types of precedences among tasks. In Section 3.3, the position of the quantified bars on the chart and the indication of precedences of the tasks on the quantified bar chart are presented. The rules on how to construct a quantified bar chart and how to modify it follow in Section 3.4. Two examples of quantified bar charts are presented in depth. The first refers to a project with well-defined precedences of tasks. The second includes tasks with loose precedences. Section 3.5 discusses the difference between temporary operations and operations that introduce constraints for future modifications. Finally, Section 3.6 describes the employment of the quantified bar chart to schedule tasks depending on the capacity of the available facilities.

3.1　THE QUANTIFIED BAR CHART

Tasks related by job code, at a specific level of a project, are grouped together in order to define their time dependencies and facilitate the allocation of resources. Those tasks are represented by quantified bars displayed in a *quantified bar chart*. The position of the quantified bars on the chart represents their time dependencies, while their shapes represent quantity, intensity and duration (Fig. 3.1). The quantified bar chart is designed to display the interchangeable intensities of its quantified bars in order to provide multiple points of view of the project.

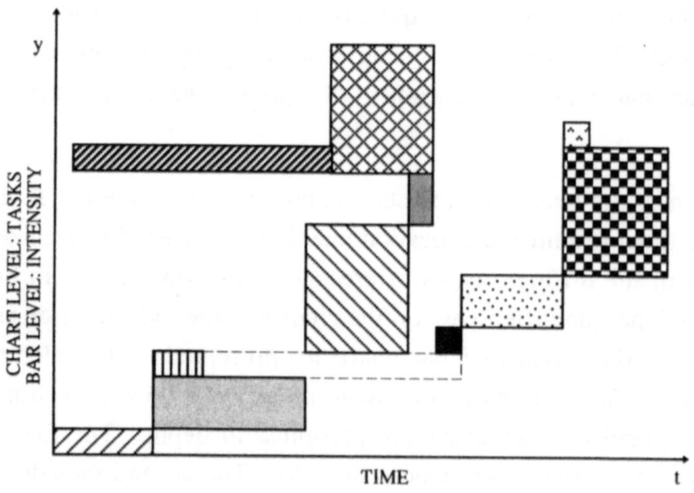

Fig. 3.1. The quantified bar chart.

The position of the quantified bars along the horizontal axis shows the time dependencies of the tasks.

The quantified bars are placed along the vertical axis of a quantified bar chart according to the following rules, in order to make the chart easier to read:

* The quantified bars representing tasks of similar constituency, or having the same resource are located on the same level.

- The quantified bars are placed so that they show progression in the execution of the tasks.

Most often, earlier tasks are placed lower and later tasks are place at the same level or higher on the vertical axis. So, combined with the time axis, tasks that are executed earlier are located at the lower left corner of the chart and subsequent tasks are placed towards the upper right corner of the chart. However, the user can override this convention as long as a systematic presentation is adapted.

The suppression of the quantity from the quantified bars in a quantified bar chart produces a *connoting bar chart*, (Fig. 3.2). A connoting bar chart inherits all the properties of the quantified bar chart, including the visual identification of the tasks and the rules for positioning the bars along the vertical axis and it can be converted to a quantified bar chart at any time.[1]

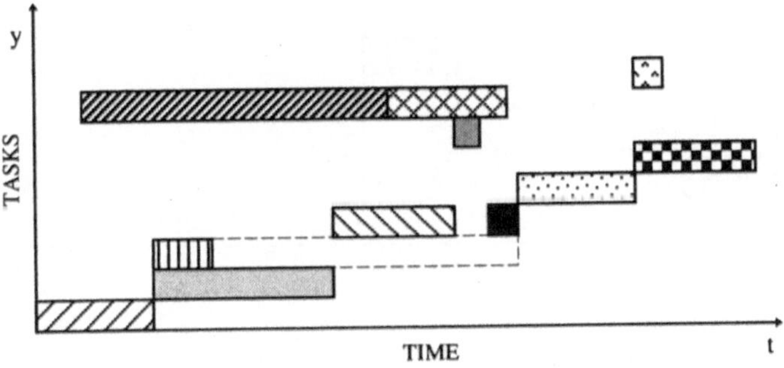

Fig. 3.2. The connoting bar chart.

---

[1]   In its simplest form, the connoting bar chart is like a Gantt chart, which is presented in Chapter 7, as part of the state-of-practice visual presentation methods.

3.2 INDEPENDENT AND DEPENDENT TASKS

The tasks on a quantified bar chart can be either independent or dependent. Two tasks are *independent tasks* when the execution of the first task does not have any relationship to the execution of the second task (Fig. 3.3). Two tasks are *dependent tasks* when the execution of the one task depends on the execution of the other task. The precedences among tasks result from time dependencies, sharing of common resources, or execution in the same location. The precedences among the tasks are treated as constraints among the corresponding quantified bars, a process that is presented in Section 3.5. Precedences are described in the form of parallel tasks, continuous tasks, overlapping tasks and forced overlapping tasks, common start tasks, and common finish tasks.

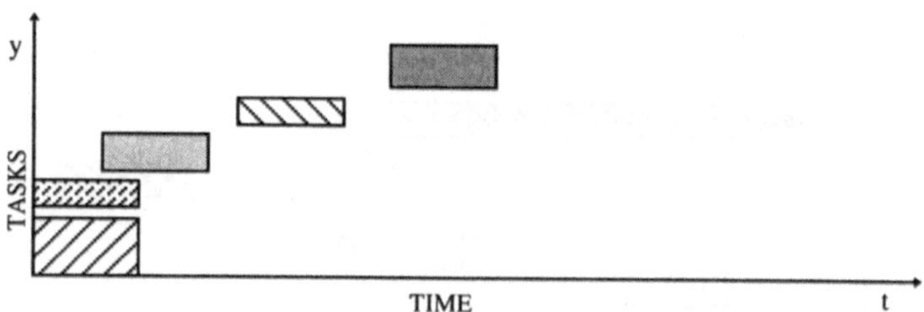

Fig. 3.3. Independent tasks.

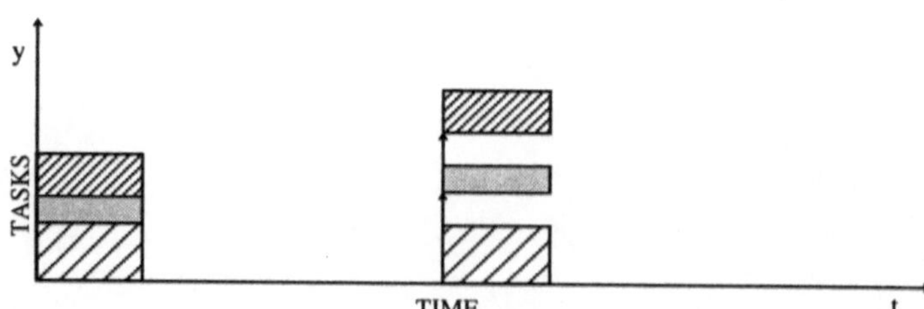

Fig. 3.4. Parallel tasks.

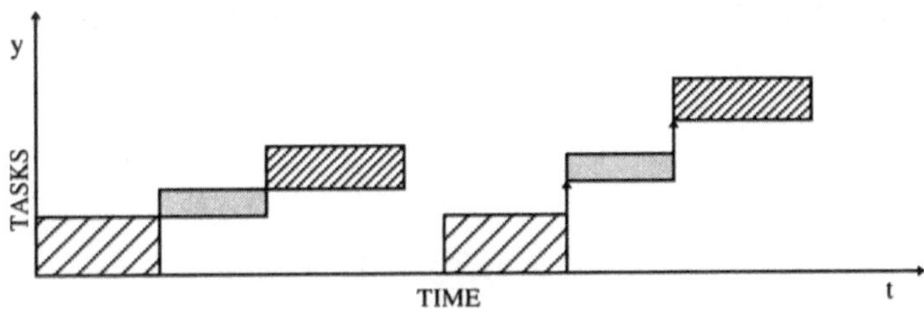

Fig. 3.5. Continuous or serial tasks.

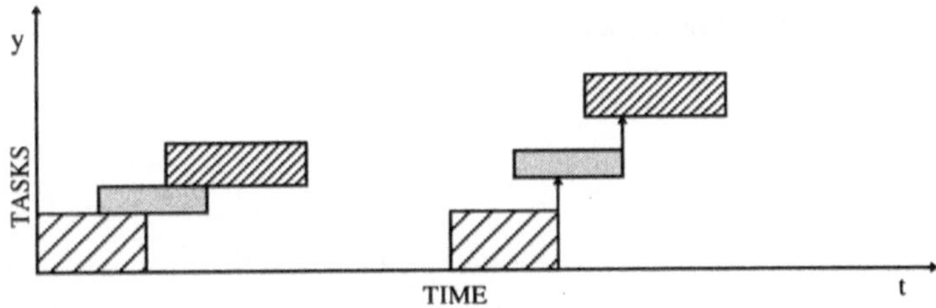

Fig. 3.6. Overlapping or forced overlapping tasks.

Two tasks are *parallel tasks*, when the two tasks must start and finish simultaneously (Fig. 3.4). Two tasks are *continuous or serial tasks* when the one task must be completed before the other starts (Fig. 3.5). Two tasks are *overlapping tasks*, when the one task cannot start before the other task has been partially completed (Fig. 3.6). Overlapping tasks can also be *forced overlapping tasks* when the second task must start at a certain percentage of completion of the first task.[2] The required level of completion of the task that precedes another task is either established in a breakdown to subtasks[3] or approximately, based on prior data and experience. Two tasks are *common start tasks* when they must start

---

2   The second task of two forced overlapping tasks can be separated into two parts. The first part is a parallel task to a portion of the first task and the second part is a continuous task to its first part.

3   This is performed with the use of microtemplates and folding-up, defined in Chapter 6 as part of the hierarchical structure of the Visual Scheduling and Management System.

simultaneously[4] (Fig. 3.7). Two tasks are *common finish tasks* when they must finish together (Fig. 3.8).

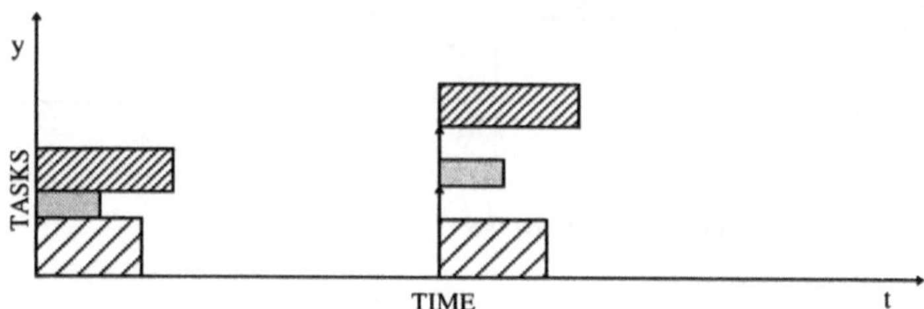

Fig. 3.7. Common start tasks.

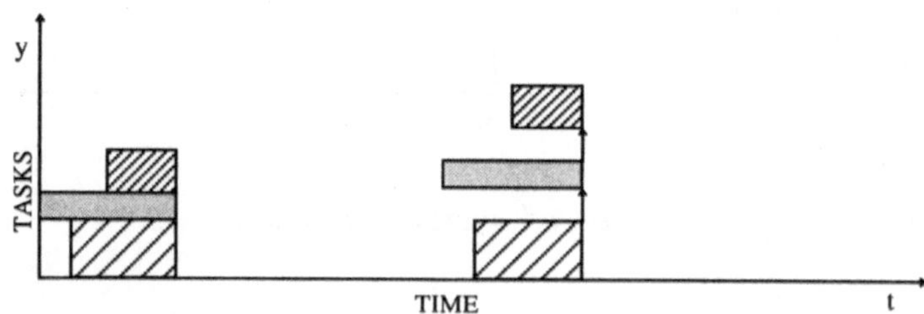

Fig. 3.8. Common finish tasks.

It is a property of each task to contain dependency information about both the tasks that precede it and the tasks that follow it. If i tasks precede the specific task, then an array $n(i)$ stores the identities of those tasks and another array $p(i)$ stores the percentage of completion of each corresponding task. A zero percent in a $p(i)$ value indicates parallel tasks, while an 100% value indicates continuous tasks. Any value between 0 and 100% indicates overlapping tasks. The information on the tasks that follow a specific task can be automatically generated from the information on the tasks that precede all the tasks in a project. Although it is redundant information, it is a property of each task to know which tasks

---

4   This is a special case of forced overlapping tasks: the required level of completion of the first task is 0% and the second task must start at that time.

follow it. The information on time interdependencies is used to define the starting and ending times of the tasks, or, equivalently, it is used for positioning the tasks along the time axis of the quantified bar chart.

3.3 QUANTIFIED BARS ON THE CHART

Parallel tasks have a strict relationship that the starting time and the ending time of both tasks must be the same. Forced overlapping tasks are also strongly interdependent, in terms of starting and ending times.

On the other hand the second (in terms of time) among two continuous tasks may be executed any time after the first task has been completed. The time between the ending of the first task and the starting of the second task is the float of the second task. The earliest possible starting time for the second task is defined as the ending time for the first task and, in that case, the float is zero. If a deadline for the second task (or the project) is also specified, then the latest possible starting time for the second task can also be calculated, based on the specific deadline and the duration of the task.[5] If the second task stars immediately after the completion of the first task, then a vertical arrow is recommended to be used to connect the two tasks, as in Fig. 3.9. Such an arrow informs visually the reader of the dependency of the tasks and that there is no float time between them. A horizontal arrow indicates the float time, if a particular task has been scheduled with a float.

---

[5]   The critical path method, presented in Chapter 7, is employed to calculate the earliest and latest starting and ending times for a group of interdependent tasks.

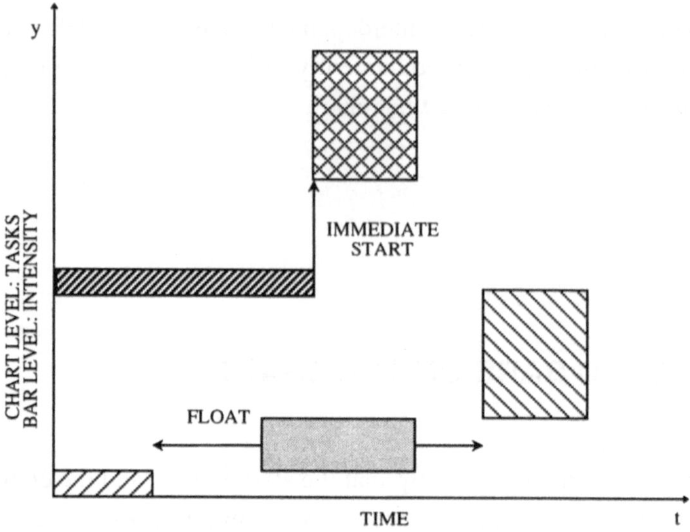

Fig. 3.9. Related quantified bars.

Similarly, the second (in terms of time) among two overlapping tasks may be executed any time after the first task has been completed by the specified percentage. The earliest starting time for the second task is when the first task has reached the specified level of completion and the float is zero. The latest possible starting time for the second task, is defined only if a deadline for the second task (or the project) has been set. If the overlapping tasks have been scheduled with no float time, a vertical arrow can show visually their inter-dependency. If a float exists, a horizontal arrow can show visually the float.

Often, the tasks displayed on the same quantified bar chart have a precedence relationship with one or more tasks that are executed by a foreign entity. Those foreign tasks should be included on the chart to define the precedences and justify certain scheduling decisions, however, their foreign nature should be maintained. The foreign tasks are represented with connoting bars drawn with a dotted line, showing the precedence relationships with the other tasks of the chart but omitting the display of quantity. Alternatively, the quantity of work may be shown but the resources should be displayed with connoting bars, since they are beyond the control of the planner.

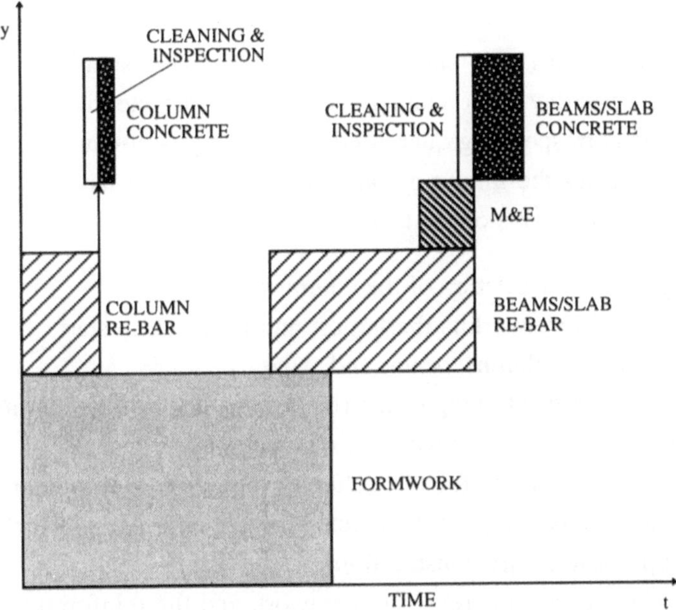

Fig. 3.10. *Quantified bar chart for the construction of a typical floor, intensity personpower.*

Example: Fig. 3.10 shows the construction of the structural skeleton of a typical floor in a cast-in-place concrete building. The following eight tasks compose the construction of the skeleton of the typical floor:
- *formwork*: making the formwork,
- *re-bar columns*: bending and positioning the reinforcing steel for the columns,
- *cleaning and inspection*: cleaning and inspection of the formwork and the steel of the columns,
- *column concrete*: placing concrete for the columns,
- *beams/slab re-bar*: bending and positioning the reinforcing steel for the beams and the slab,
- *M&E*: preparation for mechanical and electrical installations,
- *cleaning and inspection*: cleaning and inspection of the formwork and the steel of the beams and the slab,

- *beams/slab concrete*: placing concrete for the beams and the slab.

Labor (personpower) has been chosen as the quantity of display and the intensity displays workers per day. The labor intensive tasks are clearly identified by the larger size of the corresponding quantified bars. The positioning of the bars along the time axis indicates the timing of each task. The timing has resulted from the following interdependencies of the tasks:

Tasks relating to the construction of the columns:
- The making of formwork is the largest and first task to start. It includes the formwork for the columns, beams and slabs.
- The bending and positioning of the reinforcing steel for the columns can start at the same time as the formwork for the columns.
- The placing of concrete for the columns should start immediately after the reinforcing steel is ready, so the columns reach their strength early to provide partial support to future construction.
- Prior to placing the concrete, the formwork and the reinforcing steel should be cleaned and inspected by the general contractor.

Tasks relating to the construction of the beams and the slab:
- The bending and positioning of the reinforcing steel for the beams and the slab can start at a certain level of completion of the formwork.[6]
- The placing of concrete for the beams and the slab should start immediately after the reinforcing steel is ready, so the floor reaches a certain strength as soon as possible to support partially the next floor to be constructed.
- Preparation for the mechanical and electrical installations should have been completed before placing the concrete.
- The formwork and the reinforcing steel should be cleaned and inspected by the general contractor before placing the concrete.

The above tasks are scheduled to be executed by specialized subcontractors, except for cleaning and inspection that should be executed by the general contractor's personnel. So, there are no interdependencies of shared resources.

---

[6] As it will be explained in Chapter 6, the level of completion of the formwork before the work on the reinforcing bars starts is given by the microtemplate shown in Fig. 6.3.

Furthermore, there are not interdependencies resulting from a common location, as each task has its specific area of work.

The precedences among the tasks are defined according to the above relationships. Some of these precedences are derivatives of others:
- *Formwork* and *re-bar columns* have a common start.
- *Re-bar columns* and *cleaning columns* are overlapped (80% completion level).
- *Re-bar columns* and *concrete columns* are continuous.
- *Concrete columns* and *re-bar beams/slab* are continuous.
- *Cleaning columns* and *concrete columns* are continuous.
- *Formwork* and *re-bar beams/slab* are overlapped (80% completion level).
- *Re-bar beams/slab* and *M&E beams/slab* are overlapped (70% completion level).
- *Re-bar beams/slab* and *cleaning beams/slab* are overlapped (90% completion level).
- *Re-bar beams/slab* and *concrete beams/slab* are continuous.
- *Cleaning beams/slab* and *concrete beams/slab* are continuous.
- *M&E beams/slab* and *cleaning beams/slab* are overlapped (70% completion level).
- *M&E beams/slab* and *concrete beams/slab* are continuous.

The schedule shown in Fig. 3.10 represents the earliest possible starting time for each task, under the restrictions of the established precedences. The development of the schedule was visual, directly on the quantified bar chart. Alternative schedules could be developed by varying the personpower and the duration of the tasks.

3.4 OPERATIONS ON QUANTIFIED BAR CHARTS

Often the tasks of a project have well-defined precedences as in the example that was presented in the Section 3.3. In such cases, the scheduling based on precedences is meaningful. However, the planner can take into account other constraints and can modify the schedule that has been developed according to the constraints of duration and dependencies. The representation of the tasks by quantified bars allows the planner to move or alter the shape of the bars on the quantified bar chart as long as these moves do not violate the interdependencies of the tasks.

For the scheduling of tasks that do not have well-defined precedences, the planner moves and alters the quantified bars on the chart with more freedom in order to achieve a meaningful execution of the project.[7]

Four basic operations are permitted on a quantified bar chart for the purpose of changing the scheduling of tasks. Any task can be partitioned to any number of continuous, parallel or overlapping tasks following the proper sequence of these four basic operations:

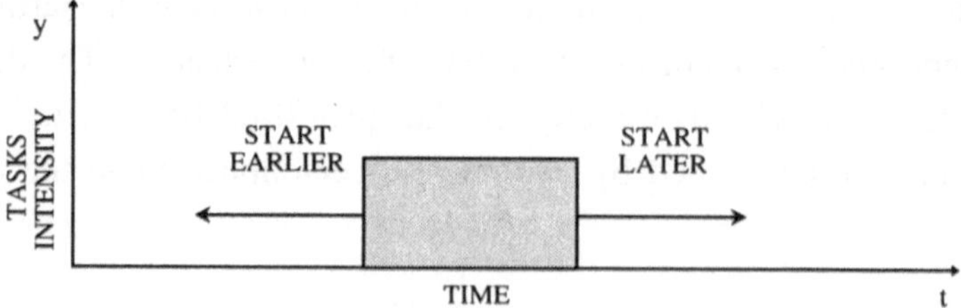

Fig. 3.11. Horizontal shift of a task.

- *Horizontal shift.* The starting time of a task can be changed. This operation will cause a horizontal shift of the task (Fig. 3.11), assuming that all the other

---

7   This provides the basis for developing the matrix-balanced chart which is presented in Chapter 5.

quantities associated with that task stay the same. Such a shift should be compatible with the interdependencies among the tasks displayed on the quantified bar chart. The float of the task defines the range that the task is allowed to be shifted, without violating the established precedences.

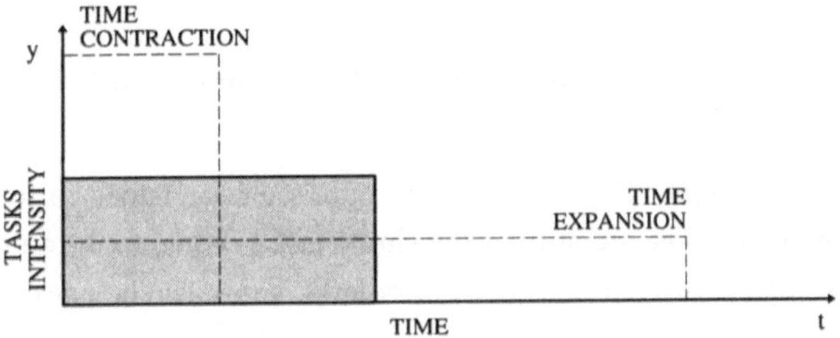

Fig. 3.12. Expansion or contraction of a task.

- *Expansion/contraction.* The duration or the intensity of a task can be expanded or contracted. Any change in the intensity of a task will cause an immediate change in the duration and vice versa (Fig. 3.12).

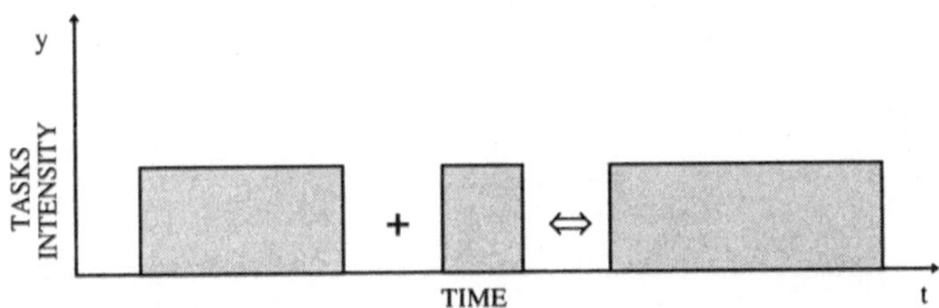

Fig. 3.13. Addition of continuous tasks and partition to continuous tasks.

- *Addition of continuous tasks.* Two continuous tasks can be added to form a single task (Fig. 3.13). The quantity of the single task is equal to the addition of the quantities of the two continuous tasks. Similarly, a task can be partitioned in two continuous tasks.

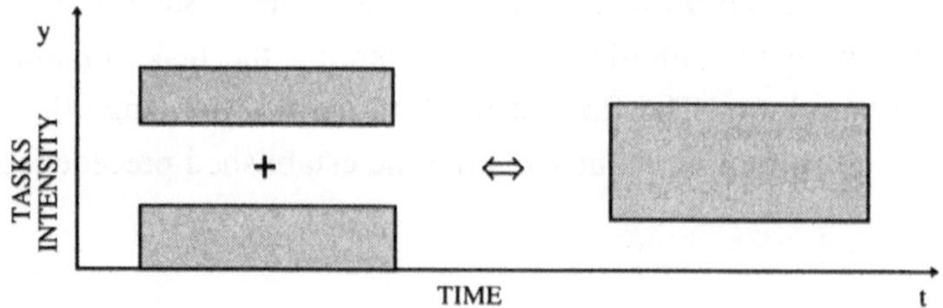

Fig. 3.14. Addition of parallel tasks and partition to parallel tasks.

- *Addition of parallel tasks:* Two parallel tasks can be added to form a single task (Fig. 3.14). The quantity of the single task is equal to the addition of the quantities of the two parallel tasks. Similarly, a task can be partitioned in two parallel tasks.

In addition to the 4 basic operations, a task can be shifted along the vertical axis in a quantified bar chart (Fig. 3.15). Such a *vertical shift* does not change any of the properties of the task but aims towards developing an easier to read quantified bar chart.

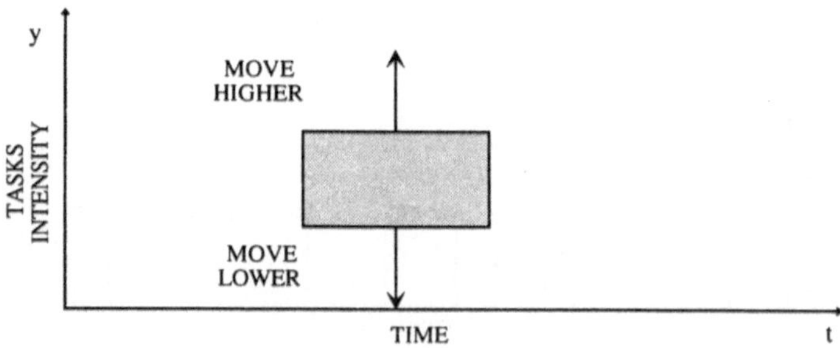

Fig. 3.15. Vertical shift of a task.

Example: The development of the quantified bar chart for scheduling the finishing tasks of a multi-storey hotel is presented. The scheduling is based on the assumption that the structural skeleton has been completed and the schedule of finishing should be optimal by itself, without taking into consideration the

repeating tasks on the different floors[8]. For a more systematic treatment, the tasks
are identified according to their physical location in a typical room of the hotel:

Tasks on the floor and between the floor and the walls:
- cleaning of the structural floor,
- main vertical mechanical and electrical installations (floor),
- preparation,
- floor screeding,
- marking (setting out),
- baseboards (skirting), and
- finishing of the floor.

Tasks on the walls and between the walls and the ceiling:
- installation of external precast panels,
- mechanical and electrical works on the walls (rough-in),
- installation of studs for the dry walls,
- installation of door frames,
- installation of glazing,
- installation of gypsum boards for the dry walls,
- mill work (curtain boxes),
- dry wall joints (painting patchy),
- painting of frames,
- painting 1st coat,
- painting 2nd coat,
- installation of door panels,
- installation of door and window hardware (iron mongery),
- fixtures/outlets (fitting),
- final coat of painting, and
- furniture.

Tasks on the ceiling:
- mechanical and electrical main horizontal ducts,
- mechanical and electrical pipes and ducts for the room (rough-in),
- construction of the ceiling grid,
- electrical wiring, and
- positioning of the ceiling boards.

---

8   The scheduling of repeating tasks in different locations of the building is presented in
Chapter 5.

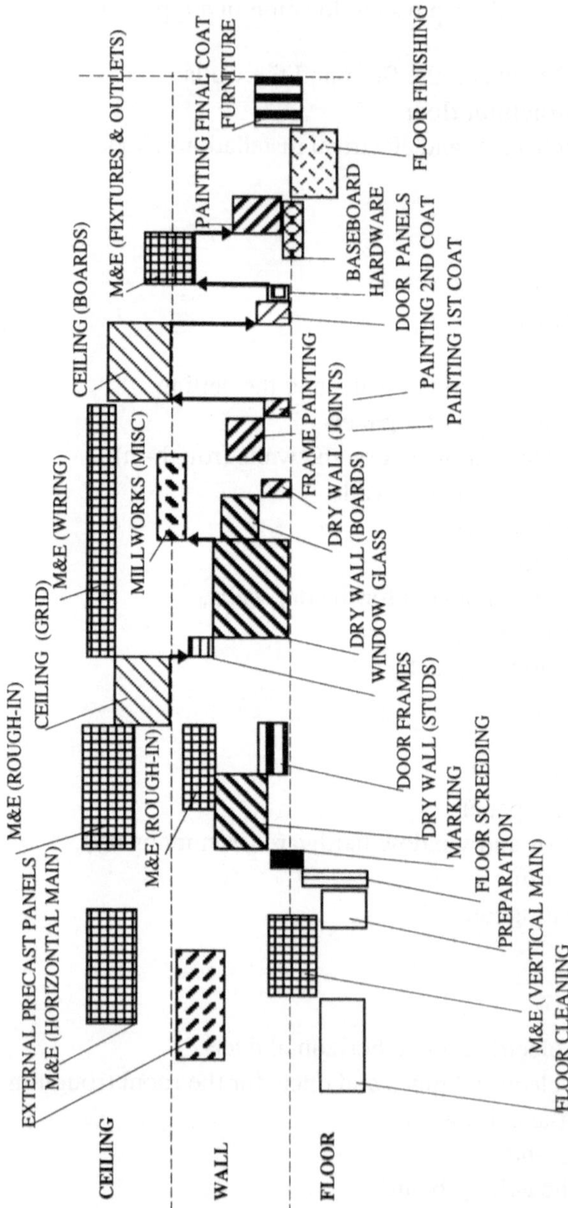

Fig. 3.16. Quantified bars for the construction of a typical room; transformed to apply to the entire floor; intensity personpower.

There are certain precedences among the 28 tasks. However, these precedences are not as strong as the precedences among the tasks for the construction of the structural skeleton of the building.

The first working quantified bar chart addresses the finishing of a single room. The tasks are represented by quantified bars with a certain sequence along the time axis (Fig. 3.16). For the convenience of the planner, the three layers of the room are included on the chart: the floor, the wall and the ceiling. The positioning of the quantified bars in any of these layers or in the overlapping area between two layers indicates the actual location of the work. Arrows indicate the interdependencies of the tasks[9]. The chart of Fig. 3.16, with amplified dimensions, represents also the finishing of the entire floor that includes many typical rooms.

Then, the planner performs a series of operations on the quantified bar chart of Fig. 3.16, illustrated in Fig. 3.17 to 3.21, to produce a meaningful and desirable schedule. All these operations are based on the four basic operations that were introduced earlier in this Section 3.4.

In Fig. 3.17, the planner examines the float time for each task and proceeds to the working schedule shown in Fig. 3.18, where the three layers have been omitted. Furthermore, the quantified bars have been re-arranged so that they maintain their precedences while similar types of tasks are shown one next to another. This is a quantified bar chart that could be used for actual scheduling. Then, the planner starts a planning procedure to impose the subjective constraint that up to two crews should work simultaneously on the same floor (Figure 3.19). This is a scheduling requirement based on the planner's experience. A constraint of having one crew or any number of crews working simultaneously on the floor would be implemented in a similar way. Fig. 3.20 shows the quantified bar chart that is derived from that constraint. Finally, Fig. 3.21 shows the final quantified bar chart where, for an even clearer schedule, the second crew is always executing mechanical and electrical work. The intensity of certain tasks was changed in the process of scheduling in order to compress or extend their duration and make a better scheduling. The sequence of Fig. 3.16 to 3.21 demonstrates the procedure of the visual development of the quantified bar chart.

---

[9]   This is a working quantified bar chart and should not be used for scheduling yet.

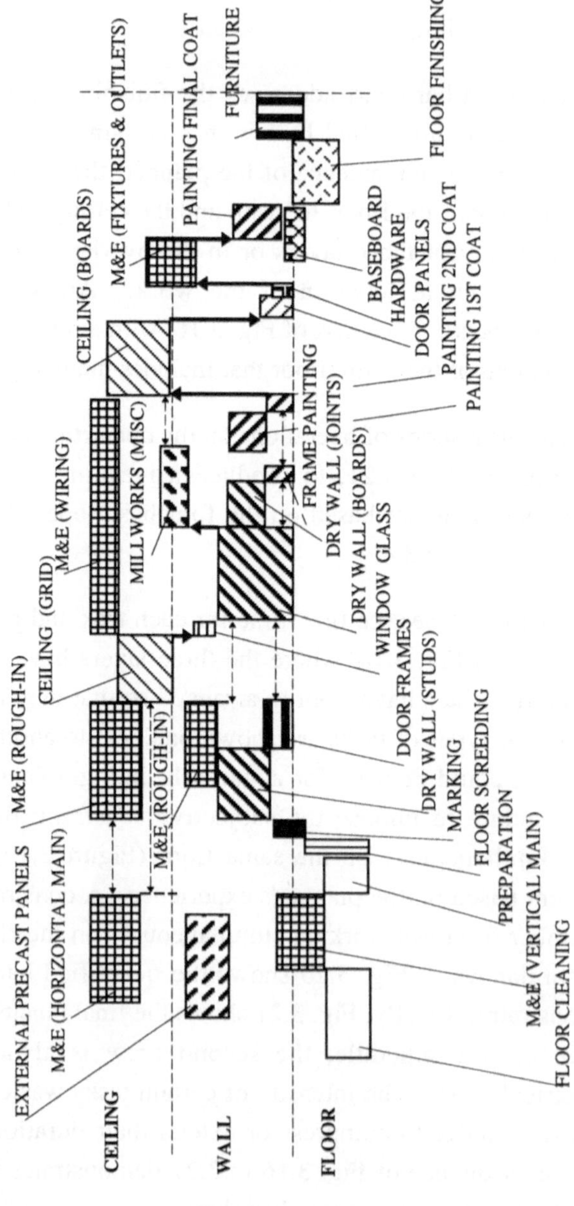

Fig. 3.17. Studies of float for the construction of a typical room; intensity personpower.

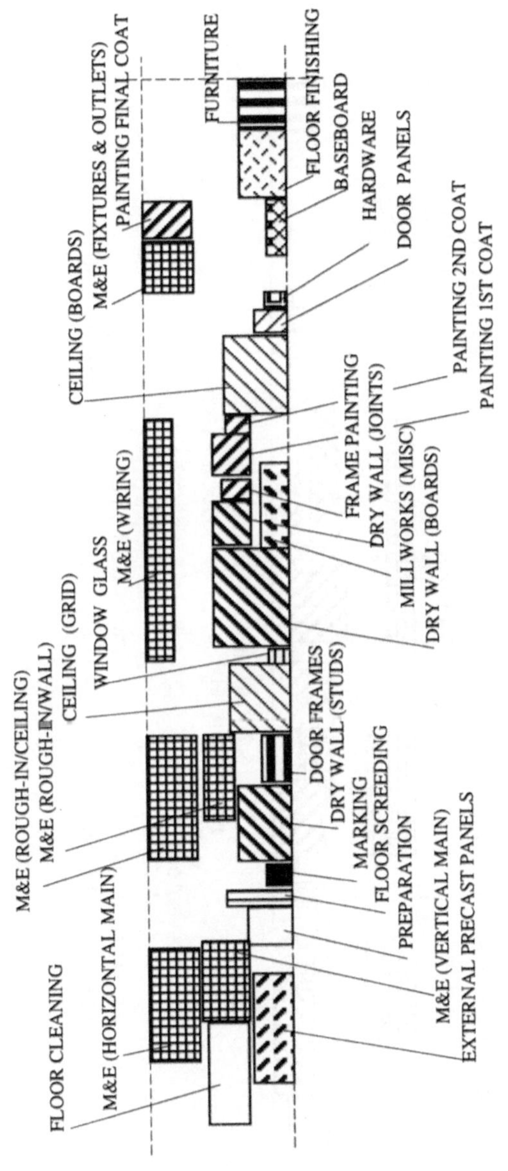

Fig. 3.18. Quantified bar chart for the construction of a typical floor; intensity personpower.

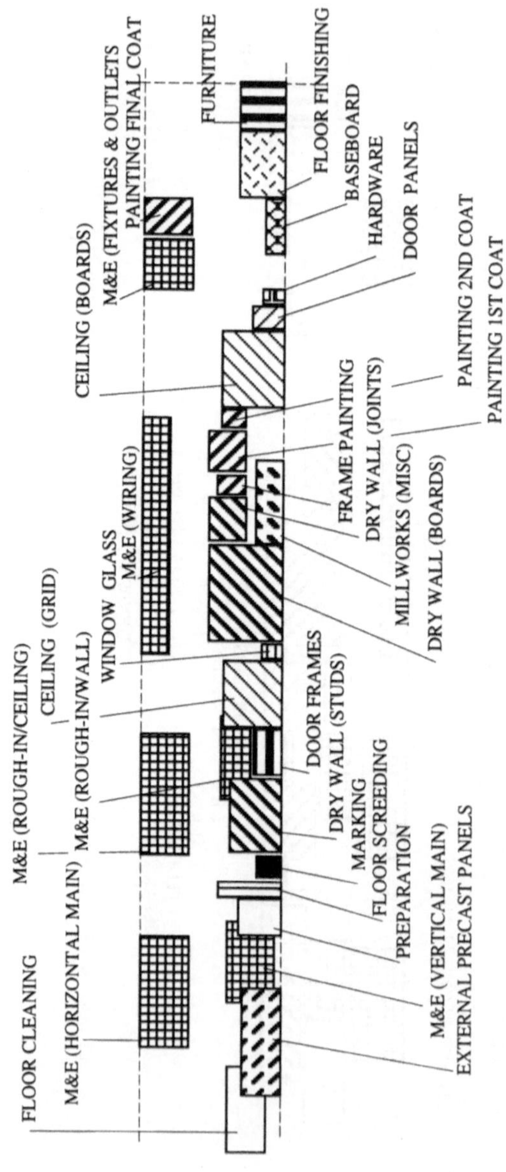

Fig. 3.19. Quantified bar chart for the construction of a typical floor; intensity personpower. Studies to introduce two crews at a time.

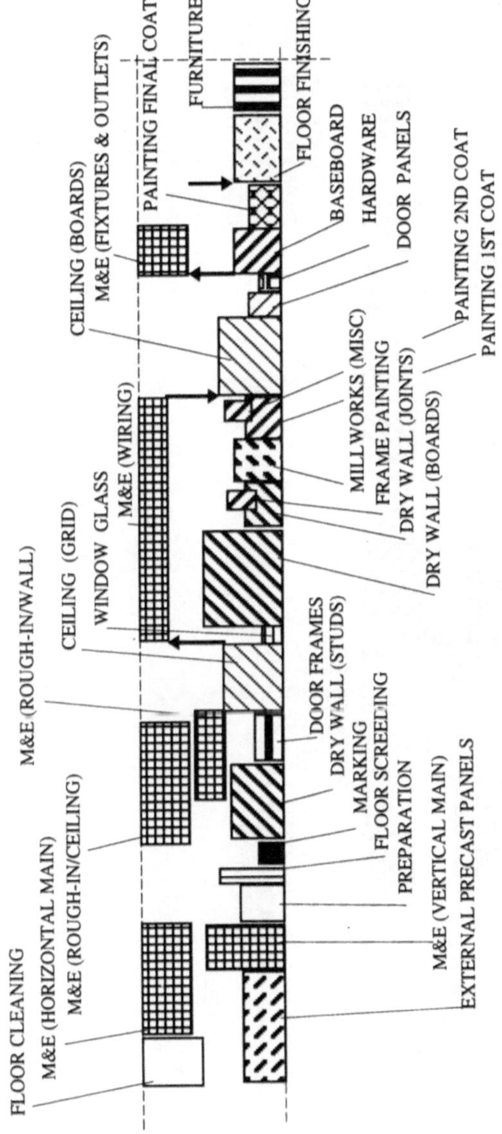

Fig. 3.20. Quantified bar chart for the construction of a typical floor with two crews at a time; intensity personpower.

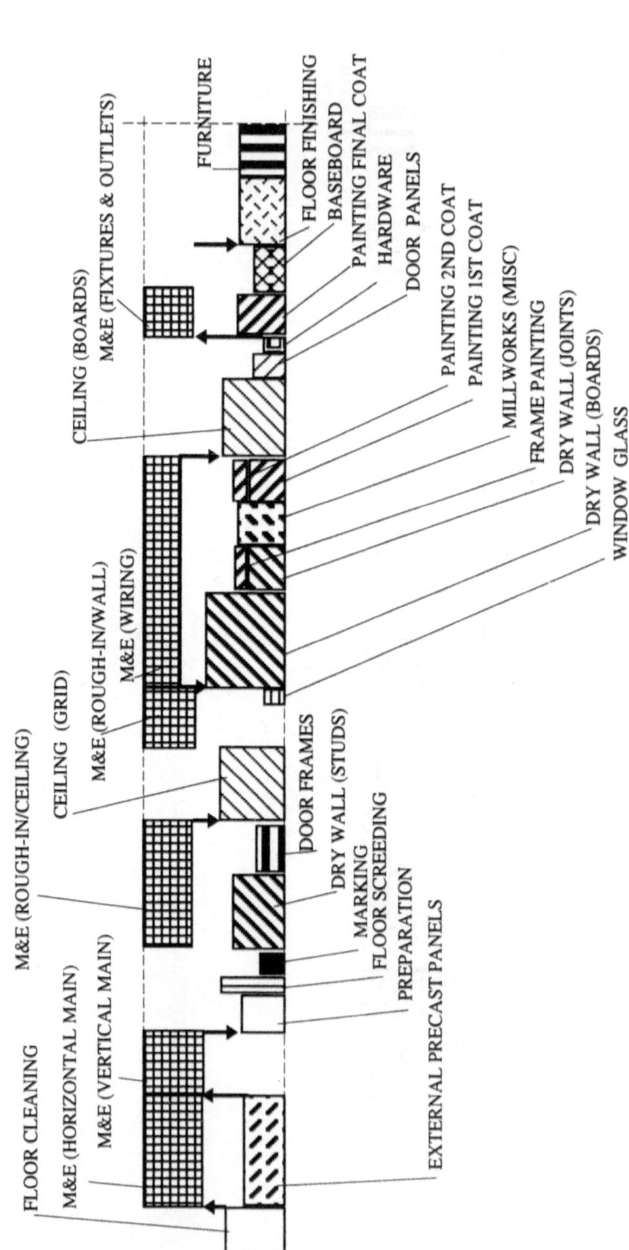

Fig. 3.21. Final quantified bar chart for the construction of a typical floor; second crew always M&E; intensity personpower.

3.5 CONSTRAINTS ON THE QUANTIFIED BARS

As shown in the presented examples, a series of operations alter the shapes and the relative positioning of the quantified bars for the purpose of making a quantified bar chart suitable for scheduling. Some of these operations are *temporary operations*: they are executed in a temporary manner, without establishing permanent constraints either on a specific task or between any pair of tasks. A translation of a quantified bar along the time axis within its float, or a change in the intensity and duration are examples of temporary operations. Most of the feasibility studies introduce a series of temporary, *reversal operations*.

However, operations on the quantified bar can be executed with a simultaneous introduction of *constraints*. Precedences establish constraints as discussed in Section 3.2. Parallel tasks, and forced overlapped tasks introduce very specific constraints that can be expressed by analytical relationships between the dependent tasks. Continuous tasks and overlapping tasks introduce boundary constraints that can be expressed by inequalities on the dependent tasks. Similarly, the definition of a specific range for the duration or a specific range for the resources of a task, an explicitly defined starting time, or an explicitly defined ending time introduce constraints. After the corresponding operations, the constraints become part of the properties of the quantified bars and future operations should be compatible with those constraints. If a future operation violates a previously defined constraint, the user should decide which is stronger to be a permanent part of the system and which should be dropped.

3.6 DISPLAY OF CAPACITY

This section portrays the display of the tasks together with the corresponding capacity of the facilities dedicated to execute the tasks. A facility for a task is a resource for that task, and the display of the capacity of the facility is an alternative display of a resource. Furthermore, it is quite useful to provide a simultaneous display of the capacity of facilities together with the other resources of a task.

Three examples demonstrate the multiple display of intensities, both of facilities and resources. The first example presents the visual scheduling of classes in a school, the second example presents the visual scheduling of an assembly line and the third example presents the display of the carrying capacity of transportation vehicles.

3.6.1   Scheduling of Classes

Class scheduling should utilize the available classrooms in a best way and should avoid conflicts of classes that address the same groups of students. The scheduling of classes at a small college is presented and, for economy of space, a single day of the week is considered only.

The available classrooms and their seating capacity are represented in Fig. 3.22 with quantified bars. Classrooms are always available, so the duration of the corresponding quantified bars extends during the whole day. The intensity of the quantified bar that represents each classroom is equal to the seating capacity of that classroom, which is also written at the right part of each bar. The name of the classroom appears on the left of each bar. Alternative intensities for the classrooms could be capacities for other uses, such as design studios, laboratories for sciences, or hands-on computer laboratories.

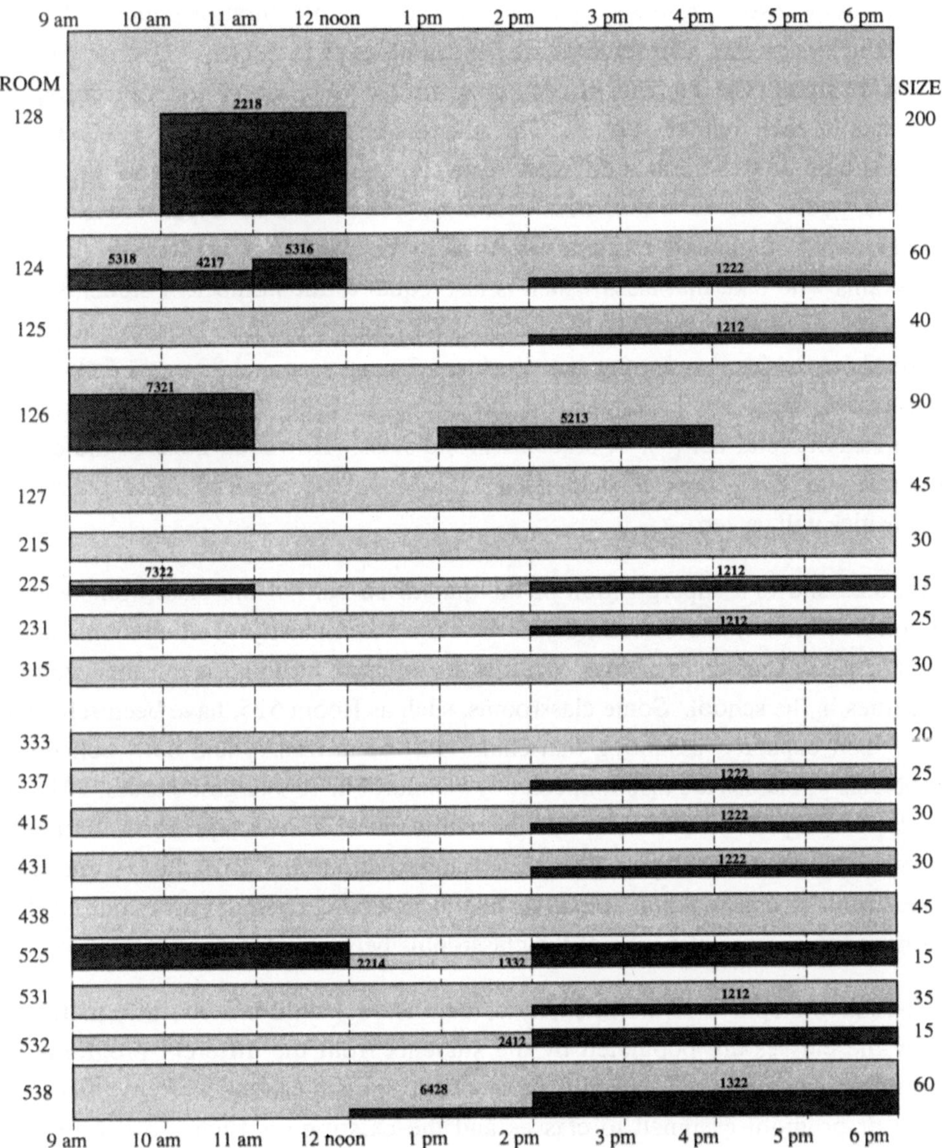

Fig. 3.22. *Scheduling of classes, intensities capacities of classrooms and all students.*

Each class is also represented by a quantified bar, with a duration equal to the time that the class meets. The students are the resources of each class. Distinctions can be made among the students of each program of the school as well as among the students of each year of studies. The students from each program who take that class should be treated as a different resource. Similarly, the students from each year of studies that take that class should be treated as a different resource. The total number of students in a class is equal to the number of students from all the programs who take that class which is also equal to the number of students of all the years of study who take that class. So, each class can be represented by several intensities. Assuming that there are 3 programs and 3 years of studies in the school, there are 9 independent intensities for each class. A 10th intensity indicates the total number of students in the class. However, most of the classes interest specific groups of students and, most likely, some of these alternative intensities will be zero.

Fig. 3.22 shows a superposition of the quantified bars of the classrooms and the quantified bars of the classes, displayed with the intensity of all students taking each class. The chart shows visually the overall utilization of the available facilities in the school. Some classrooms, such as Room 525, have been scheduled over their capacity, assuming that chairs will be moved in and out. Scheduling problems of classes are also immediately visible. The two largest classes, 2218 and 7321, overlap from 10 am to 11 am, while there is no major class scheduled between 12 noon and 1 pm. Thus, it is suggested that the 2218 class is moved to meet from 11 am to 1 pm. Finally, this chart could schedule the required daily preparation and maintenance of the classrooms between classes.

Alternative displays of the intensity of the classes could provide information on how the classes are populated by the students from the different programs and from each year of study. Specific charts could show the students from a particular year or program assigned to classes and the existing conflicts. Some of these charts will contain classes with zero intensities; those classes should be shown with connoting bars. Multiple intensities could be presented in the same chart. A visual identification should be used in the form of color or hatching for the intensities representing students from the different years of study or for the different programs.

3.6.2   Visualization of Transportation Capacity

The carrying capacity of different transportation vehicles and their range can be displayed using quantified bars. The horizontal axis is either time or distance, since speed provides a direct relation between time and distance. Fig. 3.23 displays the maximum payload carrying capacity and the corresponding range of 4 aircrafts, as well as their maximum range and the corresponding payload, based on the data shown in Table 3.1.

Table 3.1. *Characteristics of selected aircrafts, for maximum range and for maximum payload*[10].

TYPE OF AIRCRAFT	DISTANCE (MILES)	LOAD (TONS)
747-200	4330 7140	72.3 28.5
Concorde	4430 4480	12.7 10.7
A300 B4	1820 3400	35.3 18.1
737-200	1280 2740	15.9 9.7

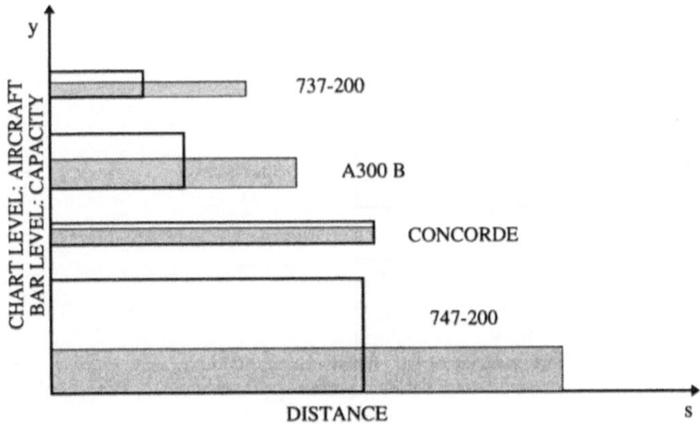

Fig. 3.23. *Visual display of the range of the aircrafts and the corresponding payload, for maximum range and for maximum payload.*

10   Source: Ashford, N., and P.H. Wright, *Airport Engineering*, 3rd edition, John Wiley: New York, 1992.

Fig. 3.24 presents the same information with the horizontal axis displaying time instead of distance, assuming that the 3 aircrafts cruise at 600 mph and the Concorde cruises at 1400 mph.

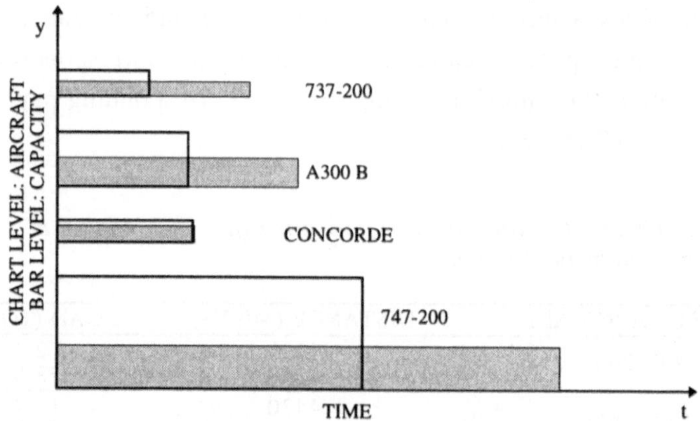

Fig. 3.24. *Visual display of the cruising time of the aircrafts and the corresponding payload, for maximum range and for maximum payload.*

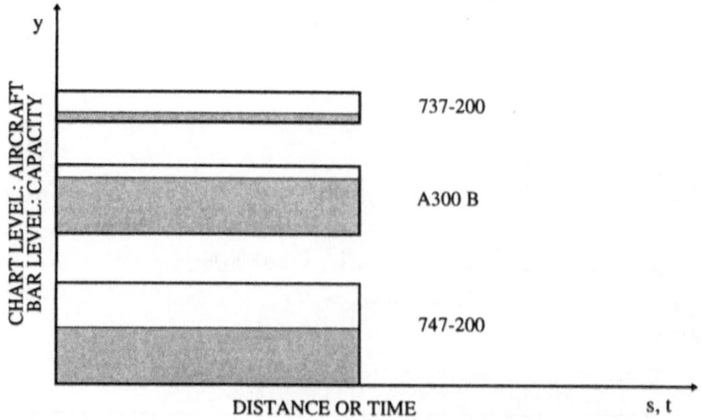

Fig. 3.25. *Visual display of the seating capacity of the aircrafts and the actual number of passengers in a specific flight.*

Fig. 3.25 displays the number of passengers actually transported at a certain distance versus the seating capacity of the 3 aircrafts. The horizontal axis represents both time and distance, assuming that the aircrafts cruise at the same speed. As long as the capacity of a vehicle or a system can be quantified and it has a certain significance as related to range or time, then quantified bars can be employed to display the scheduling of the vehicles or the systems and monitor the actual execution of operations.

CHAPTER 4

TEMPLATES

Following the definition of the quantified bar chart, the template is introduced as the next representation level of the Visual Scheduling and Management System. A template includes a quantified bar chart and alphanumeric data and has special provisions for aggregating the discrete tasks and for monitoring the project.

The definition of the template is presented in Section 4.1. The dual presentation of the information, both in graphic and alphanumeric forms is discussed in Section 4.2 and the process of input and output of data is explained. In the same section, a detailed example demonstrates the process of developing a template. Section 4.3 presents the use of templates for studying visually resource leveling and it is accompanied by two examples from the services industry. Finally, in Section 4.4, the use of control templates for monitoring the actual execution of a project is presented, accompanied by an example.

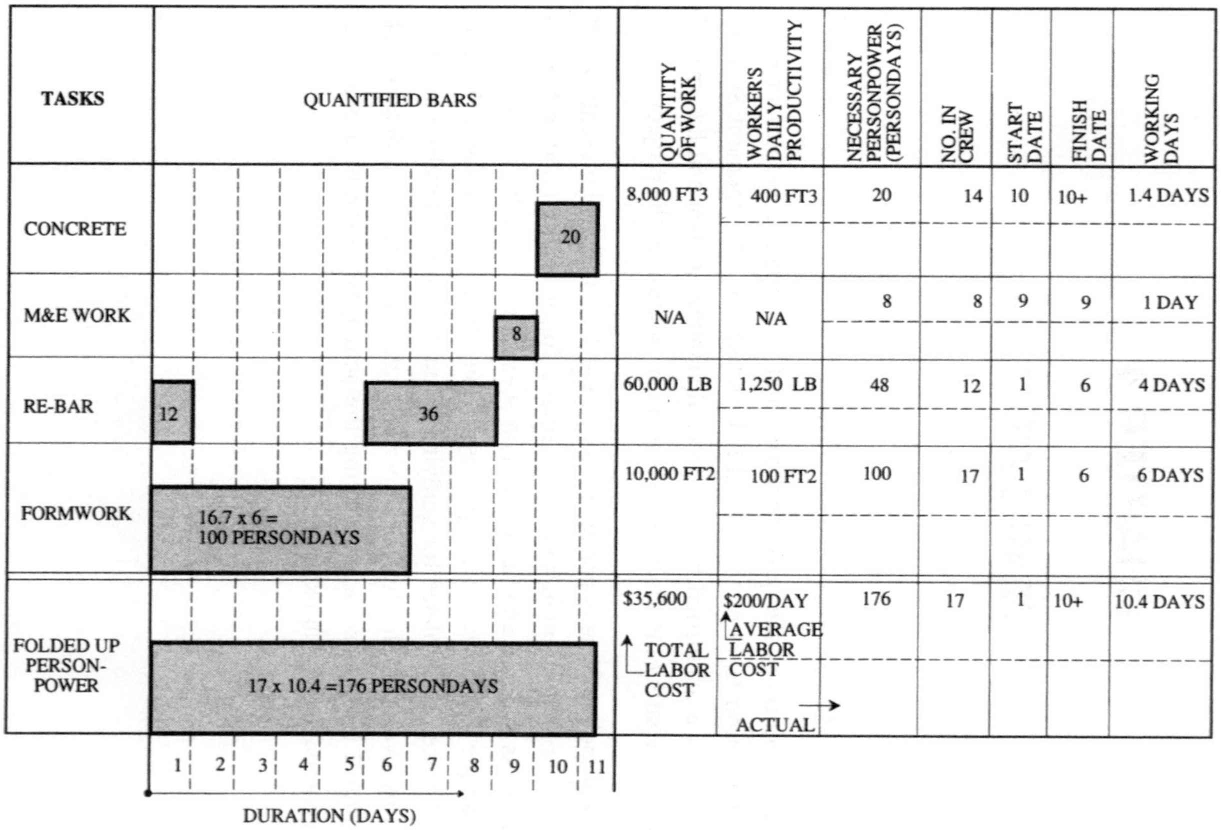
TASKS
QUANTIFIED BARS
QUANTITY OF WORK
WORKER'S DAILY PRODUCTIVITY
NECESSARY PERSONPOWER (PERSONDAYS)
NO. IN CREW
START DATE
FINISH DATE
WORKING DAYS
CONCRETE
20
8,000 FT3
400 FT3
20
14
10
10+
1.4 DAYS
M&E WORK
8
N/A
N/A
8
8
9
9
1 DAY
RE-BAR
12
36
60,000 LB
1,250 LB
48
12
1
6
4 DAYS
FORMWORK
16.7 x 6 =
100 PERSONDAYS
10,000 FT2
100 FT2
100
17
1
6
6 DAYS
FOLDED UP PERSON-POWER
17 x 10.4 =176 PERSONDAYS
$35,600
TOTAL LABOR COST
$200/DAY
AVERAGE LABOR COST
ACTUAL
176
17
1
10+
10.4 DAYS
1 2 3 4 5 6 7 8 9 10 11
DURATION (DAYS)

Fig. 4.1. Template for the planning of the construction of a typical floor.

4.1 THE TEMPLATE

A *template* is composed of a quantified bar chart, its folded-up task[1] and alphanumeric data in a spreadsheet format. A template inherits all the properties of the quantified bar chart, while the simultaneous presentation of graphics and text allows a multiple representation of information.

Example: The template in Fig. 4.1 contains a quantified bar chart for the construction of the reinforced concrete skeleton of a typical floor of a building. This quantified bar chart is a simplified version of Fig. 3.10. The cleaning and inspection operations are not shown, as they are executed by the general contractor, and the concrete is placed at the same time for the columns and the slab. The first column of the template in Fig. 4.1 contains the name of each task. The second column contains the quantified bars that make the quantified bar chart. The quantity of the work is in column 3, while the productivity, the required person-days, and the number of workers in the crews are presented in columns 4, 5 and 6. Columns 7 and 8 show the starting and finishing days and column 9 shows the duration of each task. The first row is the title row, while each subsequent row contains a task. For each task there are two subrows in the spreadsheet part of the template. The top subrow contains the information during the planning stage and the bottom subrow will contain the information of the mate quantified bar, for monitoring and updating the task. Thus, during planning, the bottom subrow is left intentionally blank. The last row of the template includes the folded-up task that aggregates the individual tasks shown on the template. The folded-up task is presented in detail in Chapter 6, as part of the hierarchical structure of the Visual Scheduling and Management System.

---

[1] The folded-up task is defined in Chapter 6, as part of the hierarchical structure of the Visual Scheduling and Management System.

4.2 INPUT AND OUTPUT

Each cell in the alphanumeric part of the template serves both as input and output of information. The data in the columns are related as shown in Fig. 2.8, or by the expressions 2.1 to 2.5. So, empty cells can be filled with information until there are enough data to generate the data in the other cells. Overwriting data in any cell will cause the changing of the data in the cells with direct relationships.

Table 4.1. Data to generate the template shown in Fig. 4.1.

	A	B	C	D	E
1	TASK	QUANTITY OF WORK	CONTRACT UNIT COST	CONTRACT TOTAL COST	WAGE RATE
2	CONCRETE	8,000 ft^3	$0.50 /ft^3	$4,000	$180
3	FORMWORK	10,000 ft^2	$2.00 /ft^2	$20,000	$220
4	RE-BARS	60,000 lb	$0.17 /lb	$10,000	$200
5	M&E	N/A	N/A	$1,600	$200
6	*TOTAL*	*N/A*	*N/A*	*$35,600*	*N/A*

	A	F	G	H	I
1	TASK	CALCULATED PERSONDAYS FROM WAGES	CALCULATED PRODUCTIVITY FROM WAGES	PRODUCTIVITY FROM RECORDS	ADOPTED PRODUCTIVITY
2	CONCRETE	22	360 ft^3	500 ft^3	400 ft^3
3	FORMWORK	91	110 ft^2	90 ft^2	100 ft^2
4	RE-BARS	50	1,200 lb	1,200 lb	1,250 lb
5	M&E	8	N/A	N/A	N/A
6	*TOTAL*	*171*	*N/A*	*N/A*	*N/A*

	A	J	K	L
1	TASK	ADOPTED PERSONDAYS	ACTUAL WORKING DAYS FOR A 10 DAY SCHEDULE	CREW SIZE FOR A 10 DAYS SCHEDULE
2	CONCRETE	20	1 + OVER TIME	14
3	FORMWORK	100	6	17
4	RE-BARS	48	4	12
5	M&E	8	1	8
6	*TOTAL*	*176*	*10*	*AVERAGE 18*

Referring to the template of Fig. 4.1, the data in columns 3, 4 and 5 are inter-related: productivity is the ratio of the quantity of the work (size of the task) divided by the necessary personpower. Thus, any two of these data can generate the third. After the data have been entered or calculated, a change in any of those will cause a change in the others. Unless overwritten by the user, the productivity is the most volatile, with the necessary personpower being second. So, if the necessary personpower is changed, the productivity will be changed while the quantity of the work will stay the same.

The quantified bars serve for input and output of information as well. As output devices, they display the information of the spreadsheet. As input devices, they are generated or modified with the help of a pointer. The modifications should result from the four basic operations on quantified bars, as defined in Section 3.4. The corresponding data in the spreadsheet change to reflect the changes applied directly on the quantified bars.

Example: There are many different ways to develop the template of Fig. 4.1. The approach of making the spreadsheet first, then produce the quantified bars and finally assemble the template will be demonstrated as an example.

The project focuses on the scheduling of labor for the construction of the structural skeleton of a single floor, in a reinforced concrete building. The four tasks are defined in column A of Table 4.1. The quantity of work and the contracted unit cost for labor are known to the project planner and entered in columns B and C. The total contracted cost is calculated in column D. The wages, known to the project manager as well, are entered in column E. The calculated personpower is shown in column F and the calculated productivity in column G. According to the data available the project planner, the productivity in similar sites in the past has been recorded as entered in column H. The project planner adjusts that productivity to reflect the specific conditions of this project and enters the adjusted productivity in column I, which is used to calculate the personpower in column J. Then the project planner defines the duration of the project as 10 days, so the duration of each task is estimated as shown in column K. Finally, the sizes of the work crews are calculated in column L.

The last task, the preparation for mechanical and electrical installations, does not have a quantity of work. This, however, does not affect the process, since the required personpower is estimated directly.[2]

The above process is just one of the several alternatives to plan the project. Other planners may choose to start with other data, such as the productivity from other sites, then calculate the size of the work crews and the duration of the tasks and finally determine the necessary contracted cost.

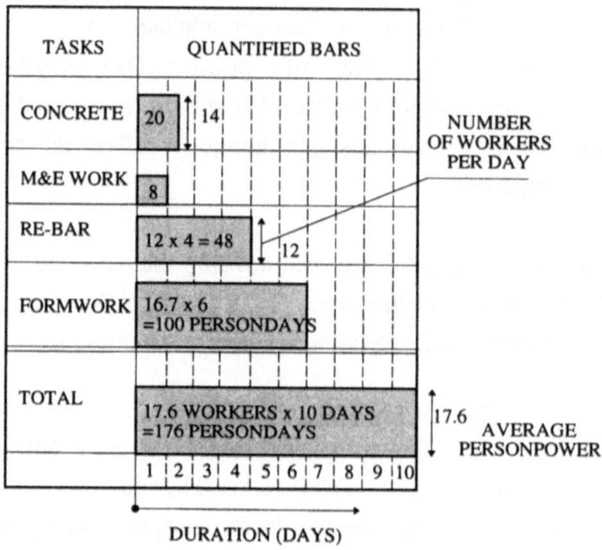

Fig. 4.2. Quantified bars without established precedences.

At this stage the starting and ending times for the 4 tasks have not been defined yet. The quantified bar chart shown in Fig. 4.2 shows the quantified bars for the 4 tasks and the folded-up task prior to establishing precedences. After the precedences among the tasks are defined, the quantified bars are positioned along

---

[2] The folded-up task that is described in the last row of the template in Fig. 4.1 is not homogeneous, since it aggregates tasks of different constituencies. However, the total cost and the personpower are meaningful for the folded-up task. The constituency of the folded-up task will be discussed in Chapter 6.

the time axis and the template shown in Fig. 4.1 is obtained, which shows selected data on its spreadsheet part.

4.3 VISUAL LEVELING OF RESOURCES

In the previous sections, it has been assumed that the tasks do not need resource leveling. This is a realistic assumption in construction, where most of the tasks are subcontracted. However, a template can be used to monitor the use of resources for a group of tasks and provides the framework for a visual resource leveling. Furthermore, it can accept a certain resource ceiling as a constraint in the visual scheduling, in a form consistent with Section 3.5.

The last row of a template is reserved for the folded-up task, which is defined in Section 6.1. In addition, the same last row can contain a quantified bar with the cumulative intensity of all the quantified bars that are displayed on the template. If the displayed intensity on the template is personpower, then the cumulative intensity is also personpower for the time period covered by the template. So, the last row can be utilized to level visually a resource by moving and altering the quantified bars in the template. This assumes that the tasks shown on the template employ the specific resource, which can be achieved with a proper hierarchical structure, as it is discussed in Chapter 6.

Two examples are presented to demonstrate the *cumulative resource quantified bar* and resource leveling. The first example refers to a software development that requires resource leveling. The second example refers to scheduling the preparations for an art exhibition, where the tasks do not require resource leveling, but where information on the cumulative resources is useful.

The template for planning the software development by a small firm is shown in Fig. 4.3, with the cumulative intensity at the bottom row of the template, depicted simultaneously with the folded-up task. The product is designed to be developed without any subcontracting and, at any time, the allocation of the personnel on the various tasks should be equal to the total number of the employees of the firm. As a result, the summation of the personpower of all the quantified bars should be smooth and should represent the members of the team at each corresponding time unit.

During scheduling, the visual modifications of the quantified bars are reflected immediately on the cumulative resource bar. Thus, the process of balancing the resources is assisted visually. A constraint, according to Section 3.5, can be also established for the cumulative intensity of all the tasks shown on the template. As a result of such a constraint, any modifications that violate the maximum allowable resources could be either rejected or temporarily sustained until a next move would balance the resources again.

Fig. 4.4 shows the template during planning for the preparations of an art exhibition at a college gallery. Sixty works of art should be displayed in the exhibition, to be selected from approximately 500 works available among the collectors. The displayed intensity is the gallery's personpower and the last row of the template contains the accumulated personpower which has several peaks and valleys. There is a time period, following the task of *framing* that none of the gallery's personnel is scheduled to work for the exhibition for 2 days. This is due to the 6 days that the framing shop requires to frame the works of art, shown as a foreign task represented with a connoting bar since its resources are foreign to the gallery. Graduate students staff the art gallery as a part-time work and their hours are flexible. Thus, the peaks and valleys in the cumulative resource quantified bar are quite acceptable and resource leveling is not required.

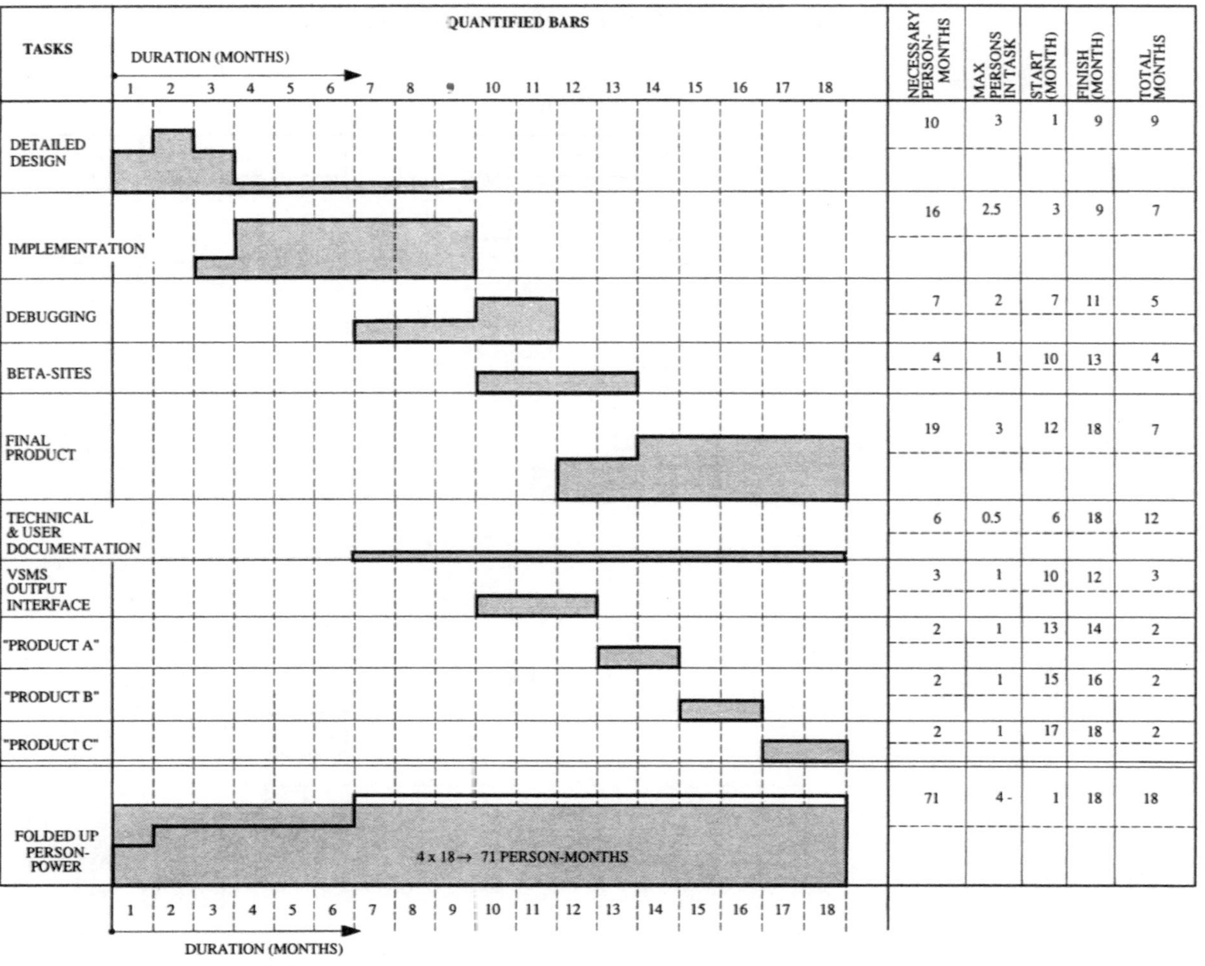

TASKS	NECESSARY PERSON-MONTHS	MAX PERSONS IN TASK	START (MONTH)	FINISH (MONTH)	TOTAL MONTHS
DETAILED DESIGN	10	3	1	9	9
IMPLEMENTATION	16	2.5	3	9	7
DEBUGGING	7	2	7	11	5
BETA-SITES	4	1	10	13	4
FINAL PRODUCT	19	3	12	18	7
TECHNICAL & USER DOCUMENTATION	6	0.5	6	18	12
VSMS OUTPUT INTERFACE	3	1	10	12	3
"PRODUCT A"	2	1	13	14	2
"PRODUCT B"	2	1	15	16	2
"PRODUCT C"	2	1	17	18	2
FOLDED UP PERSON-POWER	71	4 -	1	18	18

Fig. 4.3. The development of a software product.

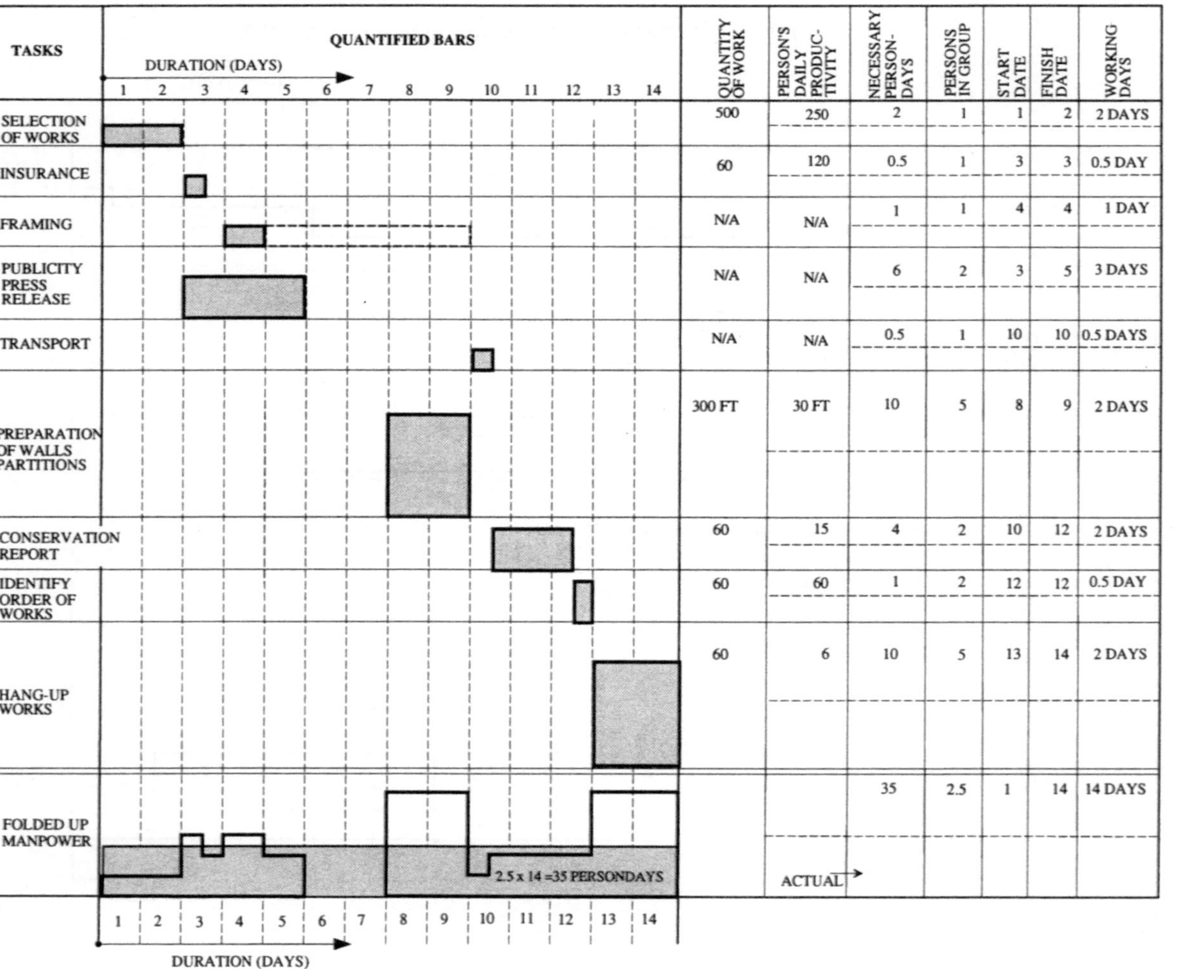

TASKS	QUANTITY OF WORK	PERSON'S DAILY PRODUC-TIVITY	NECESSARY PERSON-DAYS	PERSONS IN GROUP	START DATE	FINISH DATE	WORKING DAYS
SELECTION OF WORKS	500	250	2	1	1	2	2 DAYS
INSURANCE	60	120	0.5	1	3	3	0.5 DAY
FRAMING	N/A	N/A	1	1	4	4	1 DAY
PUBLICITY PRESS RELEASE	N/A	N/A	6	2	3	5	3 DAYS
TRANSPORT	N/A	N/A	0.5	1	10	10	0.5 DAYS
PREPARATION OF WALLS PARTITIONS	300 FT	30 FT	10	5	8	9	2 DAYS
CONSERVATION REPORT	60	15	4	2	10	12	2 DAYS
IDENTIFY ORDER OF WORKS	60	60	1	2	12	12	0.5 DAY
HANG-UP WORKS	60	6	10	5	13	14	2 DAYS
FOLDED UP MANPOWER			35	2.5	1	14	14 DAYS

ACTUAL

Fig. 4.4. Preparations for an art gallery exhibition.

4.4 MONITORING AND FORECASTING

A *control template* displays updated information as it becomes available by employing a mate quantified bar for each quantified bar that is defined during the planning stage. The display of actual data on the template requires an appropriate mechanism for collecting these data from the field.

In the construction industry, most of the standard forms for daily site report do not have a provision to include the amount of completed work. Two special forms have been developed for monitoring daily the construction site as part of the proposed system. The first form reports the activities of the employees of the construction firm and it is shown in Fig. 4.5. The second form is designed for the control of the activities of the subcontractors and it is shown in Fig. 4.6. Both forms should be used to collect the data to describe the quantified bars that represent the tasks of the project.

A percentage of the work of each task can describe approximately the completed work per time unit. This approximation is justified by the time savings of collecting data in the field. However, a measure of the actually completed work should be used at certain time intervals to adjust the percentage estimates.

Fig. 4.7 shows the superposition of the planned tasks as shown in Fig. 4.1 and their actual execution. This control template was prepared after the completion of all the tasks.

In addition to superimposing the actual quantified bars on the originally planned quantified bars, Fig. 4.7 includes the alphanumeric information on the actual execution of each task. This information has been inserted in the spreadsheet part of the template, in the lower subrow of each task.

SITE STAFF	NAME	I.D.	A.M. 5	6	7	8	9	10	11	P.M. 12	1	2	3	4	5	6	7	8	9	DESCRIPTION OF WORK
SUPERINTENDENT																				
ENGINEERS																				
ENGINEERS																				
ACCOUNTANT																				
CARPENTER FOREMAN																				
CARPENTERS																				
CARPENTERS																				
CARPENTERS																				
MASON FOREMAN																				
IRONWORKER FOREMAN																				
IRONWORKER																				
IRONWORKER																				
CEMENT FINISH FOREMAN																				
CEMENT FINISHERS																				
CEMENT FINISHERS																				
CEMENT FINISHERS																				
LABOR FOREMAN																				
LABORS																				
LABORS																				
LABORS																				
LABORS																				
LABORS																				
LABORS																				
MASON TENDERS																				
TOTAL																				

DAILY FIELD REPORT
PROJECT NAME　　　　DATE　　WEATHER　　TEMPERATURE 8:00A.M.　　4:30P.M.
INSPECTION　　　　VISITORS　　EVENTS

MATERIAL　　　　RENTAL EQUIPMENT

Fig. 4.5. Construction site daily report for the control of the company's workers.

DAILY FIELD REPORT

PROJECT NAME   DATE

SUB CONTRACTORS / COMPANY NAME	C OR D	JOB CODE	TOTAL QUANTITY	QUANTITY DONE %	PERSON POWER	LOCATION	PP	Q	LOCATION	PP	Q	LOCATION	PP	Q	COMMENTS
EXCAVATION															
PLUMBER															
HEATING															
ELECTRICIAN															
ROOFER															
METAL WORKER															
ELEVATOR & ESCALATOR															
MARBLE, CEMENT TILE															
PLASTERER															
PAINTER															
STEEL ERECTOR															
ORNAMENT IRON															
GLASS															
SPRINCLER															
FLOORING															
TOTAL C			C: CONTRACT WORK												
TOTAL D			D: DAY WORK												
GRAND TOTAL															

Fig. 4.6. Construction site daily report for the control of the subcontractors.

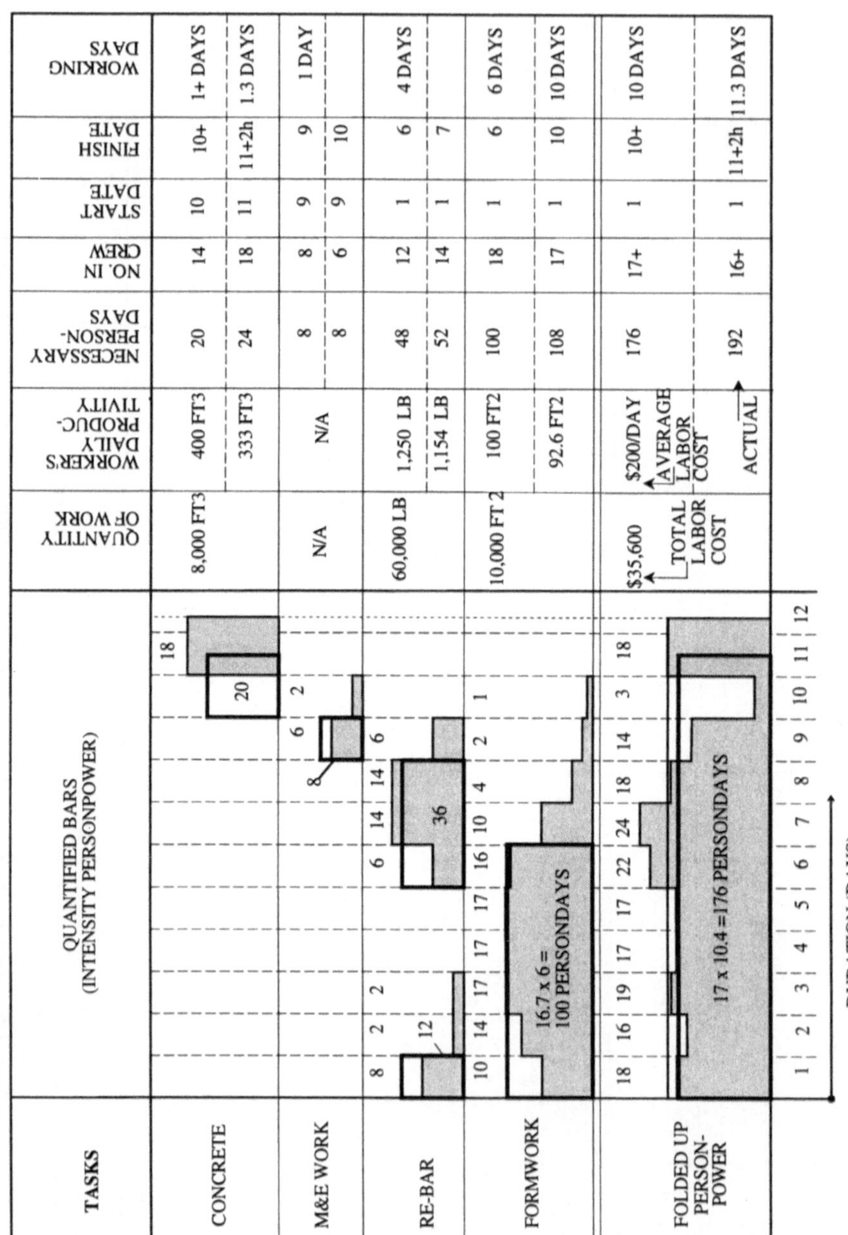

Fig. 4.7. The control template for planning and monitoring the construction of a typical floor.

Useful comments for the progression of a project can be made by observing the control template in Fig. 4.7. A visual comparison of the planning versus the actual quantified bars shows that both the formwork and the reinforcing bars were advancing in a slower than expected pace at the beginning. In addition, the completion of the formwork was delayed during the last days. This delay created a delay in placing the concrete and as a result a delay in the ending of the project. So, the delay in the completion of the project is visually presented and the cause is visually identifiable[3].

A series of control templates at intermediate stages during the process can be developed. The original schedule, the actual execution until the date of reference, and the projection for the rest of the project would have been superimposed on the intermediate stage templates, to provide a best visual update, as has been shown in Fig. 2.11.

---

[3]   The microtemplate of Fig. 6.3 displays the detailed schedule for making the formwork included in the control template of Fig. 4.7. An explanation can be given on why the completion of the formwork did not proceed according to the plan. The actual execution was closer to the detailed quantified bars of the microtemplate. Assuming that the project planner had worked with the data at the microtemplate, he made an effort to shorten the project by arbitrarily shortening the duration of the formwork. Apparently that was ambitious to achieve.

CHAPTER 5

THE MATRIX-BALANCED CHART

The matrix-balance chart follows the presentation of the quantified bar chart and the template. The matrix-balance chart is at the higher level of the quantified charts in the Visual Scheduling and Management System.

Section 5.1 presents the issue of repeating tasks and introduces the additional dimension of location in the scheduling of projects. The introduction of location sets the ground for developing the concept of the matrix-balanced chart to schedule tasks with precedences of diminishing importance. Section 5.2 presents the definition of the matrix-balanced chart and its properties. Section 5.3 discusses the slope of the line of the diagonals of the quantified bars, that compose the matrix-balance chart. The visual depiction of the learning curve is presented with the line of the diagonals, in the same section. The use of the matrix-balanced chart is presented in Section 5.4 together with a detailed example that shows the balancing process in a sequence of steps. Finally, a re-arrangement of the tasks along the vertical axis is presented in Section 5.5. That re-arrangement allows the user to study the scheduling of the tasks according to the constitution of the tasks rather than their location.

5.1 REPEATING TASKS

A task that is repeated at different physical locations of a project and requires similar resources is a *repeating task.* The finishing of a typical floor of a multi-storey building is a repeated task at those different floors of the building. The installation of the door panels in a typical room of a hotel building is a repeated task in those different rooms.

The introduction of location as an additional dimension to scheduling has a major impact on precedences. In most cases, precedences can be established for the tasks to be executed for the same project at a specific location. If these tasks should be repeated in many locations, the same precedences could apply for each location separately. If the resources are unlimited for each task of the project, then the dimension of location should not alter the scheduling at each location. However, since the same tasks are repeated from location to location, it is reasonable to be executed by the same resources in a sequential procedure. The availability of many locations simultaneously for the same resources diminishes the effect of precedences among the tasks. The scheduling becomes more complex and should provide an answer to the question *what task to execute at what location*, rising the need to schedule tasks that can be executed in a variety of sequences.

Using the example of finishing a multi-storey hotel, there are precedences for the tasks in each room. However, if many rooms are available to be finished, a decision has to be made on the order that the different tasks will be executed in each room on every floor. Thus, the scheduling should focus on which rooms to do first by which crews. The scheduling is then based less on time precedences, and more on issues like the total number of crews working in the same space and the reduction of float time for specialty workers.

A repeating task may also occur at the same location at different time intervals or for different projects. In the services industry, a weekly meeting is a repeating task that occurs at specific time intervals. In manufacturing, tasks on the assembly line are repeating tasks that occur in specific time intervals. For simplicity, in the rest of the presentation of the Visual Scheduling and Management System, the term *location* will mean either physical location at the project site or a specific time interval.

Tasks with a common location within a project make a cluster of tasks. Each cluster of tasks is represented by a quantified bar chart that corresponds to the specific location. Such a quantified bar chart is a *location-specific quantified chart*. The quantified bar chart that shows the construction of a typical floor of a building is a location-specific quantified bar chart (Fig. 3.10). A *location-specific template* is a template that includes a location-specific quantified bar chart and the corresponding data in a spreadsheet format.

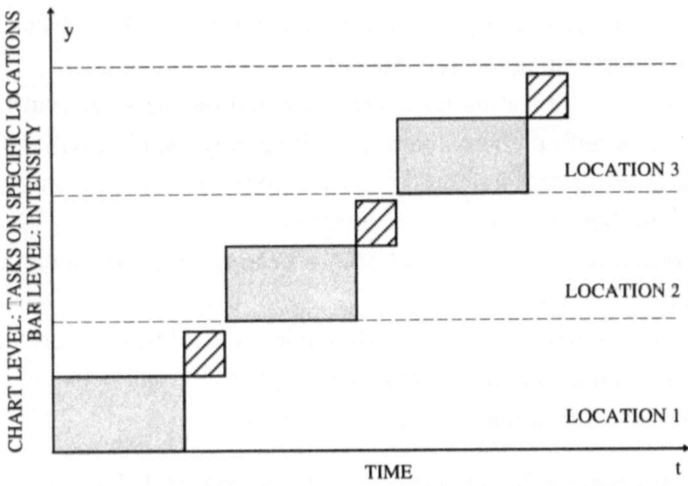

***Fig. 5.1.** The concept of the matrix-balanced chart, indicating its dimensions.*

5.2 THE MATRIX-BALANCED CHART

The *matrix-balanced chart* is used to schedule projects with repeating tasks. Thus, the *matrix-balanced chart* includes the dimension of location, in addition to the dimensions of time and intensity of a simple quantified bar chart (Fig. 5.1). In a *matrix-balanced chart*:

- there are as many location-specific quantified charts as the number of identified locations,
- the location-specific quantified charts are aligned along the time axis, so they share a common time coordinate,
- there is a meaningful progression in horizontal layers of the location-specific quantified charts along the vertical axis,
- if more than one repeating tasks are presented on the same matrix-balanced chart, the task with the maximum intensity at any location will determine the positioning of the tasks along the vertical axis; thus, a repeating task can be visually detached from location to location,
- the quantified bars that represent each repeating task have a common visual identification in all locations,
- the relative starting times and dependencies of the discrete tasks are displayed simultaneously for all locations, and the matrix-balanced schedule is optimal for all locations considered together.

The tasks are represented by quantified bars in the matrix-balanced chart. So, the vertical axis has a triple dimension: at the quantified bar level it indicates the intensity of the tasks; at the layer level it indicates the location of the tasks, and at the chart level it indicates the identity of the tasks. Thus, the matrix-balanced chart is a two-dimensional representation of multi-dimensional information of tasks: their magnitudes, resources, cost, location and time of execution.

5.3 LINE OF THE DIAGONALS

If the repeating tasks are displayed with adjacent quantified bars, the line of the diagonals of the quantified bars represents the slope of the intensity of the repeating task from location to location (Fig. 5.2). If both the quantity and the intensity of a repeated task are the same for all locations, then the diagonals of the quantified bars are aligned along a straight line. However, the matrix-balanced chart is composed of quantified bars with each representing quantity, intensity and duration which, even for the same repeating task, can vary from location to location. So, in general, the diagonals of the quantified bars will not be aligned along a straight line.

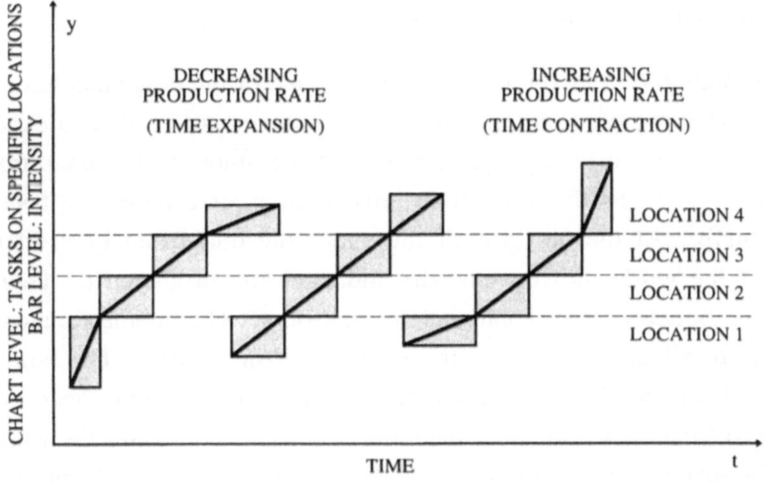

Fig. 5.2. The line of the diagonals for tasks with the same quantity in all locations.

The line of the diagonals is meaningful to the project planner only for repeating tasks that have:

• the same quantity at the considered locations (*i.e.*, Fig. 5.2), or

- the same duration at the considered locations, or
- the same intensity at the considered locations.

If the same quantity is scheduled with a different intensity (and thus a different duration) from location to location, then the line of the diagonals will be curved. An increasing slope line will depict an increasing intensity, while a decreasing slope line will depict a decreasing intensity.

If tasks of different quantity are scheduled to have the same duration, then the line of the diagonals will be curved. An increasing slope line will depict an increasing quantity of work, while a decreasing slope line will depict a decreasing quantity of work.

Finally, if tasks of different quantity are scheduled to have the same intensity, then the line of the diagonals will be curved as well. An increasing slope line will depict a decreasing quantity of work, while a decreasing slope line will depict an increasing quantity of work.

The representation of a learning curve with the line of the diagonals has a special interest. A learning curve implies that less resources are needed to execute the work from location to location, assuming that the amount of work remains the same. Fig. 5.3 shows the alternative presentations of a repeating task with a learning curve. At the left part of the chart, the quantified bars display the quantity of the work and the intensity indicates the production. There is an increase in production from location 1 to location 4. The geometric areas of the rectangles are all the same since the quantity of the work is the same for all locations. However, since the production increases, the duration decreases from location 1 to location 4. So, the same crew of workers completes the work faster, as it can be seen on the right part of Fig. 5.3, where the same tasks are displayed but the intensity is transformed to person-power. The faster execution is not a result of more resources allocated to the task, but of a more efficient execution. Thus, the quantity of the bars depicting person-time decrease from location 1 to location 4, translated to savings in resources and cost.

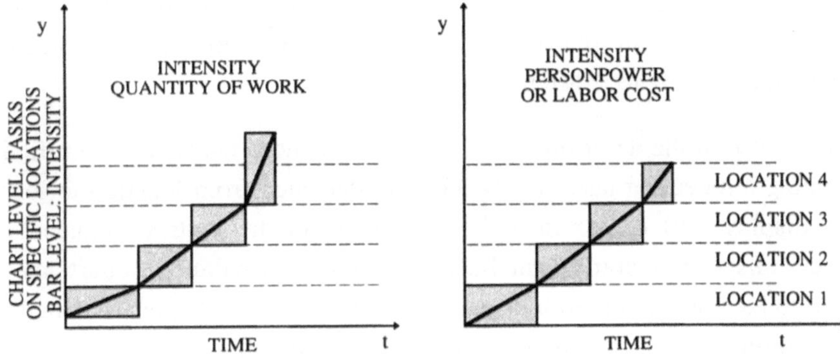

Fig. 5.3. *The line of the diagonals indicating a learning curve from location to location.*

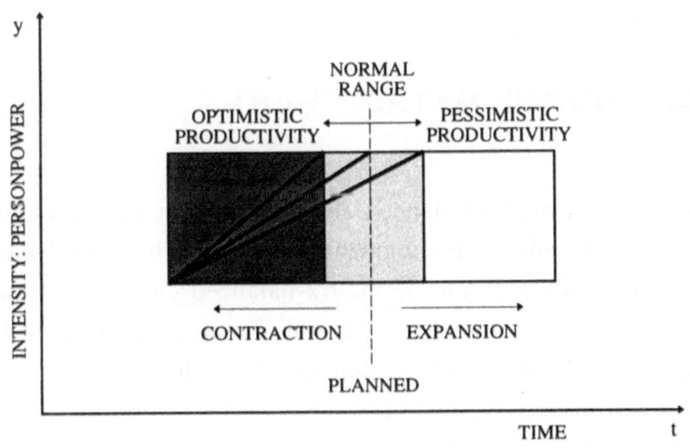

Fig. 5.4. *Productivity and the quantified bar displaying personpower.*

Fig. 5.4 shows the range for estimating the productivity for a task. High productivity means less required resources to execute the task, thus the quantified bar has a smaller area, if it displays person-time. At the same time the slope of the diagonal is steeper, reflecting the increased production rate. On the other hand, a low productivity translates to a larger area of the quantified bar and a lower slope for the diagonal. The quantified bar displays cost, if multiplied by the wage rate. Thus, the difference in size of the quantified bars depicting person-time is translated immediately to a difference in labor cost.

As it was stated in the description of the matrix-balanced chart, the quantified bars representing a repeating task may be visually detached from location to location. Such a display will discontinue the diagonals on the matrix-balanced chart. However, this is not significant because the matrix-balanced chart has been designed to include quantified bars and not their line of the diagonals. Finally, the representation of tasks not related to each other on the same matrix-balanced chart is not recommended.

5.4 BALANCING THE MATRIX CHART

The construction of a matrix-balanced chart starts with the development of the most representative location-specific quantified chart. The other location-specific charts are developed directly on the matrix-balanced chart, as extrapolations of the typical location-specific chart. In general, the quantity of work for the same repeating task could be different at each location. In addition, changes in the amount of required resources could occur even for tasks with the same quantity of work at each location. Fewer resources may be needed at later stages due to learning, or more resources may be needed to compensate for environmental conditions or other delaying causes. So, variations among the location-specific charts are expected and they are handled by quantified bars of different sizes.

The initial assembly of the location-specific quantified charts is just a *matrix of quantified bars*. The time and location interdependencies among the tasks in the various locations require a series of operations for a proper scheduling. These operations constitute the balancing of the matrix of quantified bars to become a *matrix-balanced chart* and they are based on the four basic operations described in Section 3.4. First, as an intermediate step, each repeating task is scheduled to continue at the next location after it is executed in the previous location. This step leads to physical overlapping of tasks and temporary violations of precedences at certain locations. To resolve those issues, the tasks are re-arranged on the chart:

- by moving the tasks along the time axis, preferably within their float,
- by breaking the continuity of tasks,
- by adjusting the duration, and thus the intensity, from location to location,
- and by separating single tasks to multiple tasks and then performing any of the above three operations.

As a general rule, larger tasks have a priority over the smaller tasks and they should be subject to fewer interventions. The breaking of the continuity of tasks can be achieved in two ways: either as a temporary suspension of a particular task, or as a jump to a location other than the physically adjacent location.

The matrix-balanced chart is meaningful and can be used for the scheduling of the tasks, only after it is balanced, *i.e.,* after the necessary time and location re-arrangements of the tasks are executed and there are no more physical overlapping of tasks or violations of precedences.

Example: The scheduling of the finishing of a multi-story hotel is presented as an example of using the matrix-balanced chart, based on the following assumptions:

- the construction of the structural skeleton does not interfere with the finishing of the building,[1]
- the floors from the 3rd to the 12th are identical, and
- each floor contains typical rooms only.

---

[1] An auxiliary chart that provides information on the tasks that have been executed is part of the new system and will be presented in Section 5.6.

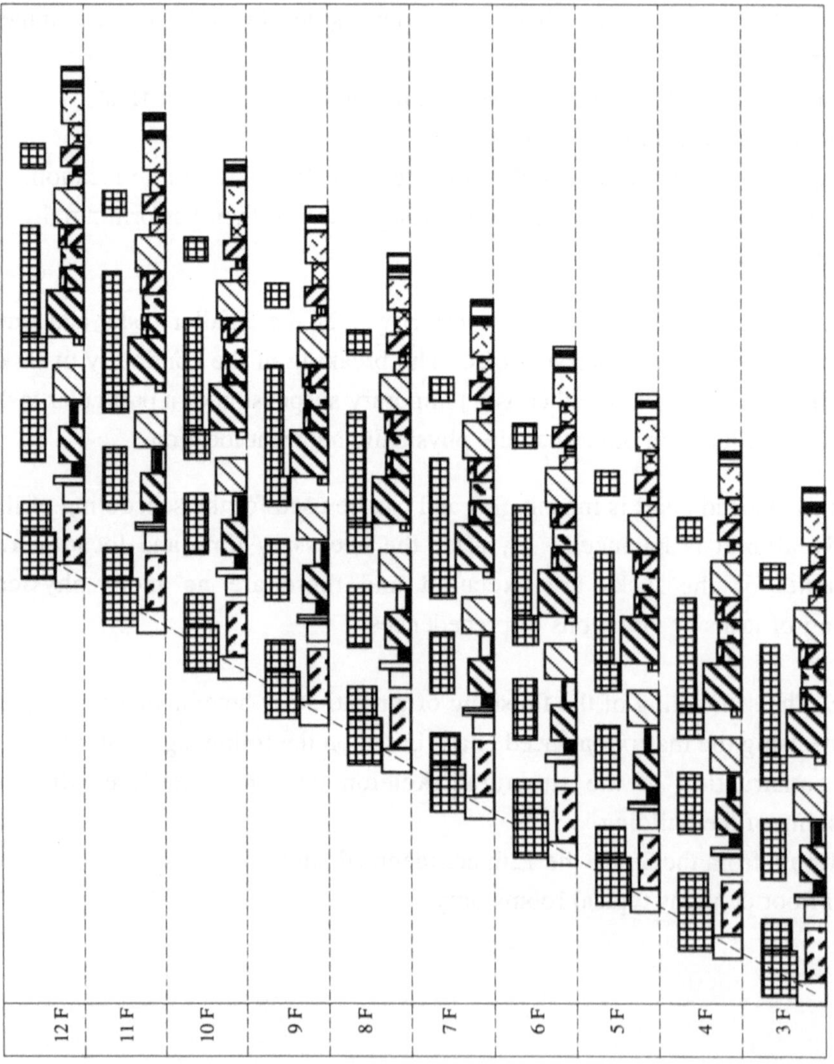

Fig. 5.5. The scheduling of all floors as it would be optimal for each individual floor; intensity personpower.

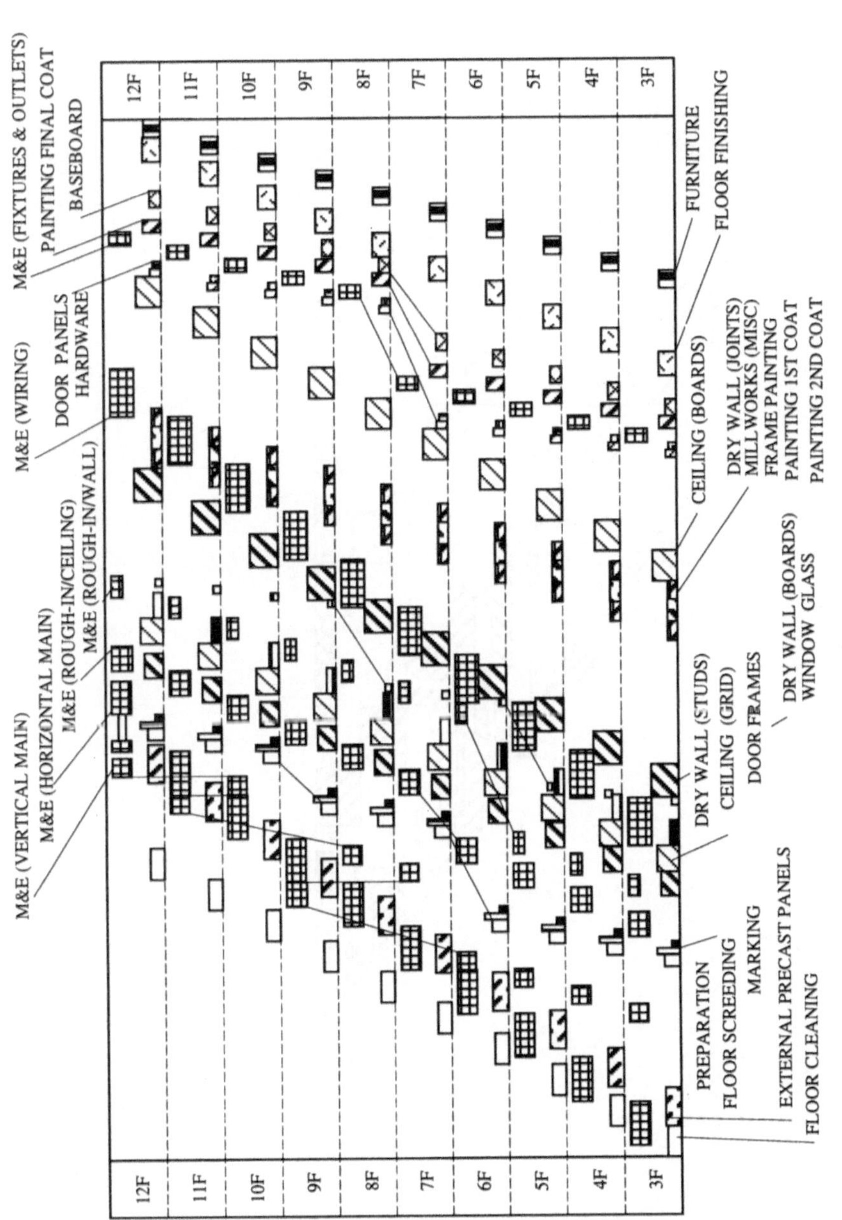

Fig. 5.6. The matrix-balanced chart; intensity personpower.

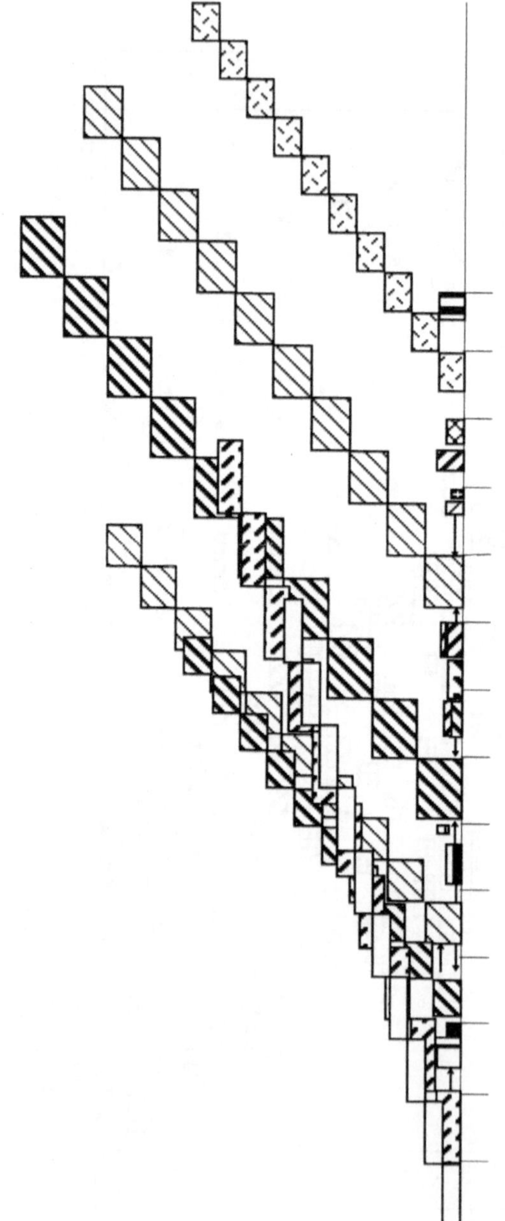

Fig. 5.7. Progression of repeating tasks from location to location; intensity personpower.

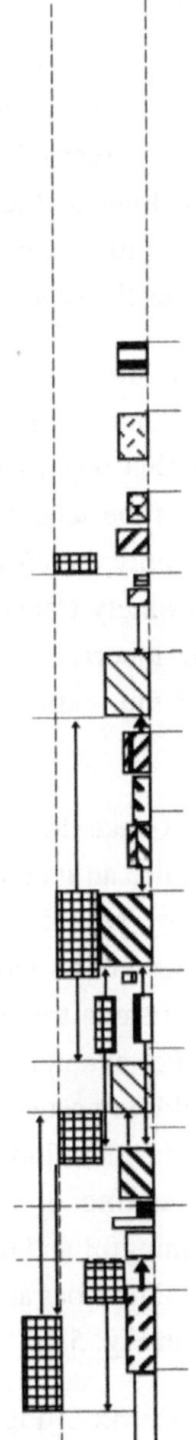

Fig. 5.8. Studies of float time among the tasks; intensity personpower.

The typical location-specific quantified bar chart was developed as an example of a quantified bar chart with loose dependencies in Section 3.4, shown in Fig. 3.21. According to the constraints and the criteria presented in Section 3.4, that location-specific quantified chart presents a best schedule for the finishing of a single floor, considered in isolation to the rest of the building. However, that schedule cannot be applied for the finishing of the complete building. This is demonstrated in Fig. 5.5, where the scheduling of the 3rd to the 12th floors of the building is presented in a similar manner as the scheduling of the typical floor.

The delay in starting each floor above the 3rd floor serves a dual purpose. First, to delay the finishing in the upper floors, assuming that the structural skeleton is still in progress. Second, to move the crew that installs the mechanical and electrical main ducts from one floor to the other. If the scheduling of the complete building would follow the chart of Fig. 5.5, then only the crew that installs the mechanical and electrical main ducts would have a timely transition from floor to floor. The sequencing of all other tasks would be incorrect. The tasks that take a shorter time to execute than the installation of the main ducts would have a consistent time lag from floor to floor.

Even more problematic, the tasks that take longer time to execute than the installation of the main ducts would require an increase of resources from floor to floor, up to a certain floor. Then, they would require a gradual decrease of resources for the rest of the floors. These tasks would not be leveled and there would be times that several crews of the same trade would be needed to work in the building for the same type of task. For example, according to the matrix chart of Fig. 5.5, up to 6 different crews would be needed for mechanical and electrical work. Thus, the planner taking into consideration the interdependencies of the repeating tasks, must correct the scheduling of this chart. After a series of balancing operations, the result is a meaningful and optimal distribution of tasks in the various floors, that systematizes the time float and avoids peaks and valleys in the demand for the resources, as shown in Fig. 5.6.

Fig. 5.6 is constructed by balancing the matrix of Fig. 5.5, following the procedure that was described earlier in this section. First, each repeating task is scheduled to continue to the higher floor after it finishes in the previous floor, as shown in

Fig. 5.7.[2] In the following step, the vertical dimension of location is re-established by separating the repeating tasks on the display and the float between repeating tasks is examined, as shown in Fig. 5.8. Finally, the physical overlapping of tasks and the violations of precedences are balanced (Fig. 5.6):

- *Translation of the tasks along the time axis.* The joints of the dry walls, the milling works and the painting (except for the final painting) are grouped together and they are scheduled with the criterion to continue immediately after the gypsum boards are installed on the 12th floor. Their rate of progression from floor to floor determines their starting time on the first floor. Since these tasks progress faster than the installation of the gypsum boards there is a float between these tasks on the first floor. The float shortens from floor to floor and vanishes on the 12th floor.
  Looking at another pair of tasks, the installation of the ceiling boards follows the completion of painting on the first floor. However, the rate of progression of the installation of ceiling boards from floor to floor is slower than painting and that creates an increasing float on the floors, with the largest float on the 12th floor. Similarly, the translation of all the repeating tasks along the time axis of the matrix can be explained.

- *Break of the continuity of tasks.* The installation of mechanical and electrical floor ducts jumps from the 6th floor to the 9th floor in order not to coincide with the crew that installs the main vertical mechanical and electrical ducts on the 7th floor. Then it continues to the 7th, 8th, 11th, 10th and 12th floors. After the installation of window glasses in the 5th floor, this relatively short task is interrupted. The installation of the window glasses at the 6th floor continues much later, after the crew is inactive at this project for a certain time period. This period of inactivity is part of the plan and it does not generate a problem because the crew is a specialized subcontractor.

---

2   Figure 5.7 demonstrates the need for keeping the location well-defined along the vertical axis. In Figure 5.7 the quantified bars representing a specific repeating task were positioned to be adjacent and have a common corner, in order to define their progression from floor to floor. However, immediately after this usage, the convention on the representation of the location should be reinstated, in order to create a readable chart.

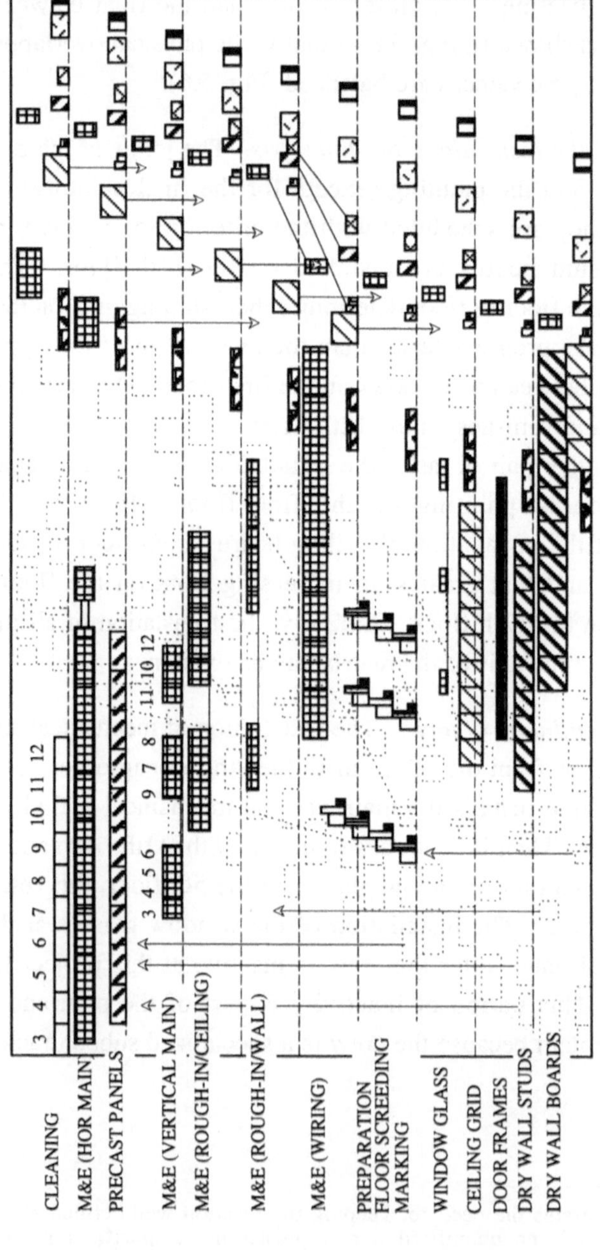

Fig. 5.9. Translation of the tasks along the vertical axis in order to develop the constituent matrix chart; intensity personpower.

- *Adjustments in personpower, and thus in duration, from location to location.* This procedure was not followed in this example, although it could be effective. An increase in the intensity of the installation of the ceiling boards or a decrease in the intensity of painting (frame, 1st and 2nd coat) could have shorten the total duration of the project (Fig. 5.6). However, such changes were not applied on the chart due to a specific availability of resources.

5.5 CONSTITUENT MATRIX CHART

By definition, the vertical axis of a matrix-balanced chart indicates location. All the tasks on the same location are displayed on the same horizontal zone within the chart, corresponding to the location-specific quantified chart. Each location-specific quantified chart includes tasks of different constituencies, identifiable by different visual codes, such as hatching, color or text. A reversal of order between constituency and location along the vertical axis can produce a useful chart, after the balancing of the matrix chart. Such a reversal is achieved by vertical translations of the quantified bars so that each repeating task is separated and it appears on the same horizontal zone. Following these translations, the vertical axis indicates the constituency of each task and the tasks at each location are identified by visual codes. The shape of the quantified bars and their positioning along the time axis remain the same after the transformation. Fig. 5.9 presents the process of the transformation of the matrix-balanced chart of Fig. 5.6 to create a *constituent matrix chart.* The left part of the figure shows the quantified bars in their new position, while their original positions are indicated by ghost images. Vertical arrows connect the ghost images with the final position, to indicate the procedure. The right part of Fig. 5.6 is not transformed yet.

The transformed representation provides the schedule of each repeating task, which is useful for communication and monitoring. However, it is a derivative chart that does not have the power to produce a schedule, as the matrix-balanced chart. A conversion of the quantified bars to connoting bars, *i.e.*, a visual suppression of their intensity, produces a connoted bar chart. However, this connoted bar chart does not contain visually the information on why the scheduling has been done in the way that it is presented.

5.6 MONITORING DIFFERENT LOCATIONS

The monitoring of the actual execution of the tasks on a matrix-balanced chart follows the same concept of the mate quantified bars, as discussed in Section 2.3 for monitoring with the quantified bars and Section 4.4 for monitoring with templates. However, additional control is needed for the matrix-balanced chart, both for planning and for monitoring.[3]

The matrix-balanced chart is built on the assumption that resources can move to different locations to execute a task. However, the infrastructure for executing the tasks may not be ready at all the available locations. Thus, an auxiliary chart that monitors the progress of the various tasks should accompany the matrix-balanced charts, especially when applied to tasks with loose precedences. This chart, shown in Fig. 5.10, provides visual information on the availability at the various locations to host the execution of tasks.

---

[3]   An example of the control matrix-balanced chart is presented in Chapter 9, Fig. 9.18.

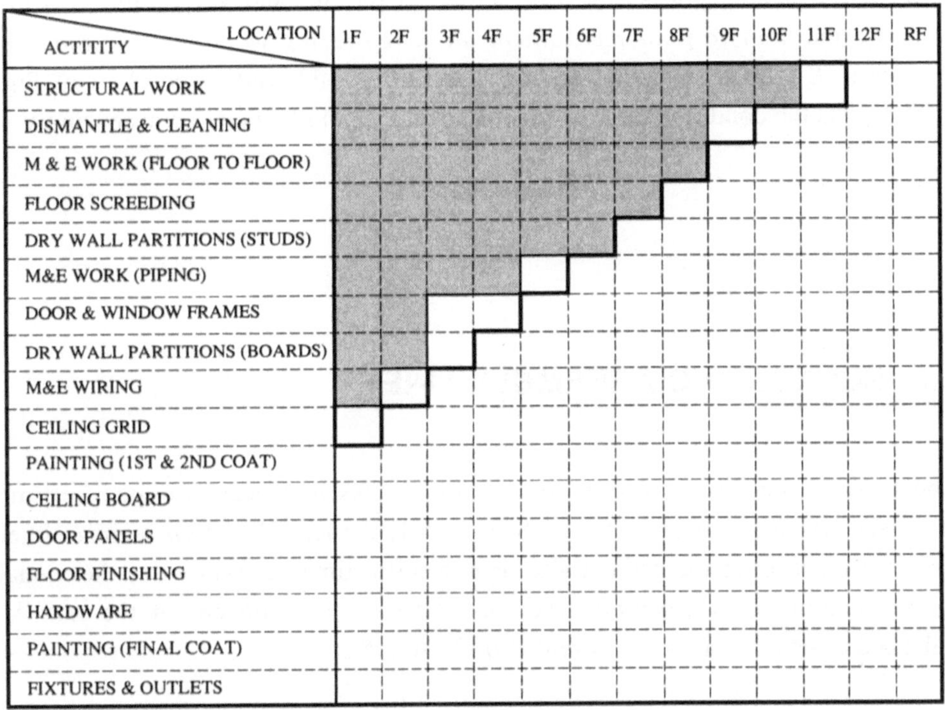

Fig. 5.10. Auxiliary monitoring chart.

In the auxiliary monitoring chart, the horizontal axis indicates the location, while the vertical axis lists the tasks to be executed at each location. The tasks are sorted according to precedence, even if those precedences are loosely defined. The first task to be executed at each location is listed at the top, while the last task to be executed is at the bottom of the list. The bold line in the chart indicates the boundary of eligibility. Only the locations left of the bold line are eligible for the execution of each task. This boundary is defined by the execution of the top task in the list and the precedences among the tasks. The gray coloring of the squares of the matrix indicates that the specific task at the specific location has been executed. Thus, in the example of Fig. 5.10, the *structure work* has been completed up to the 10th floor. A space between the vertical bold line and the gray colored square, indicates that the specific task can be executed at those floors. As an example, the *ceiling grid* can be constructed on the 1st floor and the *door and window frames* can be installed in the 3rd and 4th floors. On the contrary, the *floor to floor mechanical and engineering work* and the *studs for the dry wall partitions* cannot be executed and should wait. The chart of Fig. 5.10 depicts the condition on a specific date and should be updated accordingly.

5.7 SCHEDULING ASSEMBLY LINES

The tasks in the assembly line are repeating tasks that occur in specific time intervals. As it has been stated in Section 5.1, the term *location* means either physical location at the project site or a specific time interval. So, the visual representation of an assembly line should follow the concept of the matrix-balanced chart that has been presented in Section 5.2.

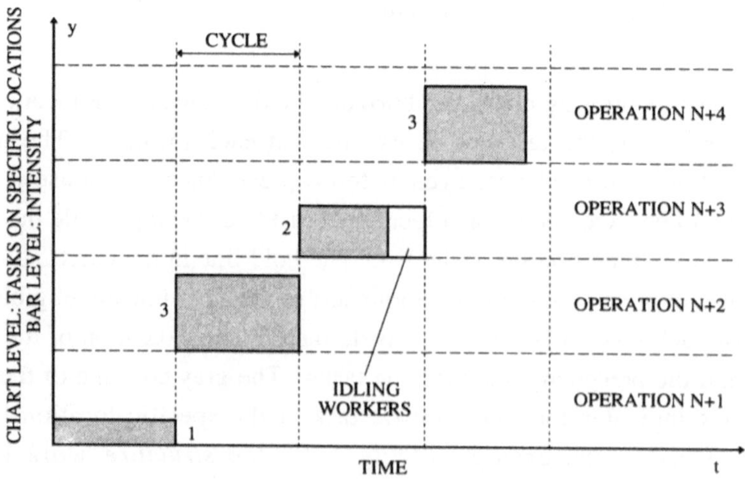

Fig. 5.11.   *Visualization of the assembly line — operations for the manufacturing of a single object.*

Fig. 5.11 represents 4 sequential operations for the assembly of a single object, using quantified bars. The timing of all the operations is equal, to allow the flow of the objects from one operation to another. The labor requirements for each operation are different. The n+1 operation requires one worker who is occupied for the full cycle of the operation, thus ensuring 100% occupancy. Similarly, the n+2 operation requires 3 workers for the full cycle. The other two operations, however, do not occupy the workers for the whole cycle. The n+3 operation requires 2 workers for 70% of the allocated time, and the n+4 operation requires one worker for 80% of the allocated time. The area on the right part of each quantified bar until the end of the cycle of the operation indicates visually the idling work force. In Fig. 5.11, for illustrative purposes, the idling person-time of the idling workers in the n+3 operation is depicted visually with an outlined quantified bar. Among the design objectives of an assembly line is the reduction if not the elimination of any idling person-time.

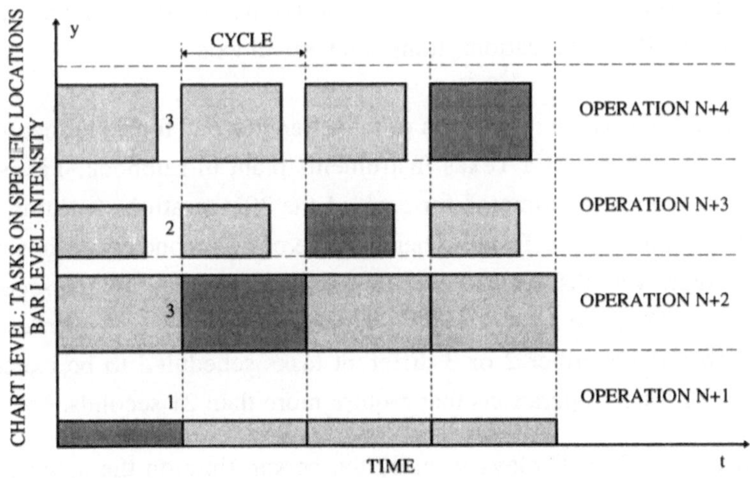

Fig. 5.12. Visualization of the assembly line — multiple operations.

A major difference between the scheduling of the assembly line and the matrix-balanced chart, as presented in Section 5.1, is the assignment of resources. In the matrix-balanced chart the scheduling is based on the assumption that the resources move from location to location. Thus, a certain continuity must be established. In an assembly line, on the other hand, there are different objects that continuously pour into the process and the resources are assigned to specific operations that have a specific time cycle. Thus, the visualization of the assembly line, at any time, is closer to the depiction of Fig. 5.12. All operations proceed simultaneously and there are as many objects on the assembly line, as there are operations.

A simplified and more meaningful representation of the assembly line focuses on monitoring a single object being manufactured from the beginning to the end of the process. Assuming that the process has n operations and the allocated time for every operation is t, then the time length to depict the whole process is equal to nxt. This is derived from Fig. 5.11 by eliminating the dimension of location or, equivalently, by compressing the vertical axis. An alternative representation of the assembly line could capture the n operations of the process for a single cycle. Thus, the duration of the observation would be equal to the duration of a single operation of the process, and the different operations could be displayed using quantified bars as different locations along the vertical axis.

Example. Table 5.1 lists the operations of the assembly line for manufacturing the TI-500 electronic watches at a Texas Instruments plant in Lubbock, Texas.[4] The required person-time was estimated for each of the 30 operations (column B) and it is given in column C of the Table. Then, a cycle of 21 seconds was chosen and a number of workers was assigned to execute each operation within 21 seconds, as shown in column D of the same Table. The assignment of 2 or 3 workers in the same operation reflects either 2 or 3 different tasks scheduled to be executed in that operation, or longer operations that require more than 21 seconds.

The top part of Fig. 5.13 displays visually the person-time on the assembly line. Each quantified bar represents a single operation with the horizontal axis depicting time and the vertical axis depicting the number of workers assigned to the operation. Thus, the area of each quantified bar depicts the required person-time for the represented task. This representation scheme follows the suggestion

---

4   Source: *Texas Instruments-Time Products Division*, Harvard Business School case study No. 9-677-043, revised 6/3/91.

to focus on a single object as it is manufactured (*i.e.*, Fig. 5.11) and to compress the vertical axis.

Table 5.1. Assembly flow, time estimates and personnel requirements for final assembly of the TI-500 electronic watch.

A	B	C	D	E
No.	Operation	Person-time (sec)	workers initially	workers balanced line
1	Prepare module	20	2	1
2	Functional test-module	21	2	1
3	Frequency test-module	21	1	1
4	Scrape novalac off the switch contacts	20	1	1
5	Clip one post from module	18	1	1
6	Apply static resistant tape on module	14	1	1
7	Remove tape tab cover	16	1	1
8	Heat-stake lens to bezel	21	2	1
9	Inspect bezel and deburr switch holes	41	3	2
10	Clean switch holes (air nozzle)	11	1	1
11	Install and press set switch in bezel and clean	18	1	1
12	Install and press command switch in bezel and clean	18	1	1
13	Check switch travel	12	1	1
14	Clean inside bezel using air nozzle	12	1	1
15	Install module in bezel	21	?	1
16	Install battery clip on module	20	2	1
17	Heat-stake battery clip on module	15	1	1
18	Install two batteries in module	21	2	1
19	Switch check (light up)	10	1	1
20	Date-code inside of watch back	10	1	1
21	Place O-ring on flange on watch back	14	1	1
22	Install back on watch	15	1	1
23	Functional test-watch	21	2	1
24	Install band on watch	42	3	2
25	Cosmetic inspection and clean	17	1	1
26	Final test/Quality control	35	2	2
27	Place watch on cuff and buckle band	36	2	2
28	Place watch and cuff in display box	19	1	1
29	Apply label and place cover on display box case	14	1	1
30	Place manual inside box and place box in tub	30	2	2
	Total	*603*	*44*	*35*

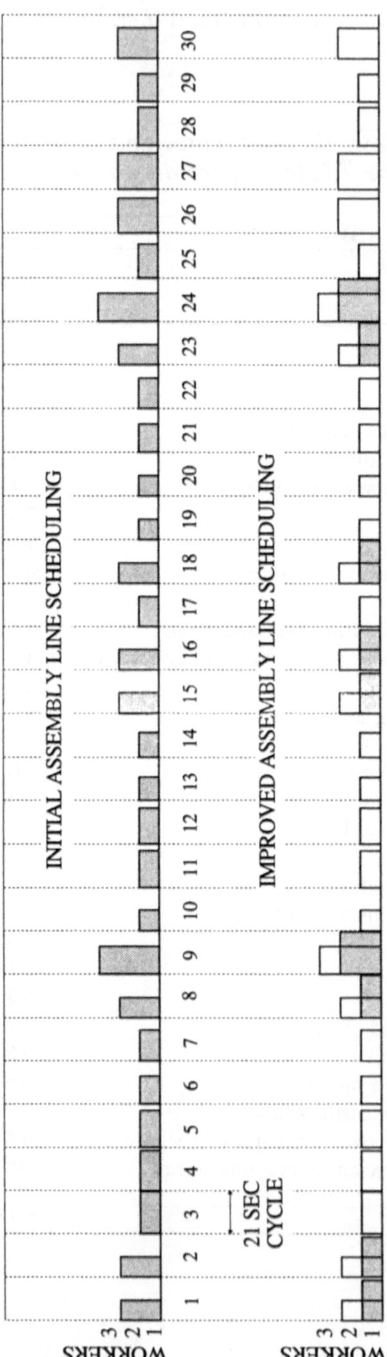

Fig. 5.13. Visualization of the personpower in the assembly line for manufacturing the TI-500 electronic watch.

After several months of operations and further studies on the assembly line, a more balanced distribution of personpower was chosen that increased the efficiency of the assembly line from 65% to 82%. The number of workers was reduced in operations 1, 2, 8, 9, 15, 16, 18, 23, and 24, either by requiring a single worker to execute 2 different tasks, within the time limit of 21 seconds, or by assigning the work of 3 workers to 2. Column E of Table 5.1 presents the new labor assignments and the lower part of Fig. 5.13 shows visually the same information. The quantified bars in gray depict the operations that have been changed, while the outlined quantified bars depict the original design of the assembly line.

In addition to personpower, quantified bars could be used to indicate the use of equipment, materials, or expenditures in an assembly line or in other manufacturing processes.

CHAPTER 6

HIERARCHICAL REPRESENTATION

This is the last chapter that describes the Visual Scheduling and Management System. The components of the system that were presented in the Chapters 2, 3, 4 and 5 are related together to assemble the new system for the scheduling and management of an entire project.

Section 6.1 defines the folding-up procedure that connects the different quantified charts of the system. Particular emphasis is given on the folding-up of tasks of a different constituency that require similar resources. Such a folding-up is necessary for building the hierarchical structure of the system at the higher levels. In Section 6.2, the hierarchical structure is presented in detail, together with the definitions of the microtemplate schedules, the template schedules, the matrix-balanced schedules and the master schedule. In the same section, an example drives the reader through the development of a microtemplate schedule, a template schedule and a matrix-balanced schedule, all inter-related. Section 6.3 presents the mechanism for changes in the scheduling of the project and how these changes can be introduced at the different levels of the hierarchical system. Finally, Section 6.4 describes the use of the system for monitoring the execution of a project: the collection of data from the field and the representation of these data on the various charts.

6.1 FOLDING-UP

A group of tasks displayed on a quantified bar chart can be aggregated to form a *folded-up task*. The folded-up task is used to represent that group of tasks in another quantified chart at a higher level. The folded-up task has the following properties:

- The folded-up task is represented by a single quantified bar.
- The starting time of the folded-up task is the starting time of the first (in terms of time) task among the tasks that they are aggregated; the ending time of the aggregate task is the ending time of the last (in terms of time) task among the tasks that they are aggregated.
- The work of the folded-up task is the summation of the work of all the tasks that have been aggregated to form the folded-up task.
- The folded-up task includes all the types of resources found in all the tasks that have been aggregated to form the folded-up task.
- Each resource of the folded-up task is the summation of that type of resources from all the tasks that have been aggregated to form the folded-up task.
- The folded-up task includes all the types of costs of resources found in all the tasks that have been aggregated to form the folded-up task.
- Each cost per resource of the folded-up task is the summation of the costs of that type of resource from all the tasks that have been aggregated to form the folded-up task.
- The total cost of the folded-up task is the summation of the total cost of all the tasks that have been aggregated to form the folded-up task.

A group of tasks that represent different types of work can be aggregated as well. In that case, the work of the folded-up task is *heterogeneous*, composed of works of different constituency, which is not as meaningful as a *homogeneous task*. However, the main purpose of such a folding-up is the aggregation of the resources and the associated costs. As shown in the template for the construction of a typical floor (Fig. 4.1), tasks of different constituency can be included in the same template. The displayed intensity is personpower, which is common to all the tasks in the template. So, the folded-up task in that template is displayed with the intensity of personpower. This folded-up task can be used as a single quantified bar to make charts at a higher level. Furthermore, a common denominator for all tasks is cost and all tasks can be aggregated on the basis of cost.

Most likely, the aggregate task will have a *variable intensity* corresponding to the summation of the intensities of the discrete tasks. However, the aggregate task is more meaningful to be presented with a *constant intensity*, so the quantified bar of the folded-up task is rectangular. Simplicity of the quantified bar charts at the higher level is one reason for such a recommendation. The second reason is to avoid details at the higher levels that may be deceiving. The choice to represent a folded-up task as a constant intensity task introduces a certain level of abstraction. Although every effort should be made to estimate each quantity as accurately as possible, the elimination of the details of the discrete tasks at a higher level of representation acknowledges the volatile nature of project scheduling. In any case, the information on the tasks that make the folded-up task is an inherited property of the folded-up task and it is always accessible to the user.

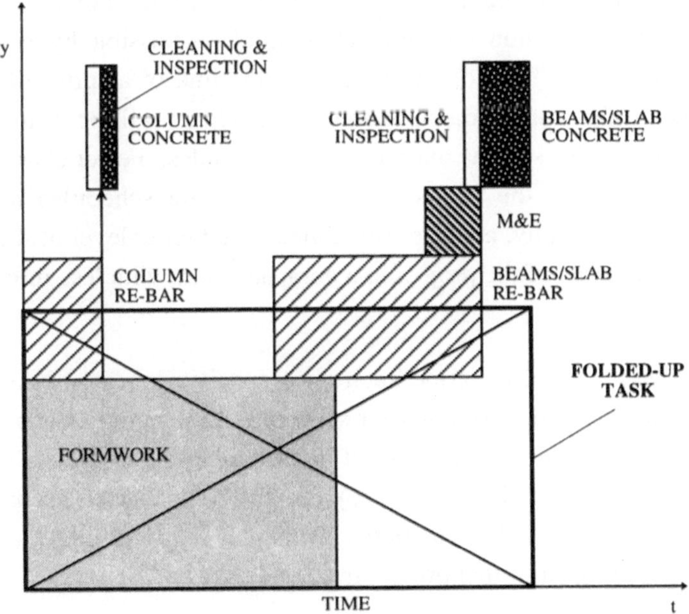

Fig. 6.1. Folding-up of a quantified bar chart, intensity personpower.

Example: The folded-up task of the tasks of the quantified bar chart of Fig. 3.10 is shown in Fig. 6.1. This new task of constant intensity can be used as a single task in a quantified bar chart at a higher level or in a matrix-balanced chart.

6.2 DESCRIPTION OF THE HIERARCHICAL SYSTEM

A quantified bar chart, a template and a matrix-balance chart are *quantified charts.*

Each quantified chart can contain a large number of tasks. However, it is impractical to include many tasks in a single quantified chart. The proposed system integrates the schedule in a hierarchical structure, as shown in Fig. 6.2, in order to make the presentation at each level as simple as possible by displaying the necessary information only. Folding-up allows the link of a series of quantified charts to schedule the same project. Some of the charts will be at a lower level showing specific details, such as microtemplate schedules. Fewer charts will show an aggregate picture of the project, such as template schedules and matrix-balanced schedules. Finally, a master schedule at the higher level of the hierarchy will include all the tasks of the project in a compact form, with less information on details.

Each chart serves a specific scope such as a specific job schedule, a weekly schedule, a monthly schedule or a master schedule. Depending on the complexity of the project, the number of the required microtemplates, templates and matrix-balanced charts varies. Furthermore, projects that do not include repeating tasks should not include matrix-balanced charts. Finally, a single template schedule can represent an entire project, if that project is composed of a few tasks.

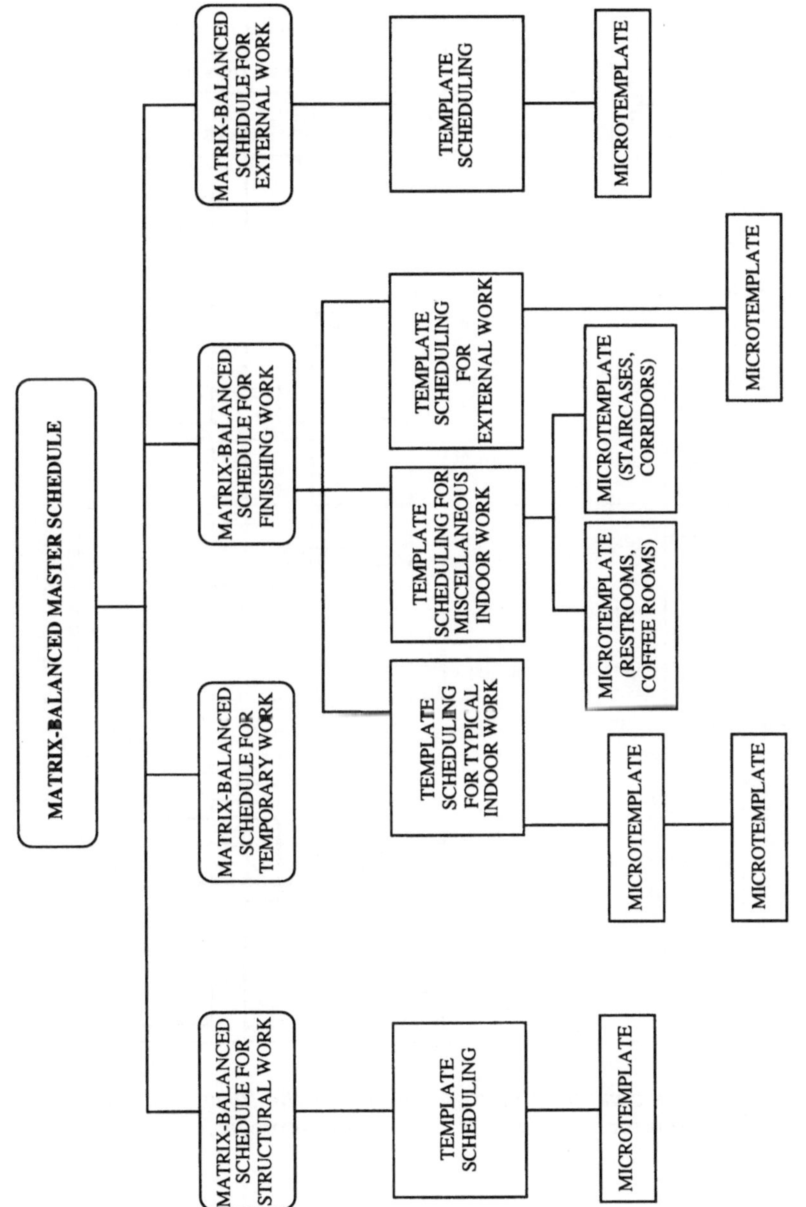

Fig. 6.2. *The hierarchical structure of the Visual Scheduling and Management System; application construction.*

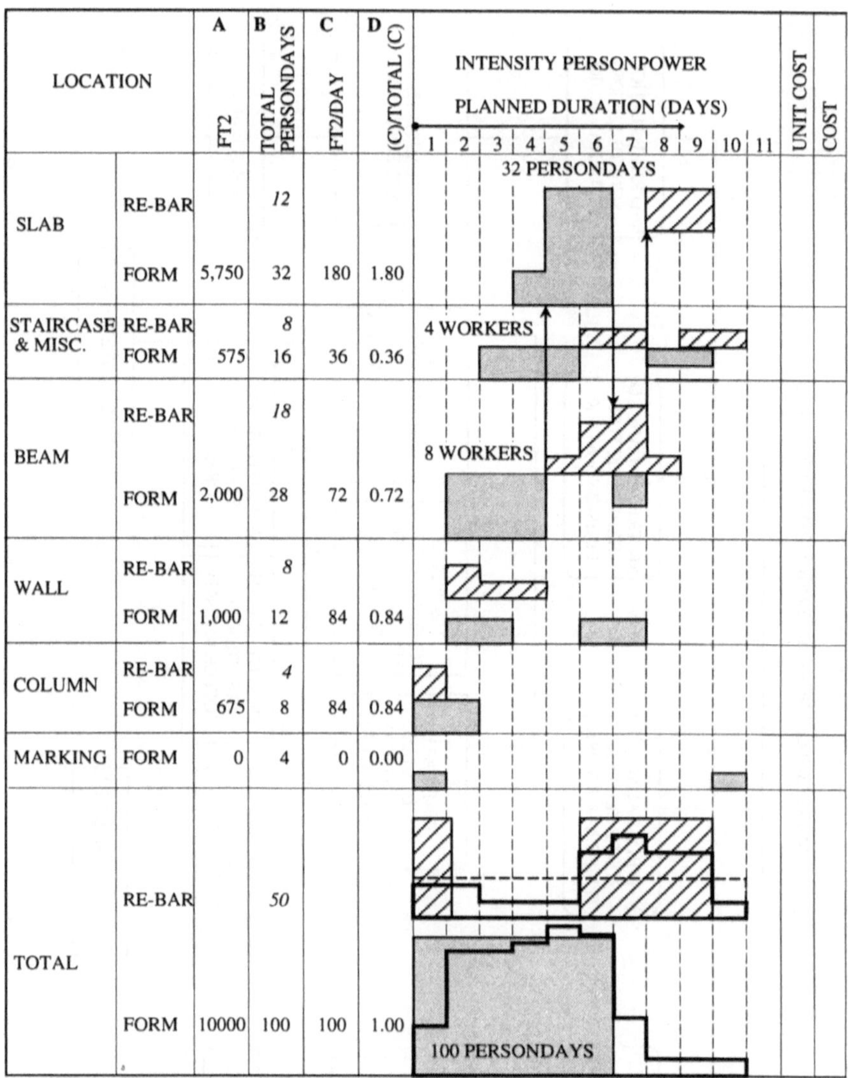

Fig. 6.3. The combined microtemplate for the formwork and reinforcing bars, intensity personpower.

6.2.1 Microtemplate Schedules

A *microtemplate schedule* consists of a template with tasks of the same constituency. As a result, the folded-up task of a microtemplate is a homogeneous task. The microtemplate is at the lowest levels of the hierarchy and serves a dual purpose. First, to make a schedule of a specific scope, to schedule and control a specific job. Second, to produce a folded-up task which, together with discrete tasks or folded-up tasks from other microtemplates, will make a quantified chart at a higher level. Such a chart could be another microtemplate, a quantified bar chart, a template, or a matrix-balanced chart.

Example: In chapter 3, it was shown in detail and for demonstration purposes how to construct the template of Fig. 4.1 with direct entries during planning. However, it is more accurate to accept that the 4 tasks shown in that template are folded-up tasks from microtemplates.

Fig. 6.3 shows the microtemplate for two of the four tasks: the positioning of the reinforcement and the building of the formwork for the various components of the structural skeleton of a typical floor. Both tasks are shown together because of their interdependencies, thus producing a combined microtemplate. The tasks are broken down to subtasks for the building of the floor: the slab, the stairways and other miscellaneous elements, the beams, the walls, the columns, and the marking. The first two columns contain the names of the tasks. Column A contains the quantity of work for each task for the formwork, while the quantities of the reinforcing bars have not been entered. Column B contains the total required persondays for each subtask. Columns C and D show the number of workers in the crew and their productivity, which is different for each subtask. The next column contains the quantified bars, and the last two columns contain the cost for each subtask. Detailed planning and expertise in breaking down the project to these low level tasks are necessary to prepare this microtemplate. An effort is made to level the resources during the development of the microtemplate. The last row contains the folded-up tasks for both the positioning of reinforcement and the building of the formwork. The folded-up tasks are shown in a dark line outline with variable intensities. Following the suggestion presented in Section 6.1 the folded-up tasks are converted to constant intensity quantified bars. These tasks contain sufficient information, given the uncertainty of the whole process and become the target to reach. However, deviations from these quantified bars are expected to occur during execution. The rectangular folded-up quantified bars are then imported as two discrete tasks in the template shown in Fig. 4.1.

6.2.2 Template Schedules

A *template schedule* consists of a quantified bar chart or a template with tasks of different type of work. The tasks shown on a template are either single tasks or folded-up tasks from microtemplates and other templates. The aggregation of the discrete tasks to a folded-up task focuses on specific resources and cost. Often, the intensity of the tasks in a template shows the required personpower, which is usually the most critical resource for planning and control. If the intensity shows personpower, then the quantity of the task represents the total person-time necessary to complete the task, which is an alternative measure of the quantity of work for a task.

There can be several levels of templates in a single branch of the hierarchical structure of the system. The folded-up tasks from the higher level templates compose the quantified bars for the matrix-balanced chart for projects with repeating tasks. If the project does not include repeating tasks, the folded-up tasks of the higher level templates make the master schedule template (Fig. 6.4).

For a typical building construction project with repeating tasks, such as shown in Fig. 6.2, there are six higher level template schedules:
- template schedule for temporary work,
- template schedule for the structural skeleton,
- template schedule for the skin of the building,
- template schedule for typical inside work,
- template schedule for external finishing work, and
- template schedule for miscellaneous inside work.

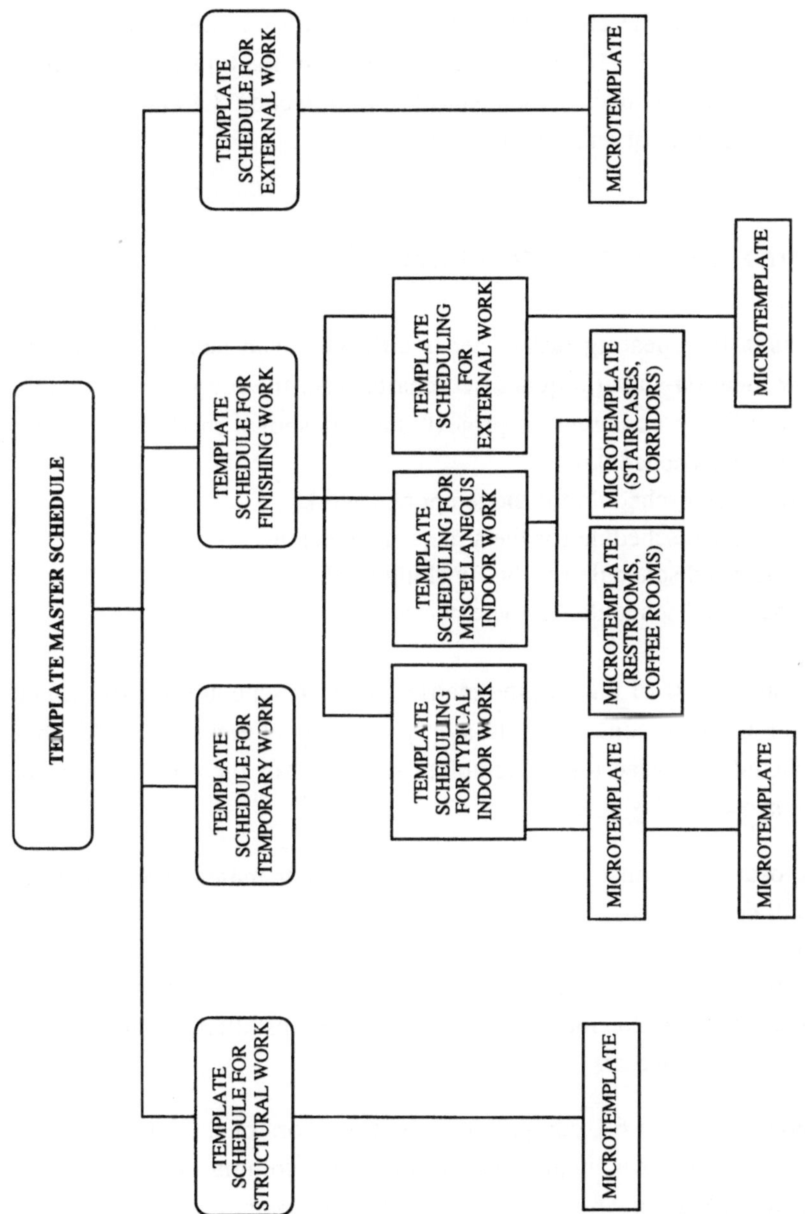

Fig. 6.4. The hierarchical structure of the Visual Scheduling and Management System for a project without repeating tasks.

The template scheduling for the structural skeleton of a typical floor has been shown in Fig. 4.1 and the example of making it from microtemplates has been presented in Section 6.2.1. The template scheduling for the typical inside work for a representative floor has been presented in detail in Section 3.4 and shown in Fig. 3.16 to 3.21, in the form of quantified bar charts.

6.2.3 Matrix-Balanced Schedules

Only projects with repeating tasks need matrix-balanced schedules, which are composed by location-specific quantified charts from the higher level templates. For a typical building construction project, such as shown in Fig. 6.2, there are four matrix-balanced schedules:
- matrix-balanced schedule for the temporary work,
- matrix-balanced schedule for the structural skeleton,
- matrix-balanced schedule for the finishing work, and
- matrix-balanced schedule for the external work.

Example: The process of making the matrix-balanced schedule for the structural skeleton of a reinforced concrete multi-storey building, is presented. This matrix-balanced schedule is based on the template schedule for the construction of the typical floor, shown in Fig. 4.1.

For the purpose of demonstrating the process, the four major tasks for building each floor will be considered:
- the making of the formwork,
- the positioning of the reinforcing bars,
- the preparations for the mechanical and electrical installations, and
- the placing of concrete.

The data shown in Table 6.1 compare the various floors of the building with the typical floor. The top rows include the titles for each column. Columns A and B include the identification of each floor and its corresponding area. Column C shows the ratio of the area of each floor over the typical floor. The 7th floor, with 5,000 ft^2 has been chosen as the typical floor and the corresponding row is shown in bold characters.

Table 6.1. *Data for the various floors of the building, task concrete.*

FLOOR DATA			CONCRETE WORK				
A	B	C	D	E	F	G	H
FLOOR	AREA (FT^2)	RATIO OF AREA TO TYPICAL FLOOR	CONCRETE (FT^3)	AVERAGE CONCRETE THICKNESS (FT)	PRODUCTION PER PERSONDAY (FT^3)	TOTAL PERSONPOWER	RATIO PERSONPOWER TO TYPICAL FLOOR
ROOF	2,000	0.4	2,000	1	330	6	0.30
12F	5,000	1	8,000	1.6	400	20	1.00
11F	5,000	1	8,000	1.6	400	20	1.00
10F	5,000	1	8,000	1.6	400	20	1.00
9F	5,000	1	8,000	1.6	400	20	1.00
8F	5,000	1	8,000	1.6	400	20	1.00
7F	**5,000**	**1**	**8,000**	**1.6**	**400**	**20**	**1.00**
6F	5,000	1	8,000	1.6	400	20	1.00
5F	5,000	1	8,000	1.6	400	20	1.00
4F	5,000	1	8,000	1.6	400	20	1.00
3F	5,000	1	8,000	1.6	400	20	1.00
2F	10,000	2	18,000	1.8	467	39	1.93
1F	10,000	2	18,000	1.8	467	39	1.93
B1F	10,000	2	20,000	2	467	43	2.14
B2F	10,000	2	20,000	2	467	43	2.14
FND	10,000	2	26,000	2.6	667	39	1.95
TOTAL	*102,000*	*20.4*	*184,000*	*1.80*	*451*	*408*	*20.39*
					ASSUME & MONITOR	ASSUME & MONITOR	

Columns D, E, F, G and H refer to the task of placing concrete:

- Column D shows the quantity of work for each floor.
- Column E shows the ratio of column D over column B and represents an average thickness of concrete per floor area!
- Column F shows the estimated productivity for each floor. This productivity is provided by the project planner, it is subjective and it will be monitored during the execution of the project (as stated in the last two rows).

- Column G shows the required manpower, for the work shown in column D and assuming the productivity of column F.
- Column H shows the ratio of the required manpower for each floor over the typical floor.

The row entitled *TOTAL* shows the summation or the average value of the data in the rows above. So, reading from column B to column H:
- the total area of the building is 102,000 ft^2,
- the building is 20.4 times larger than the typical floor,
- it will need 184,000 ft^3 of concrete,
- with an average thickness of 1.8 ft of concrete per square foot of area,
- the average productivity is estimated to be 451 ft^3 per person-day,
- 408 person-days of work are required,
- which represents 20.4 times the required work for construction of the typical floor.

Similarly, in Table 6.2, columns I, J, K, L and M refer to the making of the formwork; columns N, O, P, Q and R refer to the positioning of the reinforcing bars; and columns S and T in Table 6.3 refer to the mechanical and electrical preparations. The quantity of work of the mechanical and electrical preparations is omitted intentionally, since it is not quantifiable. Since the quantity of the work cannot be established, a productivity cannot be established either. So, the project planner estimates directly the required person-time, shown in column S and derives the ratio over the typical floor in column T.

Columns U, V, W, X, Y, Z, AA and AB present aggregate data:
- Column U shows the total person-days required for all four tasks.
- Column V shows an average ratio of required persons-days of each floor over the required persons-days of the typical floor.
- In column W the project planner decides that the overall work on the typical floor should be 10 days. This decision is based on the more detailed study of the corresponding template for the construction of the typical floor (Fig. 4.1). Based on the ratios of the floor area (column C), the rest of the cells of column W are filled. The total duration of the project is calculated at the bottom of column W to be 204 working days.
- In column X, a similar operation as in column W is repeated, based on the making of formwork (ratios of column M).

Table 6.2. *Data for the various floors of the building, tasks formwork and reinforcing bars.*

A	FORMWORK					REINFORCING BARS				
A	I	J	K	L	M	N	O	P	Q	R
FLOOR	FORMWORK (FT^2)	AVERAGE FORMWORK(FT^2) PER FT^3 OF CONCRETE	PRODUCTION PER PERSONDAY (FT^3)	TOTAL PERSONPOWER	RATIO PERSONPOWER TO TYPICAL FLOOR	REINFORCING BARS (LB)	AVERAGE RE-BARS (LB) PER FT^3 OF CONCRETE	PRODUCTION PER PERSONDAY (FT^3)	TOTAL PERSONPOWER	RATIO PERSONPOWER TO TYPICAL FLOOR
RF	3,000	1.50	90	33	0.33	10,000	5.0	1,000	10	0.21
12F	10,000	1.25	100	100	1.00	60,000	7.5	1,250	48	1.00
11F	10,000	1.25	100	100	1.00	60,000	7.5	1,250	48	1.00
10F	10,000	1.25	100	100	1.00	60,000	7.5	1,250	48	1.00
9F	10,000	1.25	100	100	1.00	60,000	7.5	1,250	48	1.00
8F	10,000	1.25	100	100	1.00	60,000	7.5	1,250	48	1.00
7F	**10,000**	**1.25**	**100**	**100**	**1.00**	**60,000**	**7.5**	**1,250**	**48**	**1.00**
6F	10,000	1.25	100	100	1.00	60,000	7.5	1,250	48	1.00
5F	10,000	1.25	100	100	1.00	60,000	7.5	1,250	48	1.00
4F	10,000	1.25	100	100	1.00	60,000	7.5	1,250	48	1.00
3F	10,000	1.25	100	100	1.00	60,000	7.5	1,250	48	1.00
2F	18,000	1.00	80	225	2.25	144,000	8.0	1,000	144	3.00
1F	18,000	1.00	80	225	2.25	144,000	8.0	1,000	144	3.00
B1F	15,000	0.75	100	150	1.50	160,000	8.0	1,100	145	3.03
B2F	16,000	0.80	100	160	1.60	160,000	8.0	1,100	145	3.03
FND	12,000	0.46	90	133	1.33	208,000	8.0	1,400	149	3.10
TTL	*182,000*	*0.99*	*94.5*	*1,927*	*19.27*	*1,426,000*	*7.8*	*1,171*	*1,217*	*25.36*
			ASSUME & MONITOR	ASSUME & MONITOR				ASSUME & MONITOR	ASSUME & MONITOR	

- In column Y, the operation of column W is repeated, based on the average ratios of column V.
- Column Z shows the adopted ratios of each floor over the typical floor, which are the same as the calculated ratios of column V.
- Column AA shows the duration for the construction of each floor, based on the adjusted duration of 200 working days.

Table 6.3. Data for the various floors of the building, task M&E installations and calculation of total duration for all floors.

A	M&E		TOTAL		CALCULATION OF DAYS					
	S	T	U	V	W	X	Y	Z	AA	AB
FLOOR	TOTAL PERSONPOWER	RATIO PERSONPOWER TO TYPICAL FLOOR	TOTAL PERSONPOWER	RATIO PERSONPOWER TO TYPICAL FLOOR	DAYS (BASED ON RATIO OF AREAS)	DAYS (BASED ON RATIO OF FORMWORK)	DAYS (BASED ON RATIO OF PERSONPOWER)	ADOPTED RATIOS	DAYS PER FLOOR	ROUNDED DAYS FOR SCHEDULE
RF	3	0.4	53	0.30	4	3	3	0.30	2.83	3
12F	8	1	176	1.00	10	10	10	1.00	9.47	10
11F	8	1	176	1.00	10	10	10	1.00	9.47	10
10F	8	1	176	1.00	10	10	10	1.00	9.47	10
9F	8	1	176	1.00	10	10	10	1.00	9.47	10
8F	8	1	176	1.00	10	10	10	1.00	9.47	10
7F	**8**	**1**	**176**	**1.00**	**10**	**10**	**10**	**1.00**	**9.47**	**10**
6F	8	1	176	1.00	10	10	10	1.00	9.47	10
5F	8	1	176	1.00	10	10	10	1.00	9.47	10
4F	8	1	176	1.00	10	10	10	1.00	9.47	10
3F	8	1	176	1.00	10	10	10	1.00	9.47	10
2F	16	2	424	2.41	20	23	24	2.41	22.80	23
1F	16	2	424	2.41	20	23	24	2.41	22.80	23
B1F	16	2	354	2.01	20	15	20	2.01	19.07	19
B2F	16	2	364	2.07	20	16	21	2.07	19.61	20
FND	16	2	337	1.91	20	13	19	1.91	18.14	18
TTL	*163*	*20*	*3,715*	*21.11*	*204*	*193*	*211*	*21.11*	*200*	*206*
			ASSUME & MONITOR		SELECT	SELECT	SELECT	DECIDE	ADJUST	FINAL

- Column AB shows the final time estimate for the construction of each floor, which are the values of column AA, rounded. The total duration of the construction of the skeleton of the building is scheduled to be 206 days.

The above aggregate data for each floor are shown in Fig. 6.5 in the form of a matrix-balanced chart, with the intensity of the quantified bars representing personpower and the vertical axis depicting the floors of the building. The quantified bars in Fig. 6.5 are the folded-up tasks for each floor of the building. Fig. 6.6 shows the matrix-balanced chart composed of the discrete tasks for the construction of every floor. After the initial setting, each of those quantified bars can be modified accordingly to reflect specific conditions.

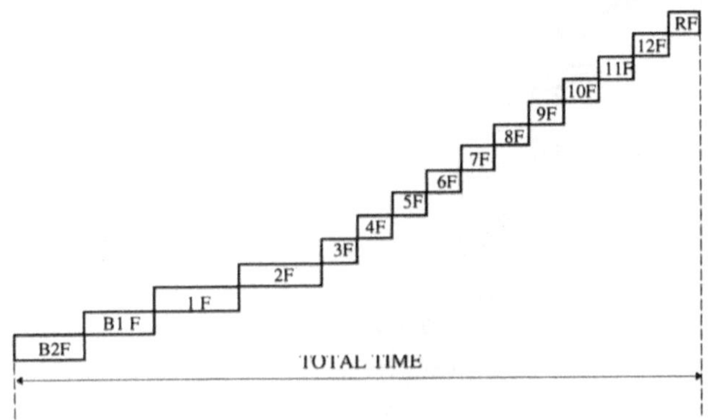

Fig. 6.5. *The matrix-balanced schedule for the structural skeleton composed of folded-up tasks, intensity personpower.*

The process of calculating the duration of the construction was based on the assumption that, on average, 17 workers will work on each floor. In an alternative planning, the construction could be scheduled to last longer by reducing the size of the crew. Fig. 6.7 indicates such a schedule with a proportional time extension for the construction of all the floors.

A planning to construct the skeleton in less than 200 days should be treated in a different way. According to the information in the template shown in Fig. 4.1, it is quite difficult to compress the schedule of floors 3 to 12, or the roof. However, floors 1 and 2 as well as the two basements are better candidates for reducing their duration because of the low slenderness ratio of the representing quantified bars. So, if the duration of these tasks is compressed, the duration of the overall schedule will be compressed as well (Fig. 6.7).

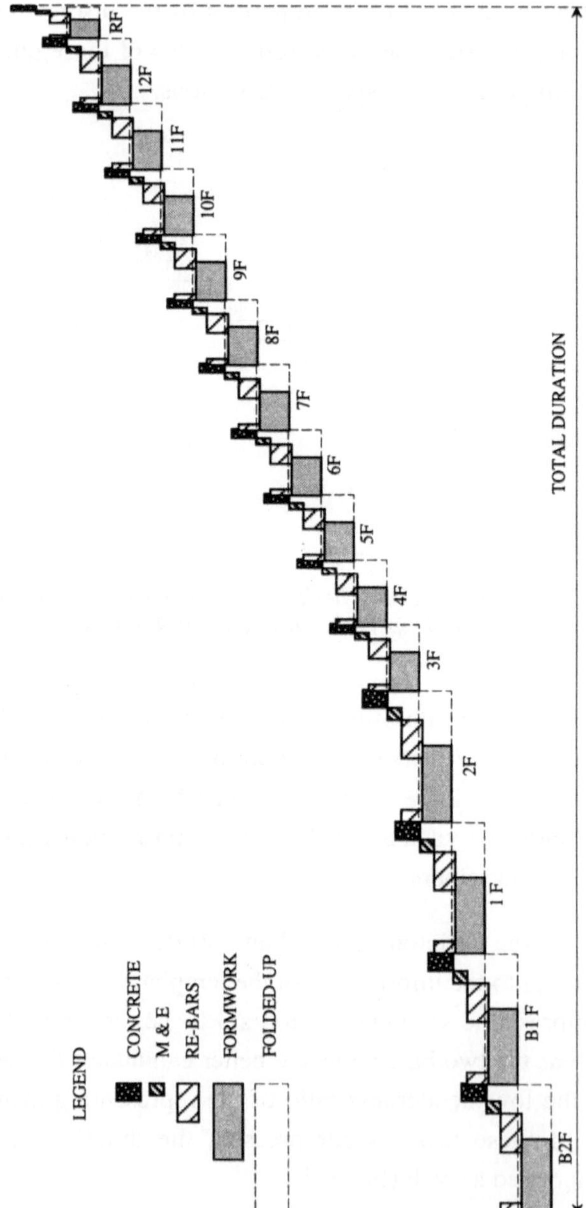

Fig. 6.6. The matrix-balanced schedule for the structural skeleton indicating the discrete tasks that make the folded-up tasks; intensity personpower.

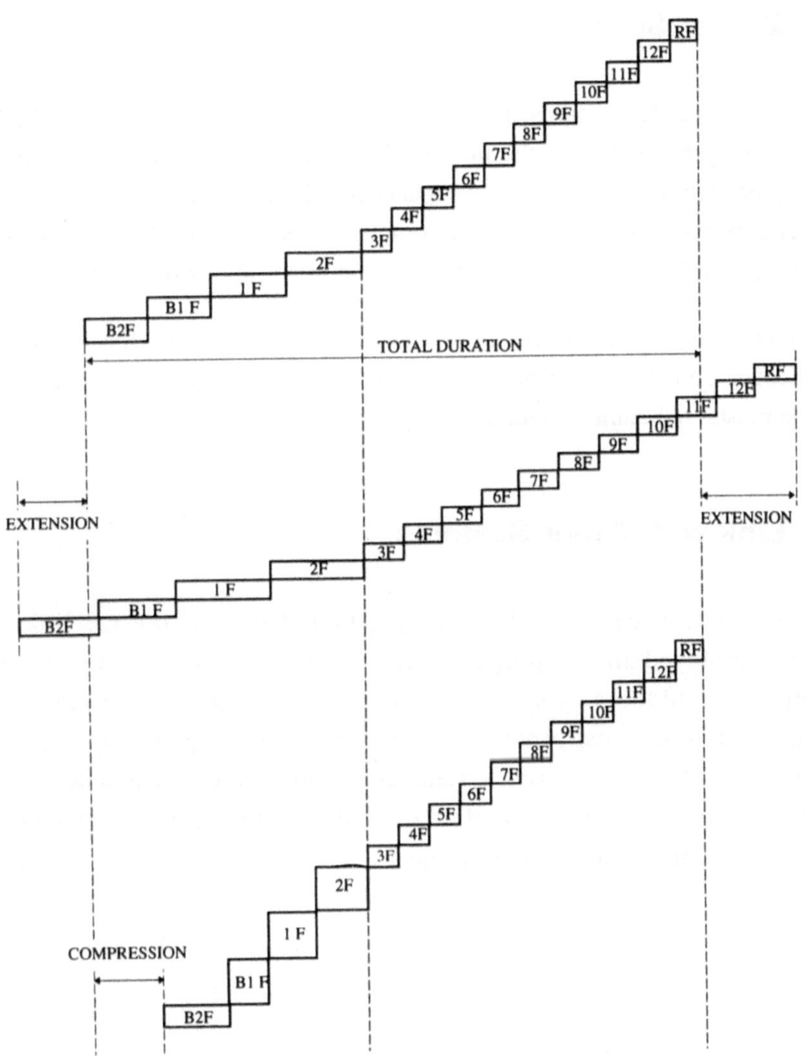

Fig. 6.7. Time expansion and contraction of the matrix-balanced schedule for the structural skeleton, intensity personpower.

6.2.4 Master Schedule

The master schedule contains, in the form of folded-up tasks, all the tasks that compose a project. It shows the master planning for purposes of communication at the higher level and it is used for supervising the flow of the project at a macro level. The master schedule does not contain the details for the discrete tasks, as these details can be seen in the schedules at the lower levels of the hierarchy.

For projects with repeating tasks, the master schedule is a matrix-balanced chart that indicates the different locations of the project. For projects without repeating tasks, the master schedule is a template.

6.2.5 Link with Other Systems

Further integration can be achieved by establishing appropriate links of the resources employed in the project to labor management, cost estimating and accounting. In addition, a systematic collection of site data on resources and productivity, through cost centers, can serve for a better planning of projects in the future. Finally, the proposed system can be employed to schedule and control several projects simultaneously after establishing the appropriate hierarchical structure for the schedules of those projects.

6.3 CHANGES IN THE SCHEDULES

The folded-up task inherits all the properties of the discrete tasks that have been aggregated. This includes timing, precedences, quantities, intensities and constraints. Modifications on any of these properties are allowed, even after the link of several charts with folded-up tasks. These modifications can be applied either on the discrete tasks that have been folded-up or on the folded-up tasks, and propagate both upwards and downwards in the hierarchical system.

6.3.1 Upward Changes

The discrete tasks are modified on the quantified bar chart that they are displayed. These modifications are translated to the folded-up task using the same rules and constraints that produced the original folded-up task. The modified folded-up task is linked to change automatically the corresponding folded-up task on the higher level chart. This change can result to further changes in the timing or the intensity of the other tasks on the latter chart. These changes could follow the rules and constraints that had been already established. For complex decisions, it is left to the user to intervene and decide how to handle the changes at the higher level.

Any changes that do not affect the starting time of the first (in terms of time) task or the ending time of the last (in terms of time) task will have no effect on the starting or ending time of the folded-up task. Furthermore, any modifications that do not change the summation of the quantities of the discrete tasks will have no effect on the quantity of the folded-up task. Finally, if the folded-up task is displayed with a constant intensity, any modifications that do not change the summation of the quantities of the discrete tasks will not even affect the constant intensity of the folded-up task.

6.3.2 Downward Changes

The direct modifications of a folded-up task in a higher level quantified chart should cause modifications to the discrete tasks in the lower level quantified charts that compose that folded-up task. Unlike the changes upward in the hierarchy, downward changes cannot be prescribed because a change in the folded-up task can be interpreted in an infinite number of combinations of changes among the discrete tasks. So, the user should intervene to specify those changes.

Alternatively and in attempt to avoid extensive interaction, a standard procedure could carry the changes at the lower levels, unless the user intervenes. The following rules constitute this standard procedure for carrying the modifications from a folded-up task to the discrete tasks at the lower levels:

- If the folded-up task is shifted along the vertical axis, then the discrete tasks will not be affected.
- If the folded-up task is shifted along the time axis, then the absolute times of the discrete tasks will change but not their relative times.
- If the quantity of the folded-up task is changed, while keeping the same productivity and the same duration, then the quantity of each discrete task will change proportionally.
- If the duration of the folded-up task is forced to change, while the quantity remains constant, then the discrete tasks will be forced to change their duration proportionally. An exemption will apply if specific constraints on a minimum and a maximum duration (or, equivalently, intensities) had been introduced for some of the affected tasks. In such a case these tasks will be extended or compressed until they reach their allowable limits and the other tasks on the chart will share the excessive time change proportionally. Any changes in the duration will be accompanied by changes in the corresponding intensities, in order to maintain the constant quantity. Often the intensity has to be modified in steps, to maintain a meaningful reading of resources such as personpower.
- If the folded-up task is forced to change its intensity, while the quantity remains constant, then the change will be handled as described above, since a change in intensity corresponds to a change in duration.

6.4 MONITORING AND UPDATING

The hierarchical structure of the scheduling system provides a framework for monitoring the execution of the project (Fig. 6.8). The quantified bars display a best estimate of how a specific task or a group of tasks will be executed. At the same time, each quantified bar in every quantified chart is paired with a mate quantified bar, as defined in Section 2.3, to display the task as it was actually executed. So, for every estimation during planning, there is a piece of information on how the task was actually executed. The same links that connect the quantified bars for scheduling, connect their mates of the actual execution. Thus, the folding-up links between the various quantified charts in the hierarchical system need not be repeated for the mate quantified bars.

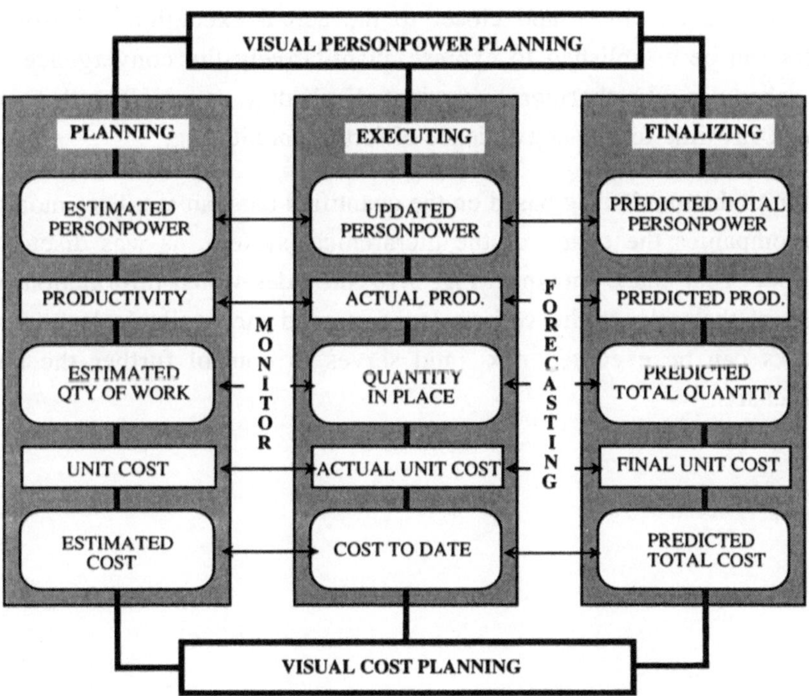

Fig. 6.8. The scheduling, monitoring and updating process.

Normally, the actual execution data are entered for discrete tasks and the information propagates to the quantified charts at the higher levels. Folded-up tasks can also be paired with actual execution data, without referencing the discrete tasks that make the folded-up task. However, these data will only propagate upward the hierarchical system. So, the quantified charts can receive information directly at any level on the actual execution, depending on the needs of the user.

Monitoring the actual information most probably will result to an updating of the remaining of the schedule, as described in Section 2.4. The updating is treated as part of monitoring. Up to the date of monitoring the mate quantified bars show the actual information from the execution of the project. After the date of monitoring, the mate quantified bars show the updated schedule. As the work progresses, mate quantified bars are expected to converge, since the updated schedule should be closer and closer to the actual execution. Performance indicators can be established to express quantitatively the convergence of the various schedules. Furthermore, an updated schedule can replace the original schedule at any time for the convenience of further monitoring.

In addition to the monitoring based on the quantified bars, an auxiliary monitoring chart accompanies the charts of the hierarchical system, as was discussed in Section 5.6. That chart, shown in Fig. 5.10, provides visual information on the execution of the tasks at the various locations and the available locations that those tasks can be executed next, and serves to control further the matrix-balanced charts.

PART II

The Visual Scheduling and Management System, and the State-of-Practice Representations

CHAPTER 7

STATE-OF-PRACTICE REPRESENTATIONS FOR SCHEDULING

The Visual Scheduling and Management System was presented in the first part of the book, without references or comparisons to other systems. In Chapter 7, the state-of-practice representation techniques for project scheduling and management are reviewed in order to proceed to comparisons in the next chapter.

Section 7.1 presents the concept of a project breakdown to discrete tasks, which is common to all the representation methods for project scheduling. Section 7.2 describes the Milestone chart, the simplest and most widely used form of project scheduling. The Gantt chart is presented in Section 7.3, acknowledged to be the most easily understood representation of project scheduling but limited because of its simplicity. The various representations of the network diagrams and the concept of the critical path are presented in Section 7.4. A brief introduction to PERT is also provided in the same section, to demonstrate a need for flexibility in the input data, although the deficiency of PERT to introduce a corresponding representation technique is acknowledged. The line of balance method is presented in Section 7.5, as the method to schedule repeating tasks at different locations. Finally, in Section 7.6, the state-of-art computer graphics are briefly evaluated, to observe that no major advancements have occurred in the representation of project scheduling, despite the proliferation of personal computers.

7.1 BREAKDOWN OF PROJECTS

The very first step for preparing a meaningful schedule for a project is to identify the set of the discrete tasks that compose that project. These tasks must fulfill the following criteria:

- The tasks should be clearly identifiable, each having a specific scope.
- The tasks should be at an equal level.
- The required resources for each task should be identifiable.
- The tasks should constitute the whole project.
- The time duration of each task could be defined.
- The direct precedences among the tasks could be defined.
- The starting time and finishing time of each task could be established.
- Each task could be subdivided further to subtasks. The subtasks of each task should follow these same criteria, as if they were the main tasks of a project.

The process of identifying the tasks that comprise a project is the *task breakdown* of the project. After the task breakdown is completed, one or more of the following representations are employed for the scheduling of projects:

- Milestone chart.
- Gantt chart or bar chart.
- Networks with nodes and connecting arrows with the tasks represented by the nodes.
- Networks with nodes and connecting arrows with the tasks represented by the arrows.
- The line of balance method, for repeating tasks at several identifiable and meaningful locations of the project.

7.2 MILESTONE CHART

The simplest scheduling of a project is the *milestone chart*. The milestone chart presents a list of the tasks, who is responsible for the task and the expected finishing times (Table 7.1). The finishing times of the tasks are determined by the project planner and the interdependencies of the tasks are implied but not indicated. Due to its simplicity, the milestone chart is widely used. However, the applicability of the milestone chart is limited to a handful of tasks. In addition to the text form, a milestone chart is often presented on a time scale as well (Fig. 7.1).

Table 7.1. The milestone chart.

	PROJECT TASK	LABOR	TARGET
1	Formwork	Carpenters	Feb, 12
2	Column re-bars	Bar benders	Feb, 8
3	Cleaning and inspection	General Contractor	Feb, 8
4	Column concrete	Concreters	Feb, 9
5	Beams/slab re-bars	Bar benders	Feb, 16
6	Cleaning and inspection	General Contractor	Feb, 16
7	M & E installations	Electrical Company	Feb, 16
8	Beams/slab concrete	Concreters	Feb, 17

As a management tool, the milestone chart is weak. It provides the project executer with the estimated finishing times. During the execution of each task there is only qualitative information on the progress of each task. It is only at the end of each task that the accuracy of the planning is tested: the task is either completed as planned or not.

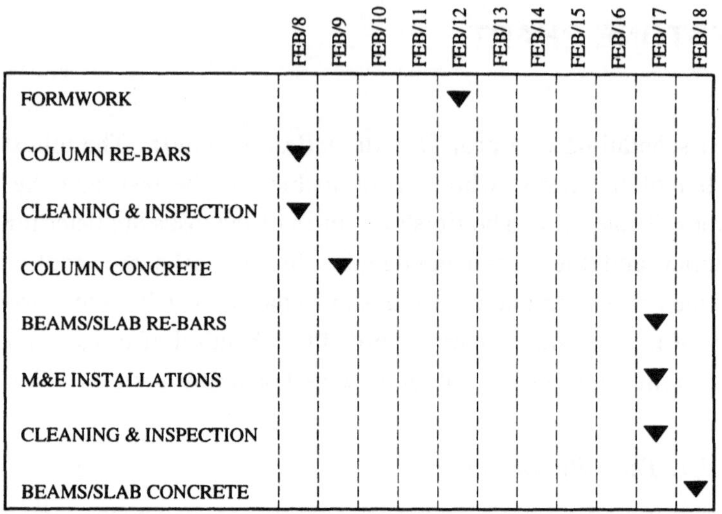

Fig. 7.1. The time scaled milestone chart.

7.3 GANTT CHART (BAR CHART)

In 1919, Gantt presented the scheduling chart that bears his name. The Gantt chart is an one-dimensional chart with the horizontal axis representing time. The tasks are presented on the chart as parallel horizontal bars of constant width. The starting time of each task is defined as the left side of the corresponding bar while the ending time of each task is defined as the right side of the corresponding bar. The relative positions of the bars on the same chart display the time interdependencies of the tasks (Fig. 7.2).

The drawbacks of the Gantt chart result from its simplicity. The interdependencies of the tasks are not explicitly represented. The assumptions on how the bars are placed along the time axis are not displayed either. In addition, tasks that require less effort are shown by the same notation as the tasks that require more effort. Thus, there is a tendency to include only tasks with a similar effort on a Gantt chart, omitting other tasks. Such a practice often is misleading.

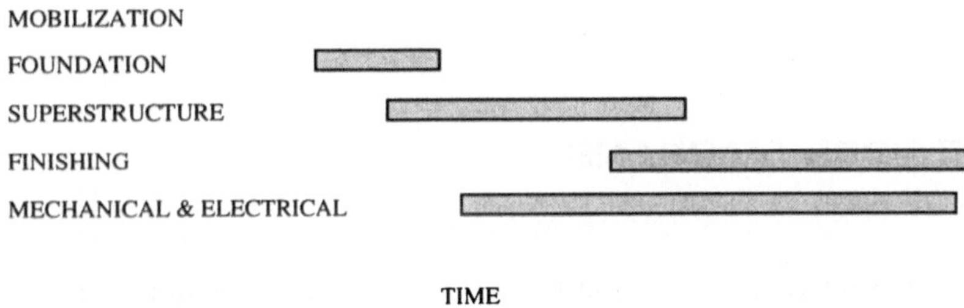

Fig. 7.2. The Gantt chart or bar chart.

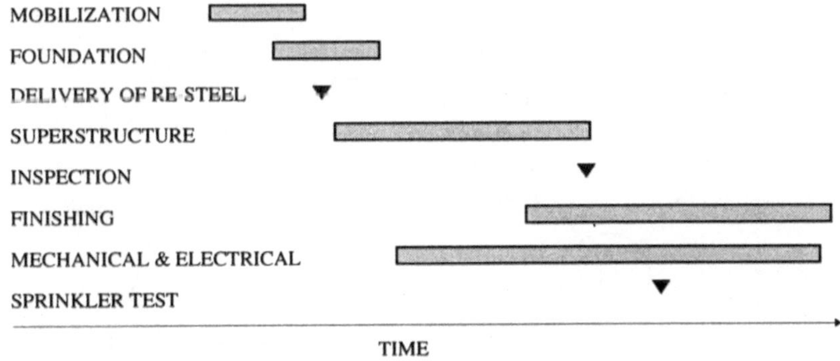

Fig. 7.3. A combination Gantt chart with milestones.

Despite its drawbacks, the Gantt chart is used in practice more than any other scheduling system. It is a remarkable communications tool and by far the easiest chart to understand by the non-specialists. A Gantt chart accompanies the scheduling of most projects, even if more detailed representation techniques are employed.

Often, a milestone chart is combined with a Gantt chart to produce a Gantt chart with milestones. The milestones in such a case are the important deadlines of the project and they are not related necessarily to each task of the project (Fig. 7.3).

7.4 NETWORK DIAGRAMS

A network presentation of a project uses a node and arrow notation (Fig. 7.4). It can be seen as a direct representation on how a computer receives the input for the tasks and their dependencies. Each task of the project should be properly identified for a network representation, and its expected duration and precedences must be explicitly described.

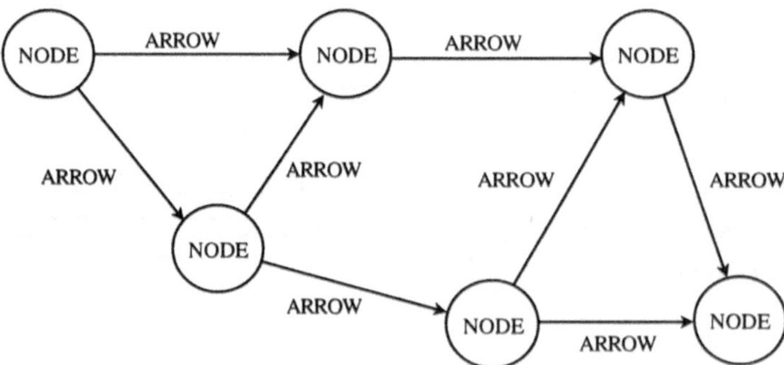

Fig. 7.4. The node and arrow notation.

7.4.1 Task Precedences on a Network

The tasks in a network can be either independent or directly dependent. The direct dependency is expressed by the constraint that a task can start only after another specific task has finished. Thus, the one task constitutes a *precedent* on the other task. Precedences relate to two actual constraints. First, when the completion of a task provides the framework for the execution of the other task. Second, when the resources dedicated to one task must be released in order to be employed for the execution of the other task. Often a task could be started while the other task is still executing. This can be represented on a network by splitting the preceding task in two subtasks and establishing the necessary precedences. However, such a splitting of a task may be problematic if the newly generated subtasks are not at the same level as the other tasks on the network.

Dummy tasks are included in a network diagram, for the convenience of the representation. Dummy tasks are artificial and they do not correspond to an actual task. They take no time but they are needed to define precedences and to mark on the diagram events of special interests such as milestones.

There are two variations of the network representations of projects. In the first variation, the nodes represent the tasks and the arrows connecting the nodes represent the direct relationships of these tasks. In the second variation the arrows represent the tasks and the nodes that define the nodes represent the direct relationships of the tasks. Each representation has its own merits.

7.4.2 Tasks on the Nodes Networks

When the nodes represent the tasks of the project, a connecting arrow between two nodes defines a direct precedence relation between these two tasks (Fig. 7.5). Thus, these diagrams are often referred as *precedence diagrams*. Any two nodes that are not connected by arrows imply that the corresponding two tasks are not directly related by a precedence relation. However, they may be indirectly related through other tasks.

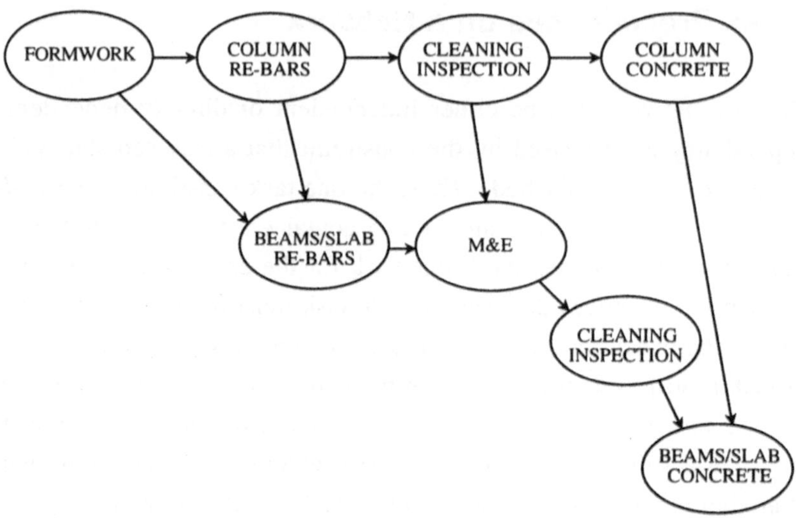

Fig. 7.5. Nodes and arrows notation, tasks on the nodes network (precedence diagram).

On a such a network, time is indicated with text. Usually the starting time, the finishing time and the time duration are shown next to each node. Similarly, resources or cost are indicated with text next to the nodes.

Tasks on nodes networks are easier to sketch by hand, especially at the starting of the planning. So, they are used primarily for smaller projects.

7.4.3 Tasks on the Arrows Networks

In this alternative representation of a network, the tasks are presented by the arrows. Thus, the nodes between arrows indicate directly interdependent tasks (Fig. 7.6). As in the other network notation, only direct dependencies are displayed, although tasks may be indirectly related through other tasks. In its generic form, the tasks on the arrows network representation does not display time. However, the network can be modified to display time and become a *time scaled network*. The nodes in a time scaled network are properly positioned on the network diagram along a horizontal axis indicating time (Fig. 7.7). Thus, the horizontal projection of the arrows indicates the time duration of the corresponding task.   For easiness of reading, arrows are drawn to have a horizontal component to indicate time and a vertical component to spread the diagram and make it readable.   The use of arrows representing dummy tasks to introduce the float between connecting nodes is necessary in such a case.

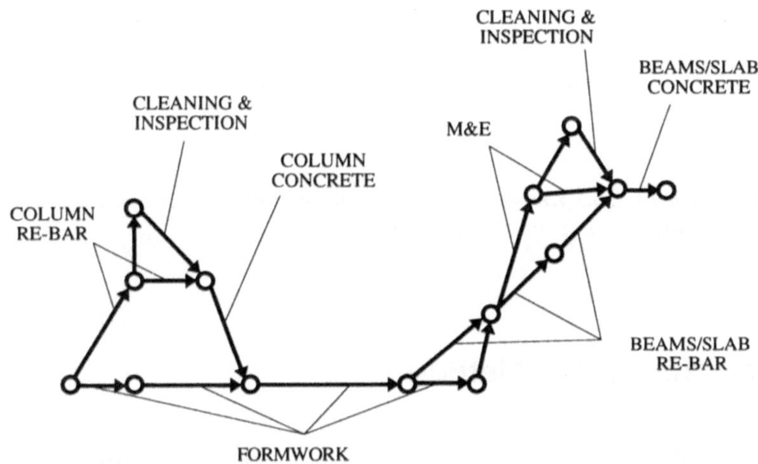

Fig. 7.6. Nodes and arrows notation, tasks on the arrows network.

The preparation of time scaled networks is quite laborious to be executed by hand and it requires the calculation of the starting time and ending time for each task, which is usually automated.   Thus, such diagrams are employed for complicated projects and they are almost always generated by a computer.

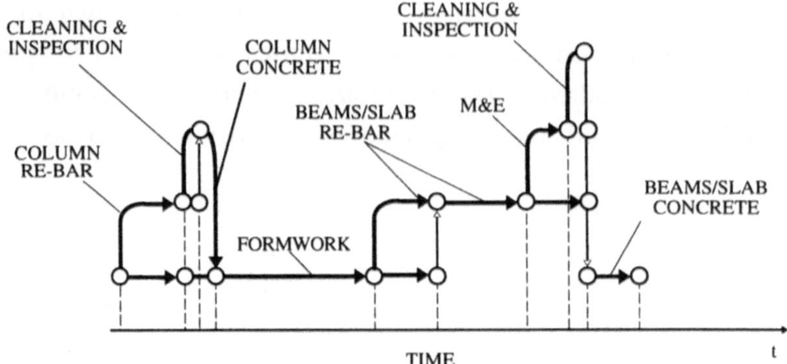

Fig. 7.7. Nodes and arrows notation, tasks on the arrows network with time dimension (time scaled network).

7.4.4 The Critical Path Method

The critical path method (CPM) is always associated with the network presentation. However, the CPM is a scheduling algorithm, which is independent of representations. The required data for the CPM are the tasks that comprise the project, their estimated time duration and the precedence relations among the tasks. The precedence relations are given for pairs of tasks and in the constraint that a specific task must be completed before another task can start.

The critical path method identifies the critical path, or the sequence of the tasks that must be executed sequentially with no float between any two of them in order to achieve the minimum total duration of the project. The summation of the time duration of all the tasks along the critical path defines the minimum duration of the project. Furthermore, it determines the starting and ending time for each task, under the assumption of a zero float for all the tasks on the critical path. So, the starting and the ending times of the tasks on the critical path are precisely calculated. The tasks that are not on the critical path have a float: they can start later and finish later without affecting the total duration of the project. The time length of the float depends on the precedence relations. An early starting time and the corresponding early ending time are specified for those tasks, which are not on the critical path. The late starting time is calculated as the addition of the early starting time and the float. A corresponding late ending time is equal to the late starting time plus the duration of the task.

Most often, a date to complete the project is also specified, implying a total allowable duration of the project. If the time along the critical path is less than the total allowed duration of the project a float can be added to all the tasks of the project. If the time along the critical path is more than the total allowed duration of the project a negative float exists. In such a case, the project planner should either reduce the time duration of the tasks along the critical path or seek an extension to finish the project.

In network representations, the tasks on the critical path are marked clearly to distinguish from the other tasks of the project in order to attract the appropriate attention.

The deterministic nature of the critical path method for a process that is highly variable and uncertain is a major drawback. The requirement to specify the exact duration of each task and the exact precedences among the tasks is quite unreal, especially before the project starts. Furthermore, changes in the input data can result to a different critical path for the project.

The Performance Evaluation and Review Technique (PERT) was invented to face these issues[1]. A PERT network describes the duration of each task in three ways. The average execution time of each task is accompanied by the shortest estimated execution time and the longest estimated execution time. The critical path is calculated using a similar algorithm to the critical path method but all the calculated time durations include average, shortest and longest estimated times. As far as the representation of the network, the only difference between a CPM network and a PERT network is that the PERT network includes the additional numerical values for each task, specifying average, shortest and longest estimated duration.

---

[1]   The PERT and the CPM were developed in parallel by two groups of scientists.

The CPM or PERT methods can be applied by hand for a few tasks only. Almost always, they are executed by computers which can calculate the critical path for a quite large number of tasks. Since the information is available in the computer, the network diagrams are also plotted following the calculation of the critical path, with the simultaneous display of corresponding text information (Fig. 7.8).

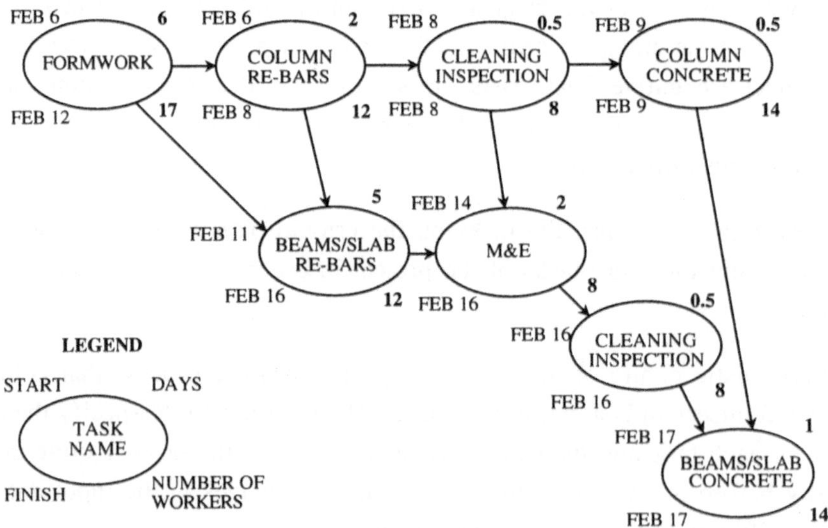

Fig. 7.8. Network with text information.

7.4.5 The Gantt Chart as Complementary Representation

Gantt charts always accompany the network diagrams as a complementary representation. If the network diagram is generated by a computer, then the corresponding Gantt chart is also plotted by the computer, based on the network information. While the network diagrams contain information desirable to the experts, a Gantt chart is unsurpassed for a quick understanding of the project and as a communications tool. The decision to include multiple representations for the same project in practice is an indicator that none of those representations is the most desirable or universally accepted.

7.5 LINE OF BALANCE CHART

The *line of balance chart* is employed to represent repeating tasks in different physical locations of a project site. The chart is two-dimensional. The horizontal axis indicates time and the vertical axis indicates the location. A straight line represents the planning of a task that is repeated in the various locations with a constant production rate. The slope of the straight line represents that production rate (Fig. 7.9).

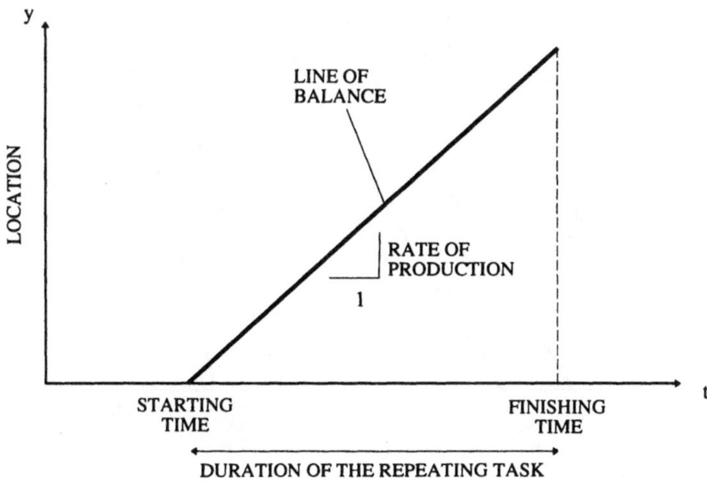

Fig. 7.9. The line of balance chart.

The line of balance chart depicts changes in the production rate by replacing the single straight line segment by a series of straight line segments. Curved lines are difficult to employ, and they are rarely used in practice. The line of balance representation is used mostly for a higher level analysis rather for representing or monitoring day-to-day operations.

Different tasks are represented with different straight line segments on the line of balance chart. Continuous (serial) or overlapping tasks can be represented by segments of straight lines that do not cross. In Fig. 7.10, tasks 4 and 5 are continuous, while tasks 2, 3 and 4 are overlapping. Tasks 4 and 6 have been scheduled with a float, indicated in Fig. 7.10. On the other hand, parallel tasks cannot be represented visually unless they are aggregated into a single task. Furthermore, independent tasks may result to crossing lines, as tasks 1 and 2 in Fig. 7.10. The line of balance method cannot display the required quantity of work or the critical path of the schedule. Thus, the use of single lines often leads to simplified representations that cannot capture actual non-trivial situations in the scheduling of a project.

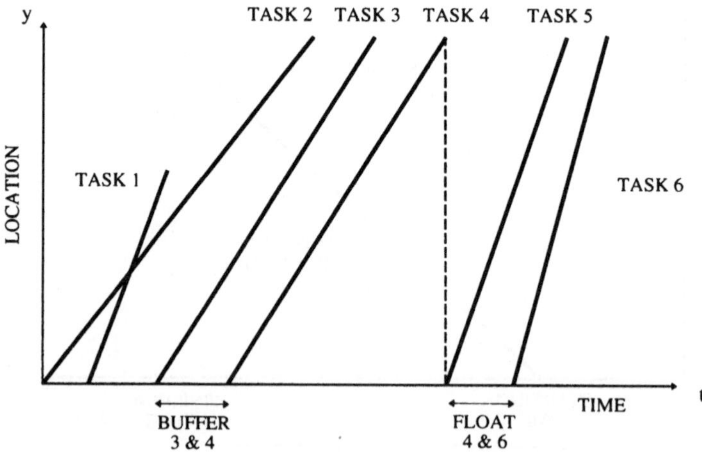

Fig. 7.10. Different repeating tasks represented on a line of balance chart.

A point that two line segments are crossing each other indicates that the two tasks are executed on the same location at the same time. Furthermore, a crossing point indicates that the tasks are scheduled to be executed in a reverse order for the locations that correspond to the locations above the crossing point than they are scheduled to be executed below that point. In general, it is desirable to have one task executed at a single location at any time and reversals of order in the execution of the tasks should be avoided. This is displayed by a series of line segments that do not cross. During planning, crossing points among the line segments can be avoided in several ways. First, by increasing the slope of the line segments, which implies more resources for the execution of the tasks. Second, by spreading the line segments along the time axis, which causes a longer execution time for the entire project. Finally, by discontinuing the execution of a certain task by splitting a single line segment into two or more parallel line segments, which causes a longer execution and, most probably, a discontinuity in the use of resources (Fig. 7.11).

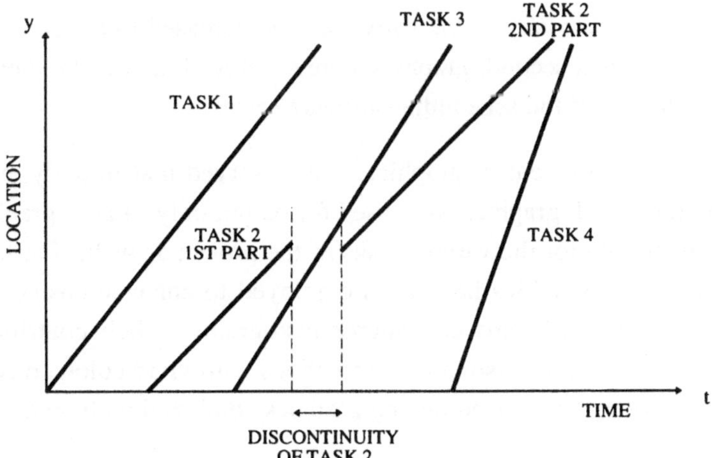

Fig. 7.11. Alternative scheduling for repeating tasks with the line of balance.

7.6 GRAPHICS IN PROJECT SCHEDULING SOFTWARE

Initially, the major contribution of computers in project scheduling was the execution of the critical path algorithm. The CPM algorithm calculated the critical path of the project, as well as the starting and ending time for each of the tasks. Both the input and the output were in the form of text.

At a second priority, the network diagrams were plotted using a nodes and arrows notation. Gantt charts at that stage of computerization were less emphasized. Major projects, mostly construction and shipbuilding for the government, were required to be planned and they were planned according to the CPM or PERT algorithms.

During the transition from the mainframes to the personal computers, these algorithms were downloaded and they were available to be used by a much wider spectrum of users. Further development was necessary and occurred in three directions. First, the capacity of the software was increased to handle more tasks and more data per task; second, graphics were employed; and third, there was an effort to make the use of the scheduling software easier.

Focusing on the employment of graphics, it is observed that initially, and at the personal computer level, graphics were used for output only. Later, graphics were employed to enter data for the various tasks of the project as well. For both input and output, however, graphics have been employed to enhance cosmetically the Gantt charts, network diagrams or resource histograms. Their contribution has been limited in beautifying existing representations with vivid colors, nice-looking symbols and notations, and for producing graphics combined with text.

CHAPTER 8

COMPARISON OF THE VSMS WITH THE STATE-OF-PRACTICE REPRESENTATIONS

The objective of a representation system of projects is dual. First, it should represent the projects in a way that it supports the project planner to make a best schedule, before actually the project starts. This schedule should be as close to reality as possible, built on reasonable assumptions and with good judgment. This representation should be also easy to understand by the parties involved in the project, some of them being non-specialists in project scheduling. Section 8.1 compares the Visual Scheduling and Management System with the state-of-practice representations for the scheduling of projects.

Second, a representation system should display the actual information from the project site during execution. This information should be represented in such a way that allows the project executer to make visual comparisons between the scheduled and actual data and control the project. Corrections for the non-executed part of the project, based on the actual data, should be invited by the properties of the representation system. Finally, this representation should be a communications device, easy to understand by the parties involved in the execution of the project. The visual display of the actual status of the work as compared to the schedule and the consequences of delays are fundamental issues for the representation of projects. Section 8.2 compares the Visual Scheduling and Management System with the state-of-practice representations for the management of projects, during their execution.

8.1 COMPARISON FOR SCHEDULING

The comparison focuses on the preparation of the initial schedule, before the project starts, and it addresses the following issues:
- visual display of work,
- visual display of resources,
- visual scheduling of repeating tasks,
- hierarchical structure,
- visual identification of the critical path, and
- feasibility studies during scheduling.

8.1.1 Visual Display of Work

None of the project scheduling methods that are employed in practice provides a visual display of the quantity of work of each task. However, this information is almost always available to the project planner, as a key element in the scheduling process, and it is often included as text information on the network diagrams.

The Visual Scheduling and Management System represents the tasks as quantified bars. In one of the alternative displays, the area of the bars indicate the work of the corresponding task while the intensity of the bars indicate the production per time unit. The quantified charts show the quantities of work and time relations of all the tasks together. The absolute magnitudes of the work of the tasks are drawn to scale and their relative magnitudes are visually observed and compared by the user. Compared to a Gantt chart or a network diagram, the display of the quantities of work on the same quantified chart introduces a totally new dimension to the visualization of the project. Fig. 8.1 provides a juxtaposition of the quantified bar chart to a Gantt chart and a network diagram. The comparison demonstrates clearly the visual richness of the new system.

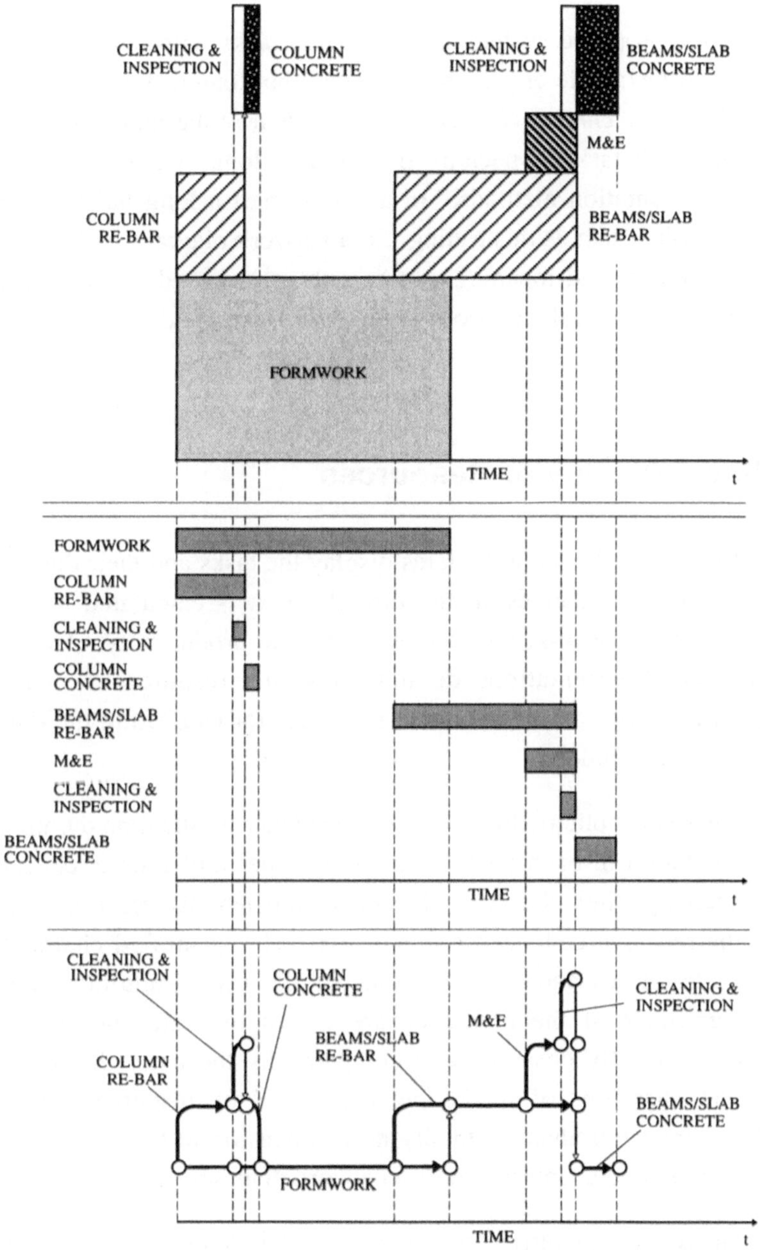

Fig. 8.1. *Juxtaposition of a quantified bar chart to a Gantt chart and a network diagram.*

Furthermore, the proposed system displays small tasks with quantified bars of a low intensity. An example of presenting a small but long task has been shown in Fig. 4.3, as the task *technical & user documentation* in the template for software development. Such tasks, especially if they take long, are not shown in most scheduling representation methods. In a Gantt chart a long bar with the same "weight" as the other bars is misleading. In a network diagram such a task would be either a different (and meaningless) branch or it would be broken down to many tasks interwoven in the network and would make the diagram unnecessarily more complicated.

8.1.2 Visual Display of Resources

The state-of-practice scheduling systems display the tasks and their duration. The duration of a task is either estimated directly or it is calculated based on the quantity of work of the task, the resources and the productivity. However, the state-of-practice representations do not show the resources visually. The underlying assumptions on the available resources for estimating the duration of each task are visually hidden.

The VSMS displays explicitly the resources together with the time duration as part of the representation of each task. If a resource per unit time is chosen as the displayed intensity, then the area of each quantified bar represents the total amount of the resource dedicated for that task. The quantified charts show the quantities of resources and time relations of the tasks simultaneously. The absolute magnitudes of the resources are drawn to scale and their relative magnitudes are visually observed and compared by the user. Similarly to the display of the quantities of work, the display of the resources on the same quantified bar chart introduces a totally new dimension to the visualization of a project, as compared to a Gantt chart or a network diagram.

Fig. 8.2 compares the quantified bar chart with the Gantt chart as they relate to the assumptions on resources and time duration. The brick laying task for a construction project is shown by a Gantt chart to last 6 days, with no further visual explanation. Below, the quantified bar shows the underlying assumption that 4 workers will accomplish the task in 6 days. Alternatively, if 6 workers were available, 4 days would suffice for that task. If such a change is accepted, the Gantt chart will change significantly. The quantified bars show the planning constraints of resources together with the time duration, so they provide a more complete picture of the project.

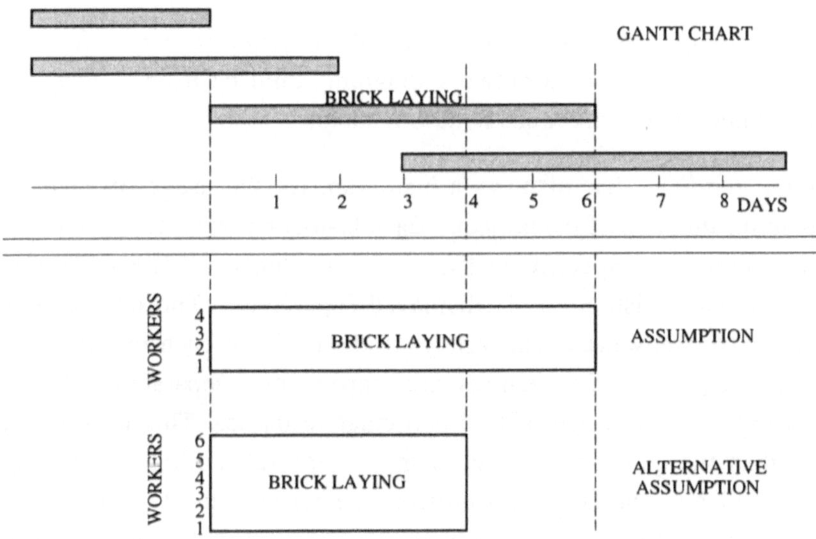

Fig. 8.2. Juxtaposition of a bar in a Gantt chart to quantified bars displaying the assumptions on the resources.

Since the Visual Scheduling and Management System requires as input the quantity of work, the dedicated resources and the productivity for visual display, it forces the project planner to think along those terms. The quantity of work is always available to the planner. So, the planner must estimate the productivity and determine the required resources prior to making the scheduling. Then, the time duration of each task is determined, which leads to the schedule of the project. A change in the available resources or the productivity will immediately affect the duration of a task. Alternatively, a change in the duration of any task can be achieved by changing the dedicated resources.

The process of scheduling based on productivity generates more confidence for the derived schedule. The accuracy of estimating the duration of each task is governed by the accuracy of estimating the available resources and their productivity. So, in the Visual Scheduling and Management System, it is quite important to record the actual productivity as early as possible. If the actual productivity is different than the estimated productivity, then the time schedule could be maintained by adjusting the dedicated resources accordingly.

If the productivity cannot be estimated and the required resources for a task are unknown, a Gantt chart or a network diagram could be used. However, their usefulness under those conditions is questionable.

A *resource loading view* displays a histogram for the usage of each resource throughout the duration of the project. Each histogram refers to a single resource, without reference to specific tasks, so it can apply to one or more tasks. Furthermore, each histogram is displayed separately. The objective of such histograms is to study peaks and valleys in the usage of each resource along the duration of the project. So, each resource appears on a separate display with the intention to study the usage of that particular resource. This is fundamentally different than the quantified charts of the Visual Scheduling and Management System that display the tasks of a project together with their resources and time interdependencies, functions which cannot be realized with the resource loading view. The visual representations of histograms and Gantt charts exist for more than 70 years. However, the Visual Scheduling and Management System is the first to propose visual presentations such as the quantified charts.

The distinction between the resources of each task versus the cumulative resources for all the tasks of the project is particularly useful for scheduling subcontracted tasks. In subcontracted tasks, similar resources may be used for different tasks. So, it is important for the project planner to visualize these resources as part of their corresponding tasks, rather than accumulate them on a single histogram. At the same time, it is important to visualize them as similar resources, so the project planner can mix or redistribute those tasks if such an action leads to a better execution of the project.

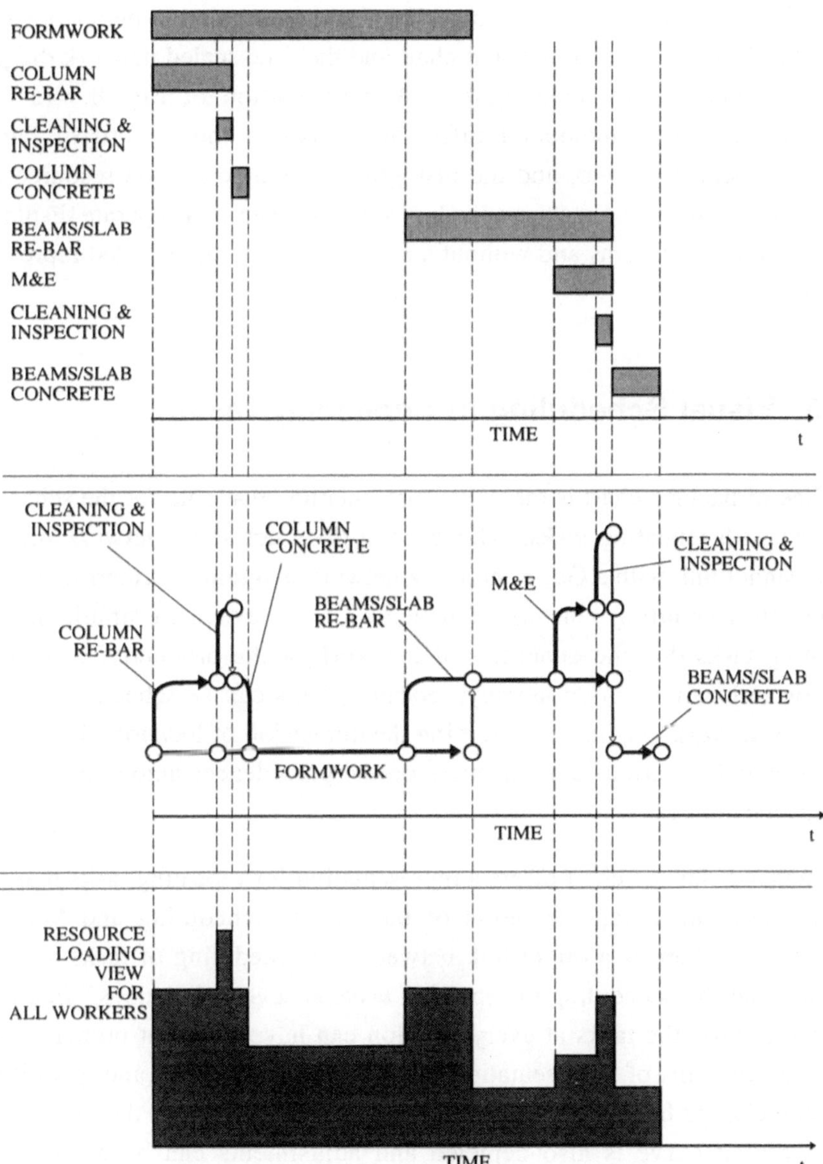

Fig. 8.3. Resource loading view for all the workers of the tasks shown in Fig. 8.1.

Fig. 8.3 presents a resource loading view for the cumulative personpower of all the tasks. The corresponding Gantt chart and the time scaled network diagram are also presented in the same figure. A juxtaposition of Fig. 8.3 to Fig. 8.1 demonstrates the fundamental difference between the quantified bar chart, indicating persons-power, and the histogram generated for the resource loading view. Furthermore, the resource loading view is given in a separate display in the state-of-practice systems and without a reference to the time scaled representation of tasks.

8.1.3   Visual Scheduling of Repeating Tasks

The line of balance chart is the only representation available for the scheduling of projects with repeating tasks. However, it does not show network information and it cannot link with a Gantt chart or a network diagram. Furthermore, it is quite limited in scheduling clusters of repeating tasks executed simultaneously, or repeating tasks that the quantities of the work or the productivity change from location to location. Alternatively, repeating tasks can be scheduled using Gantt charts or network diagrams by omitting the dimension of location. However, such an omission has serious consequences on the precedences among the tasks in the various locations.

The matrix-balanced chart offers a representation for repeating tasks that is a part of the hierarchical representation of the Visual Scheduling and Management System. So, there is a direct link between the scheduling of tasks at a specific location and the scheduling of repeating tasks at several locations. In addition to this direct link, the tasks at every location can have different properties without creating problems of representation. The duration, intensity and quantity of any task can change from location to location, giving freedom to the project planner. The learning curve is also depicted and adjustments can be made for a best schedule. Furthermore, the matrix-balanced chart has the same advantages as any quantified chart, such as the visual display of work, resources and cost; it displays the critical path visually as it will be discussed in Section 8.1.5; and it makes feasibility studies easier during scheduling, as it will be discussed in Section 8.1.6.

8.1.4 Hierarchical Structure

Both the Gantt chart and the network diagrams do not provide a hierarchical visual representation of projects. So, many tasks are shown simultaneously on the same chart, resulting to charts that are complicated to understand and to adjust. In practice, a way to avoid large charts is to classify the tasks of a project at different levels and show the tasks of each level separately. The different methods that have been applied to facilitate the classification of tasks, emphasize the use of meaningful identification codes for classes and subclasses of tasks.

The Visual Scheduling and Management System has a built-in hierarchical structure that links the quantified charts, as it was discussed in Chapter 6. This hierarchical structure permits the assembly of charts of varying details and distinct uses to compose the schedule of the entire project. Furthermore, the VSMS incorporates the scheduling of repeating tasks into the same system. On the contrary, the existing representation methods would have used charts of a different nature, such as a Gantt chart and a line-of-balance chart, to display the scheduling of repeating tasks.

8.1.5 Visual Identification of the Critical Path

In the existing methods, the total duration of a project is determined by the critical path method. Such a calculation is precise and systematic. However, the concept of the critical path is utopian. The critical path depends on the time duration of the tasks and their precedences. The duration of each task is so variable and depends on so many factors that, almost inevitably, most tasks will be shorter or longer that initially estimated. Furthermore, rarely in practice the precedences of the tasks can be so rigorously and in-detail defined as it is required for the calculation of the critical path, especially in complicated, not well-structured work. Changes in the amount of resources or their productivity will change the duration, possibly precedences and, consequently, the critical path. Both the Gantt chart and the network diagrams cannot display any of those changes. They can only recalculate the critical path, based on the new data. Under the best conditions, the same tasks will comprise the critical path but with a different time duration. However, such a recalculation may surface a completely different critical path than before, having serious consequences.

Often, the precedences among the tasks are not well-defined, as in the finishing work of construction projects or in the services industry. In such cases the concept of the critical path is of an even lesser importance and the network diagrams are less applicable. The use of probability to describe duration in the PERT diagrams allows for a margin of error but, in practical terms, it is equally problematic.

The treatment of the critical path is quite different using quantified charts. Although the CPM algorithm may be used to produce the initial sequence of the tasks, the tasks and their properties are displayed visually. Thus, the critical path is visually identifiable, together with the assumptions on work, resources and productivity. Similarly, changes on a quantified chart may change the critical path or its duration.

Even more important, the quantified chart provides the framework for a different way of thinking. It by-passes the concept of a rigorous critical path and displays the scheduling sequence with the underlying assumptions. Thus, it is equally suitable for scheduling tasks with or without well-defined precedences. Changes are performed on the quantified chart itself and the various implications of those changes are immediately seen on the display. Task precedences can be in various forms, such as parallel, continuous, overlapping or forced overlapping, common start, or common finish. Finally, the project planner can enforce a sequence of the tasks in an arbitrary way, to take into account external factors. The final schedule is the result of these interactive changes on the quantified chart and the critical path is part of the chart. The hierarchical structure of the VSMS captures the critical path for the detailed operations and for the total project, as the assembly of a series of quantified charts.

8.1.6 Feasibility Studies

The simultaneous display of tasks, resources and time allows the user to interact with the quantified bar chart without a need to retrieve hidden data. It is quite the opposite with feasibility studies on the state-of-practice representation methods. The critical path method can perform computerized feasibility studies to study the effects of precedences and duration's on the schedule. However, the results of these studies cannot be superimposed graphically to see the advantages of the one over the others. Resources or productivity are not visually displayed and a change in time duration is the only change that can be seen on a Gantt chart or on a network diagram.

Visual interactive feasibility studies can be carried out in a quantified chart, after the first schedule has been prepared. Such studies could focus on the estimates of productivity, on the size of the dedicated resources, on the duration of the tasks, as well as on the starting times and the precedences of the tasks. The tasks with a relatively low intensity and the tasks with a relatively low slenderness ratio are the prime targets for what-if questions for the project planner. A relatively low intensity bar indicates a relatively small production per unit time of that task, less allocated resources, or a lower production cost. Such a task should be considered to shorten its duration by increasing the dedicated resources, by paying more per unit time, or by reconsidering the production method (see Fig. 2.8). Furthermore, among the tasks with a similar intensity, the ones with the longer duration (relatively low slenderness ratio) are the best candidates to inquiry for shortening their duration. All possible intensities (quantity of work, resources and cost) should be closely examined during the feasibility studies.

8.2 COMPARISON FOR MANAGEMENT

The Visual Scheduling and Management System is an effective management tool for the execution of projects, because of its quantitative displays and its built-in monitoring and forecasting capability. It is also a useful communication device for technical information, easily understood by the non-specialists. On the contrary, the Gantt chart, the network diagrams and the line-of-balance chart are particularly weak as management tools because of their inability to juxtapose graphically the planned versus the actual data.

The new system is compared to the state-of-practice representations for the management of projects during execution, where the initial schedule is used for control and it is updated with new information. The comparison focuses on the following issues:
- control of the project,
- updating the project,
- visual recognition of errors, and
- communication.

8.2.1 Control of the Project

The user of a network diagram concentrates on the starting time and completion time of each task, that have been calculated based on the critical path method. The user focuses with even more attention on the tasks of the critical path, because their proper and timely execution will affect the duration of the project. Although network diagrams are used for the master schedule at the starting of the project or they are employed to agree on a time extension, they are rarely used to update a project during its execution. This is explained by the absence of a method to superimpose visually the planned versus the actual data as well as the inherent problems of the critical path concept, as discussed in Section 8.1.5.

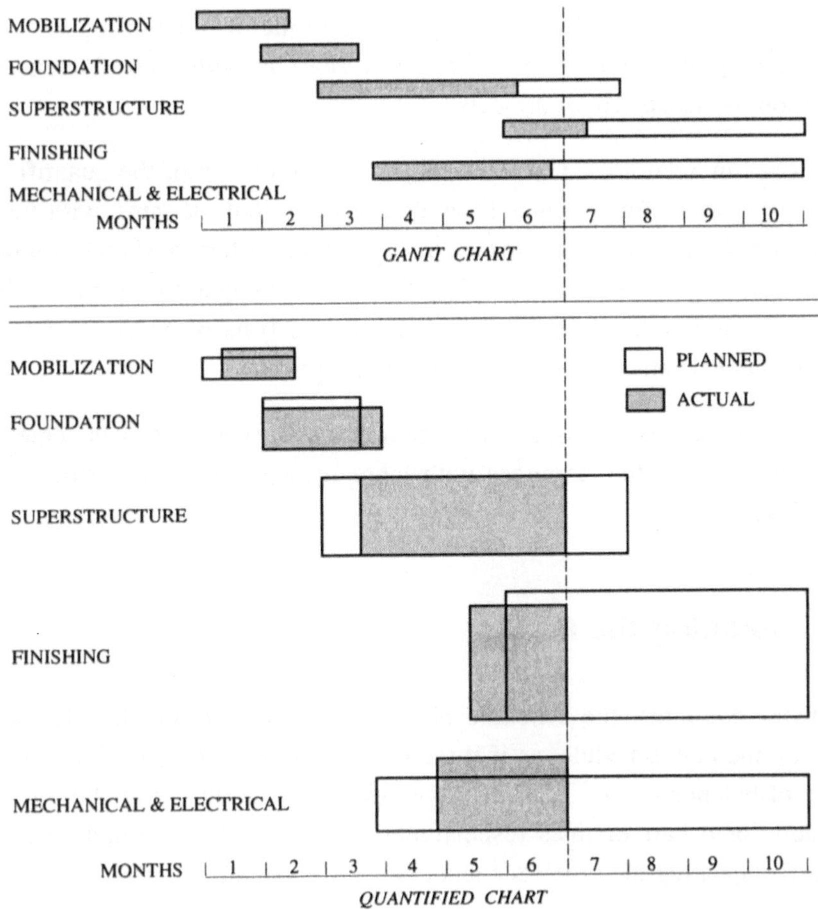

Fig. 8.4. Juxtaposition of a quantified bar chart to a Gantt chart for the control of the project.

Fig. 8.4 juxtaposes a quantified chart to a Gantt chart for monitoring a project. The Gantt chart displays the executed part of the task as a percentage of the task, either in a separate bar below the bar that describes the specific task, or within the bar of the task itself, as in Fig. 8.4. However, the visual information on a Gantt chart does not inform the user when that part of the task was executed, or if there are any modifications to be made on the schedule of the project. Furthermore, tasks appear to be completed to the right of the time of monitoring, as with the task *finishing* in Fig. 8.4.   So, the Gantt chart provides insufficient visual information for the control of projects.

As discussed in Sections 2.3, 4.4 and 6.4, the superposition of the quantified bars that represent the estimated quantities during the initial planning with the mate quantified bars that represent the actual quantities offers a visual comparison between the two, demonstrated in Fig. 8.4.   This comparison occurs at all the levels of the hierarchical structure, permits an analysis of delays and supports management decisions during the execution of a project.

In addition, as it was discussed in Section 6.2.5, further control is achieved by appropriate links of the resources with labor management, cost estimating and accounting.

8.2.2   Updating the Project

In network diagrams, the schedule is updated by correcting the old data and displaying the new schedule, as if it refer to a new project.   The Gantt chart and the line of balance chart can display the new schedule on top of the old one by using additional bars or lines respectively.   However, the assumptions and the reasons for updating the projects cannot be shown visually.

The updating of schedules in the Visual Scheduling and Management System is a natural extension of its monitoring capability.   The actual data are superimposed on the planned data, thus depicting visually the accomplished amount of a task. Then, the non-completed tasks can be updated to reflect the reality of the completed part of the quantified chart, as discussed in Sections 2.4 and 6.4.   The updating of the project is facilitated by switching among the alternative displayed intensities of the tasks (quantity of work, resources, cost).   Fig. 8.5 juxtaposes a quantified chart to a Gantt chart for updating a project, based on the example of Fig. 8.4.   The updating of the Gantt chart (tasks: *superstructure, finishing,* and *mechanical and electrical*) is based on the information on the project but it is not visually justified on the Gantt chart alone.   Furthermore, there is an unanswered question on the Gantt chart: why the *finishing*, which is ahead of schedule at the time of monitoring, is not going to finish earlier. The answer is visually shown on the quantified chart: *finishing* started earlier with fewer resources. So, it has reached an advanced stage but the rate of production is less than originally expected, so it will finish just on time.

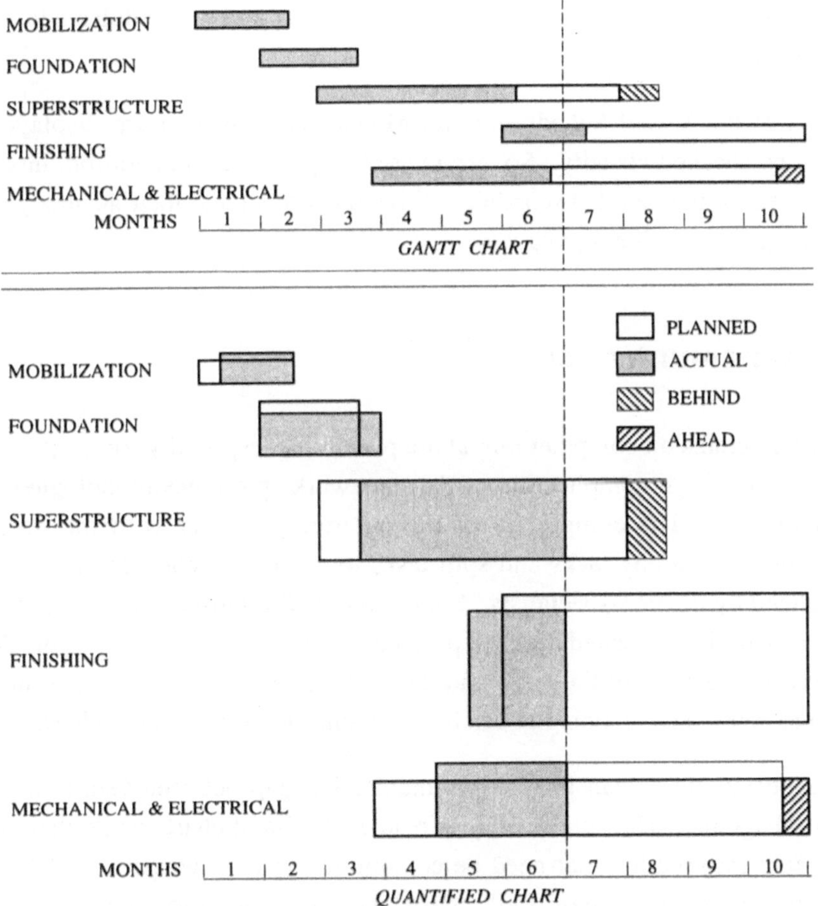

Fig. 8.5. *Juxtaposition of a quantified bar chart to a Gantt chart for updating the project.*

8.2.3 Visual Recognition of Errors

The input data are expected to be, and should be, as accurate as possible. The procedure of data input in the computer implementations of networks is monotonous and prone to errors, while understanding the computer output requires effort and special skills. So, the data could include errors either from calculation or from overlooks that can be disastrous to the schedules and project management.

The data of the Visual Scheduling and Management System are displayed and they can be checked visually. So, errors are less probable. In addition, input data are required for the detailed schedules at the lower level and their accuracy can be evaluated prior to being aggregated.

8.2.4 Communication

Network diagrams on computer output are persuasive, especially for large projects. However, the visual complication of these networks promotes monologues rather than dialogues. The complexity of the notation, together with the necessary introduction of dummy tasks and split tasks to make the schedule, is difficult to comprehend by the non-specialists. So, despite its limitations, the Gantt chart has found a niche in the scheduling of projects: usage as a communication device. However, the identity of the tasks and their time interdependencies, as scheduled, is the maximum information that can be communicated with a Gantt chart.

The quantified charts can fill the communication gap between Gantt charts and network diagrams. They are as easy to read as the Gantt charts while they display much more information that need be communicated to other parties. There is a multiple role of the quantified charts as communication devices: deliver information to the external stakeholders of the project, communicate with colleagues either locally or remotely, and manage subordinates.

Completion time, personpower planning and cash flow are visually depicted on quantified charts and provide valuable information to the owner and higher level managers. These visual displays can be also employed for payments, progress reports, company reports and safety reports.

Communication with colleagues on the site is facilitated by the displays of the Visual Scheduling and Management System. However, its real power is for communication with remote sites or the headquarters, especially with on-line interactive computer communications. The visualization of the resources make the schedules faster to understand and test the implied assumptions, while the displays of the control quantified charts depict the actual execution in a comprehensive way.

The quantified charts provide the project planner with persuading power to justify the course of action to subordinates who understand the schedules with a minimal effort, due to their strong visual representation. In addition, the amount to be paid to the subcontractor (cost-to-date) is visually displayed as a function of the completed work (quantity-in-place). So, the subcontractor's certification for payment claim can be verified and recorded, thus making the quantified charts effective for the control of subcontracting work (see Fig. 2.9, 2.10, and 2.11).

The quantified charts are also intended to be employed for scheduling professionals and facilities. Easy communication and precise information are required in those cases. An example could be the scheduling and managing of surgical units in hospitals. Each medical doctor or group of doctors, nurses, and assistants can be displayed throughout the operations, as well as the usage of the available facilities. Different visual codes on the quantified bars can display the nature of the different tasks, the available facilities, and their utilization.

PART III

The Visual Scheduling and Management System in the Construction of Buildin

CHAPTER 9

SCHEDULING THE CONSTRUCTION
OF A HOTEL

The proposed Visual Scheduling and Management System has been retroactively fitted to analyze the scheduling of the construction of a hotel building. The upper part of the hotel consisted of a repetitive floor layout that provided a best example for using the matrix-balanced chart, both for the structural frame and for the finishing work.

Section 9.1 presents the project and provides the necessary design information. Section 9.2 focuses on the construction of the reinforced concrete frame of the identical floors, including a detailed analysis of the quantities to be built. Following that analysis, the construction workers are assigned on the floor. Section 9.3 demonstrates the use of the Visual Scheduling and Management System for scheduling the construction of the frame of the building. First a microtemplate is employed for scheduling the construction of the specific reinforced concrete elements of a single floor. Then, a structural template is derived from the microtemplate, using the folding up method. Finally, in the same section, a matrix-balanced chart depicts the construction of all the identical floors, including the use of formwork and scaffolding from floor to floor. Section 9.4 demonstrates the use of the matrix-balanced chart to depict the construction of the finishing work for the identical floors. Finally, in the same section, the matrix-balanced chart is employed to recover a delay in finishing by re-scheduling the tasks in several floors.

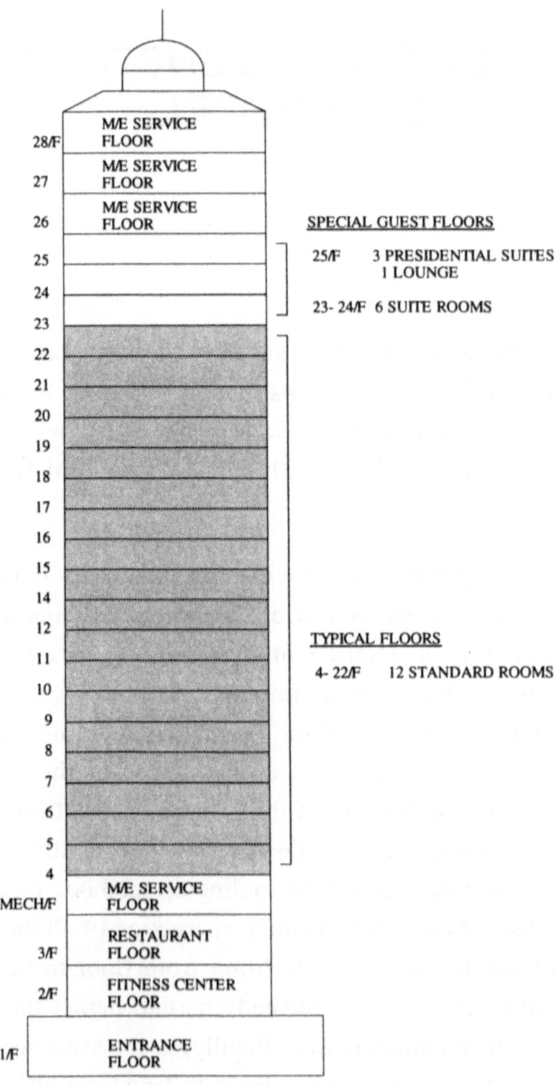

Fig. 9.1. *Schematic elevation of the hotel, showing the use of floors and the identical floors from the 4th to the 22nd.*

9.1 THE PROJECT[1]

The hotel was erected on a small lot of approximately 15,000 sq. ft. (almost 1,400 m²). The basements and the first three floors include a garage, public areas, common facilities and mechanical services. The next 18 floors, from the 4th to the 22nd, have an identical layout and contain guest quarters only. The 23rd, 24th and 25th floors contain several suites and lounges, and the top floors of the building are reserved for additional mechanical services. The structural skeleton of the building was designed to be reinforced concrete with flat plate slabs and shear walls. Fig. 9.1 shows a schematic elevation of the hotel.

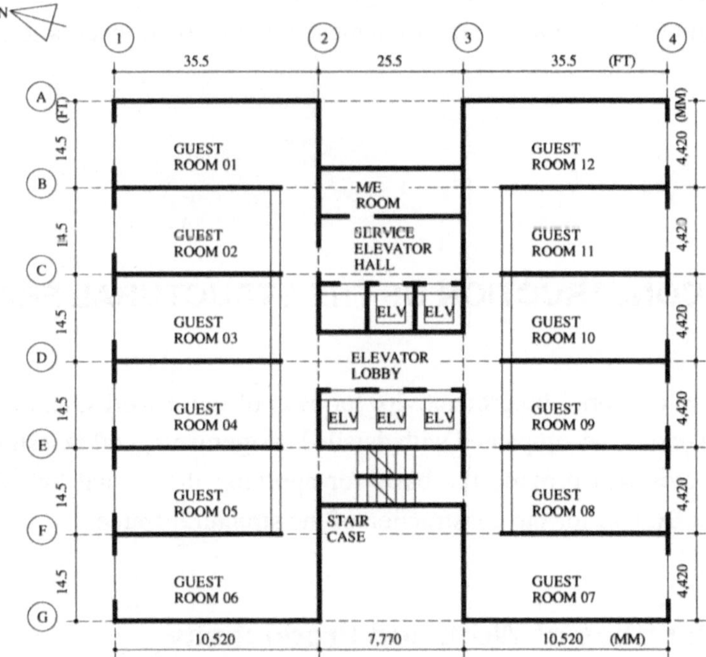

Fig. 9.2. *Plan of the identical 18 floors (4th to 22nd floor), showing the shear walls, the beams and the core of the building.*

---

1   Most of the data have been disguised.

This chapter focuses on the construction of the identical 18 floors. Fig. 9.2 shows the floor plan for these 18 floors. The established grid of 7 rows, numbered from A to G, and 4 columns, numbered from 1 to 4, facilitates the book-keeping of the works on the floor. Each typical floor includes 12 guest rooms, 6 at the north side and 6 at the south side of the building, and the north and south connecting corridors. The central core of the building consists of a staircase well, three guest elevators and their lobby, two service elevators and their lobby, a janitor's room next to the service elevators, and a mechanical and electrical room with space for vertical ducts.

Thick lines represent the shear walls from floor to floor. The slab is a flat plate with only two deep beams, defining the end of the guest rooms at the corridor side. The location of the beams is shown in Fig. 9.2 with a double line. Gypsum boards on concrete make the ceiling of the guest rooms, while the bathrooms have dropped ceilings to accommodate mechanical and electrical installations and light fixtures.

9.2 THE CONSTRUCTION OF THE STRUCTURAL FRAME

The quantities of work, the productivity for each of those works, and the required number of workers, accompanied with detailed assignments, will be estimated first. These estimates will provide the basis for applying the Visual Scheduling and Management System for the construction of the structural frame.

9.2.1 Quantities of Work and Productivity

The connoting bar chart of Fig. 9.3 was constructed first, based on experience. This chart presents a first-cut schedule for the construction of the structural elements of a typical floor, and it is subject to revisions after the detailed study of the scheduling and before starting construction. As shown on the chart, six distinct tasks comprise this construction:

- marking the floor layout,
- mechanical and electrical preparations (M&E),
- fixing of the reinforcing steel bars (re-bar),
- construction of the formwork,
- placement of concrete, and
- inspections during construction.

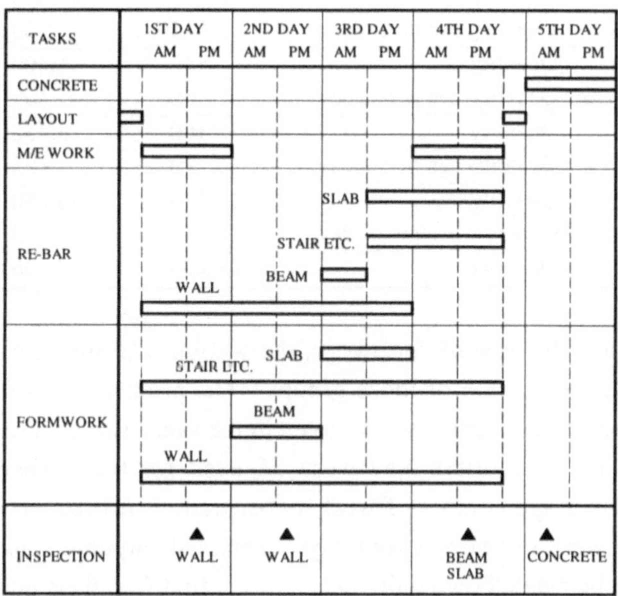

Fig. 9.3. Preliminary connoting bar chart for the construction of a typical floor.

The construction time for a single floor is estimated to be five working days, with the fifth day reserved for the placement of concrete. The marking of the layout is carried out after hours, reflecting its low labor intensity, in an effort to reduce the construction time of each floor.

The connoting bar chart shows separately the construction of the four groups of the reinforced concrete elements, shown schematically in Fig. 9.2:

- the shear walls,
- the staircase and other miscellaneous elements,
- the beams, and
- the flat plate (slab).

Table 9.1. *Quantities of materials and productivity, per element, for each floor.*

ELEMENT		FORMWORK (ft^2)	RE-BARS (lb)	CONCRETE (ft^3)
SLAB	Quantity	6,070	25,800	3,070
	Quantity per personday	217	1,720	480
STAIRCASE &	Quantity	540	1,400	170
MISCELLANEOUS	Quantity per personday	68	467	240
BEAMS	Quantity	360	3,450	420
	Quantity per personday	90	863	430
WALLS	Quantity	11,930	36,850	4,080
	Quantity per personday	139	1,152	300
TOTAL	*Quantity*	*18,900*	*67,500*	*7,740*

Table 9.1 displays the area of formwork, the weight of reinforcing steel and the volume of concrete for each of those groups. The productivity of each trade for the specific structural elements, is also given in the same Table, based on data from other construction sites, after they were adjusted for this project. From that information, an average number of workers per trade is estimated, with the target to complete the work in five working days. Thus, 34 carpenters and 14 bar fixers are estimated to be needed on a daily basis for the first four days and 18 concreters for the fifth day.

9.2.2 Assignment of Workers

Fig. 9.4, 9.5, 9.6, 9.7, 9.8, and 9.9 show in detail the assignment of the estimated number of workers for each task for every day of construction. Marking workers, formwork carpenters, reinforcing bar fixers, and mechanical and electrical workers are assigned on the specific areas that they work during the first four days. During the fifth day, concrete workers place the concrete for the shear walls, the beams, the slab and the staircase. The normal working hours are from 8 am to 4 pm.

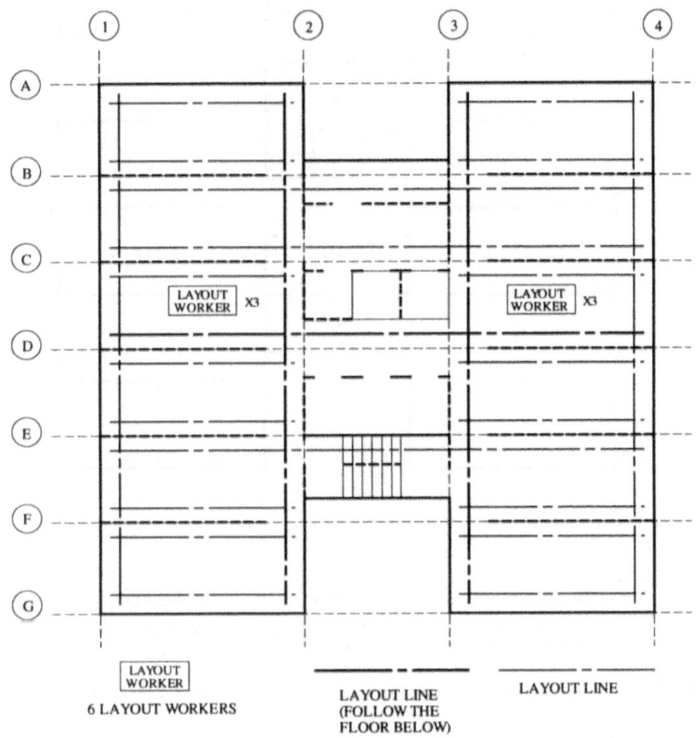

Fig. 9.4. The assignment of workers for marking the layout of the floor — Day 1 (6 am - 8 am).

Before the first day. The marking of the layout is estimated to take two hours. Scheduled to be completed before the first day, it should start at 6 am to be ready by 8 am. Six workers mark the top of the slab of the previously constructed floor, as shown in Fig. 9.4. The thicker lines mark the location of the shear walls, while the thin solid lines mark a *base line* at a distance of 4 feet (or 1 meter) from the centerline of the walls.

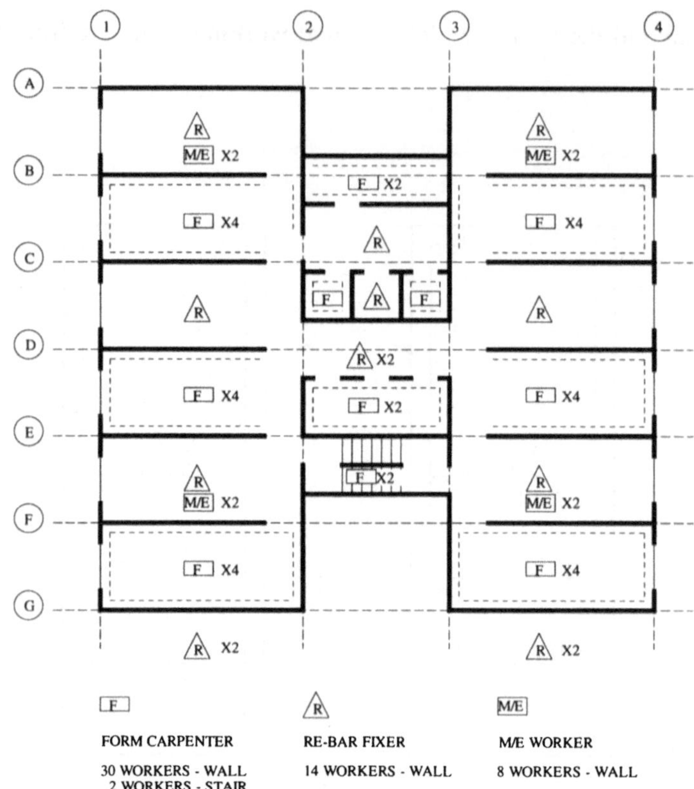

Fig. 9.5. The assignment of workers — Day 1 (8 am - 4 pm).

First day. Fig. 9.5 shows the tasks scheduled to be completed during the first day of construction. The building of the formwork, the fixing of the reinforcing steel bars, and the mechanical and electrical preparations are scheduled to proceed simultaneously. However, no more than 2 tasks are scheduled to be performed at the same time in the same working space, as it is defined by the location of the shear walls. A dotted line parallel to a shear wall represents the building of the formwork on that side of the wall, while the steel worker fixes the reinforcing bars on the other side. During the first day, 6 crews, of 4 carpenters each, are scheduled to complete the formwork of 6 guest rooms. Furthermore, a crew of 2 carpenters should complete the shear walls of the main elevator well, and a crew of another 2 carpenters should complete the shear walls of the services room. Finally,

2 carpenters should complete the formwork in the south service elevator well and in the janitor's room. Another crew of 2 should start the building of the formwork of the staircase, a task that is scheduled to continue until the 4th day of construction.

Thus, a total of 32 carpenters are scheduled to work during the first day of construction for each typical floor. In addition, 14 reinforcing bar fixers are scheduled to be distributed on the floor, as shown in Fig. 9.5. Six workers should fix the bars in the other 6 guest rooms, where wall formwork is not being built, with one person working in each room. Two crews, of 2 bar fixers each, are scheduled to work on the west side of the exterior wall and 3 more workers are allocated in the elevator lobbies. Finally, 8 M&E workers, working in crews of 2, are scheduled to prepare all the mechanical and electrical installations in the shear walls during the first day of construction. The reinforcement of the walls, the completed formwork and the M&E installations should be inspected at the end of the first day before they are covered by the formwork on the other side of the walls.

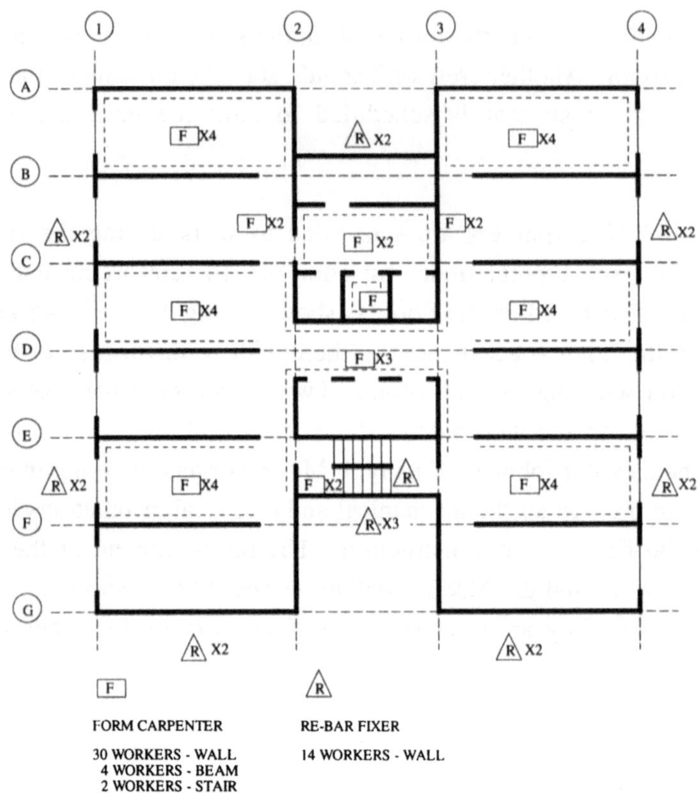

Fig. 9.6. *The assignment of workers — Day 2 (8 am - 4 pm).*

Second day. The tasks to be executed on the second day of construction are shown in Fig. 9.6. The 6 crews of carpenters working on the formwork of the shear walls that define the guest rooms should proceed to the remaining 6 rooms. The carpenters working on the core should continue the formwork on the remaining parts of the core and the walls of the long corridors. Furthermore, 4 additional carpenters should prepare the formwork for the 2 beams in the corridors. The 2 carpenters should keep working on the staircase, joined with a bar fixer. The other bar fixers should work on the exterior walls, in crews of 2, except for a crew of 3 that should work on the west side of the core. The second day, there is no more work for M&E workers on the floor. The formwork of the walls is scheduled to be inspected at the end of the second day.

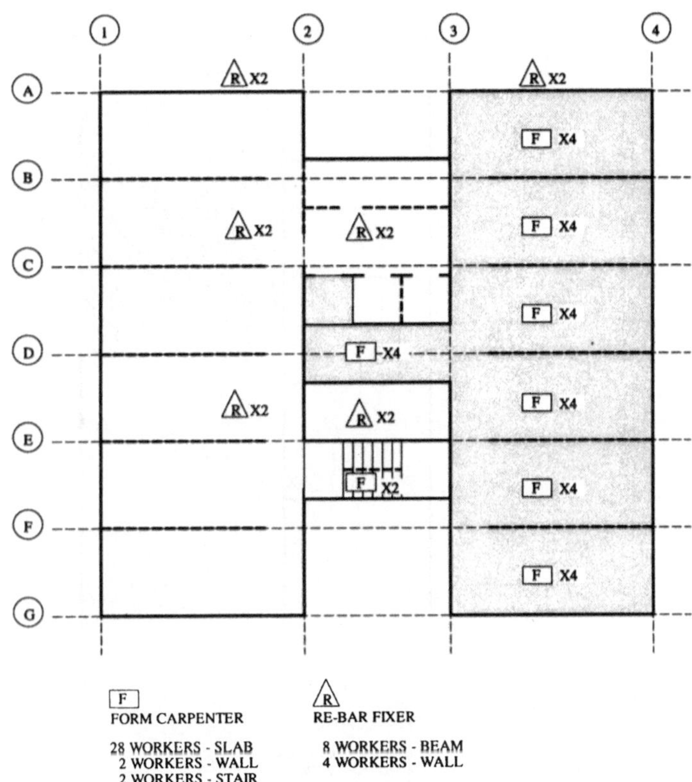

Fig. 9.7. *The assignment of workers — Day 3 (8 am - 12 noon).*

Third day. In the morning of the third day of construction, 28 carpenters should prepare the formwork for the slab on the south row of guest rooms and part of the core, as shown in Fig. 9.7. The 2 carpenters should keep working on the formwork of the staircase. Twelve bar fixers are scheduled to be on the floor during the third day. Eight should prepare the reinforcement for the 2 beams and 4 more should work on the east side of the exterior wall.

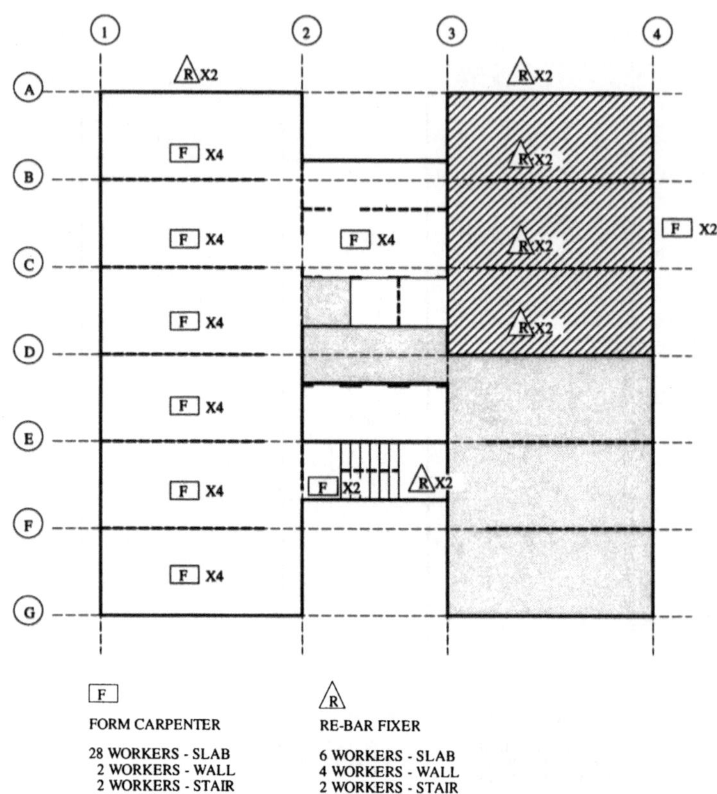

Fig. 9.8. The assignment of workers — Day 3 (12 noon - 4 pm).

In the afternoon of the third day, the carpenters are scheduled to be moved to the north part of the floor and part of the core, as shown in Fig. 9.8. Two carpenters should complete the formwork of the eastern part of the south exterior wall. At the same time, 6 bar fixers should place the reinforcing bars on the southeastern quarter of the flat plate, and 4 bar fixers should place the reinforcement on the eastern exterior wall, while 2 more should work on the staircase.

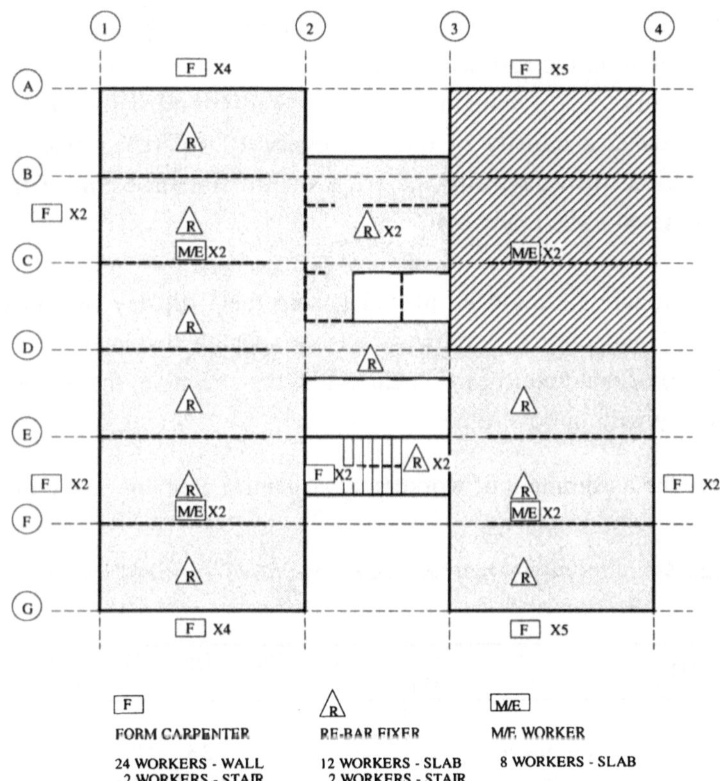

Fig. 9.9. The assignment of workers — Day 4 (8 am - 4 pm).

Fourth day. During the fourth day of construction, the carpenters should work and complete the formwork for the exterior walls of the hotel, as shown in Fig. 9.8. The bar fixers should work and complete the remaining reinforcement of the slab. The staircase should be also completed and M&E workers are scheduled to enter the site to prepare the slab prior to placing concrete. They work in crews of 2, each on a quarter of the floor. At the end of that day, the formwork, reinforcing bars and mechanical and engineering preparation should be ready for placing the concrete, and should be inspected at the end of the fourth day.

After the fourth day. The same workers who mark the layout before the first day are scheduled to position vertical steel rods in the formwork to define the top level of the concrete slab. These rods are attached to the reinforcing steel and guide the placement of concrete in the following day, ensuring that the required thickness is achieved. Six workers are scheduled to work individually for two hours to position these rods at a density of one rod every 10 sq. ft. Scheduled to be completed before the fifth day, this operation should start at 4 pm of the fourth day and it is estimated to be ready by 6 pm.

Fifth day. The concrete should be placed during the fifth day of construction, under continuous inspection. A crew of 18 is expected to place the estimated 7,740 ft^3 (220 m^3) of concrete for the shear walls, the staircase, the beams and the slab in a single day, without overtime.

Table 9.2 shows the assignment of workers by structural element on a daily basis.

Table 9.2. Assignment of workers per structural element, on a daily basis.

ELEMENT		before Day-1	Day 1	Day 2	Day 3	Day 4	after Day-4	Day 5
MARKING		3					3	
SLAB	Formwork				28			
	Re-bar				0/6*	12		
	M&E					8		
STAIRCASE	Formwork		2	2	2	2		
& MISCELLANEOUS	Re-bar				0/2	2		
BEAMS	Formwork			4				
	Re-bar				8/0			
WALLS	Formwork		30	30	2	24		
	Re-bar		14	14	4			
	M&E		8					
TOTAL	*Formwork*		*32*	*32*	*32*	*26*		
	Re-bar		*14*	*14*	*12*	*14*		
	M&E		*8*			*8*		
	Concrete							*18*
WORKERS ON THE FLOOR		*3*	*54*	*46*	*46*	*48*	*3*	*18*

* 0/6: no workers in the morning, and 6 workers in the afternoon.

9.3 SCHEDULING THE CONSTRUCTION OF THE FRAME

After the daily assignment of the workers on the floor, the Visual Scheduling and Management System is employed to represent the schedule of the construction and test the implied assumptions. First, the microtemplate schedule is constructed, followed by the development of the template schedule for the structural work on each floor. Then, the construction of the structural frame for the 18 identical floors is presented in the matrix-balanced chart, including the assembly and dismantling of the formwork and the scaffolding.

9.3.1 The Microtemplate Schedule

Fig. 9.10 shows the microtemplate schedule with a highly detailed description of the construction of the reinforced concrete elements. This microtemplate depicts four trades: layout markers, carpenters, bar fixers, and M&E workers. However, only the assignment of the carpenters and the bar fixers requires that detailed level of scheduling, since those trades need be scheduled and balanced among the various structural parts of the floor. Furthermore, a simultaneous representation of both trades on the same microtemplate allows a better understanding of their interaction. This combined microtemplate schedule is similar to the microtemplate schedule of Fig. 6.3, and shows the quantities of each element (column A), the total persondays (column B), the daily productivity (column C), and the ratio of the productivity to the average productivity (column D). Column D shows that the tasks on the wall have a slightly below average productivity, while the productivity of the tasks on the staircase is almost half, the beam averages about 65%, and the slab has an increased productivity of 40% above the average.

Column E shows the number of workers working on the site and on the particular elements, both in the morning and in the afternoon. The total number of workers for each task in column E is equal to the number shown in column B. Notice that column E had been hidden in the microtemplate schedule of Fig. 6.3.

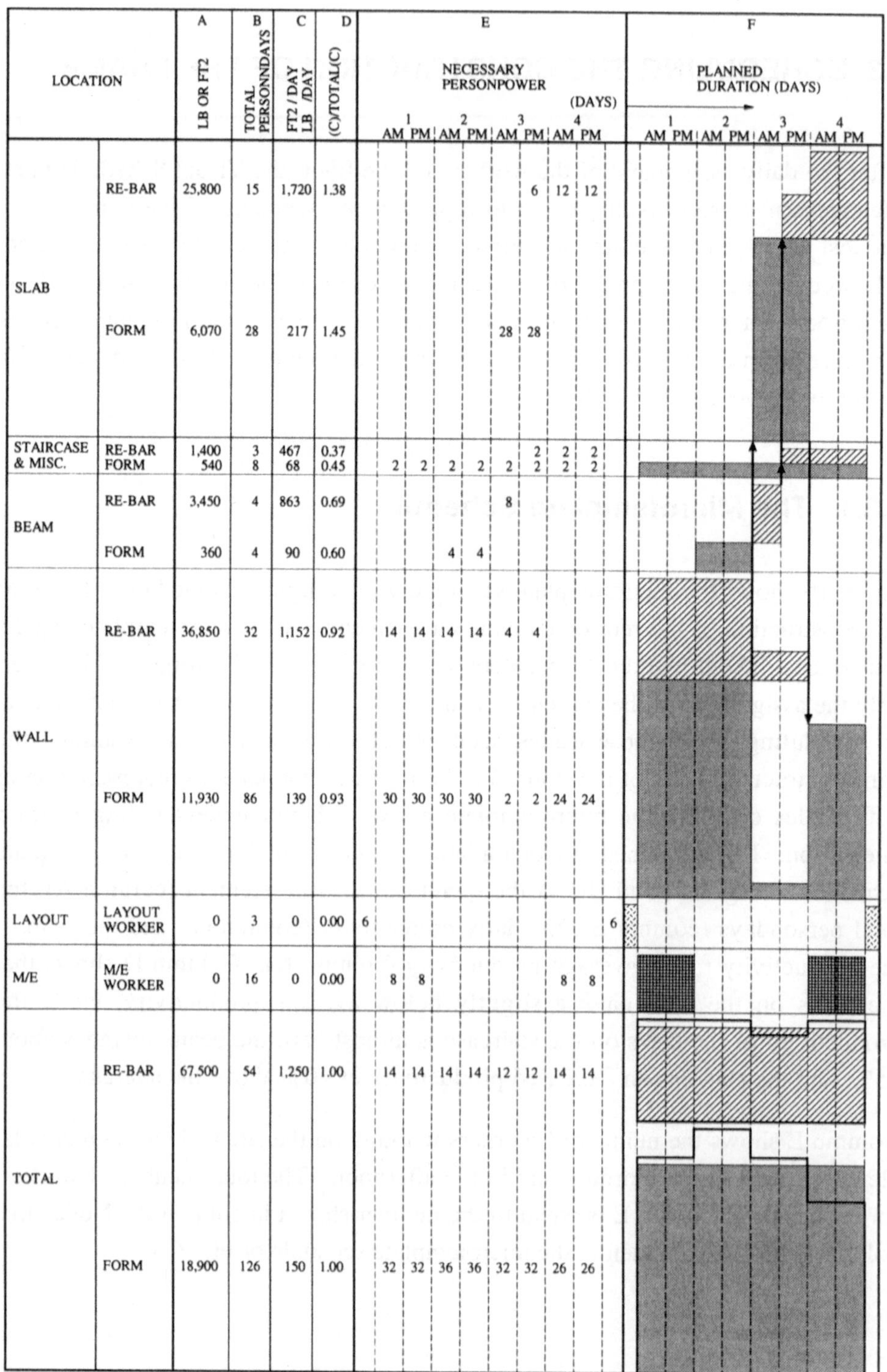

LOCATION		A LB OR FT2	B TOTAL PERSONNDAYS	C FT2/DAY LB/DAY	D (CV/TOTAL(C))	E NECESSARY PERSONPOWER 1 AM	1 PM	2 AM	2 PM	3 AM	3 PM	4 AM	4 PM	F PLANNED DURATION (DAYS)
SLAB	RE-BAR	25,800	15	1,720	1.38						6	12	12	
	FORM	6,070	28	217	1.45					28	28			
STAIRCASE & MISC.	RE-BAR	1,400	3	467	0.37						2	2	2	
	FORM	540	8	68	0.45	2	2	2	2	2	2	2	2	
BEAM	RE-BAR	3,450	4	863	0.69					8				
	FORM	360	4	90	0.60			4	4					
WALL	RE-BAR	36,850	32	1,152	0.92	14	14	14	14	4	4			
	FORM	11,930	86	139	0.93	30	30	30	30	2	2	24	24	
LAYOUT	LAYOUT WORKER	0	3	0	0.00	6							6	
M/E	M/E WORKER	0	16	0	0.00	8	8					8	8	
TOTAL	RE-BAR	67,500	54	1,250	1.00	14	14	14	14	12	12	14	14	
	FORM	18,900	126	150	1.00	32	32	36	36	32	32	26	26	

Fig. 9.10. Microtemplate for reinforced concrete elements.

The total daily number of workers for the bar fixers and the carpenters, shown at the bottom of the microtemplate schedule, indicates that the work is not leveled off. The average number of bar fixers is 13.5 and the average number of carpenters is 31.5. However, the carpenters and the bar fixers have parallel work on secondary structures in the lower floors of the same building. Thus, it is accepted to schedule the construction of the floor as it is shown on the microtemplate schedule.

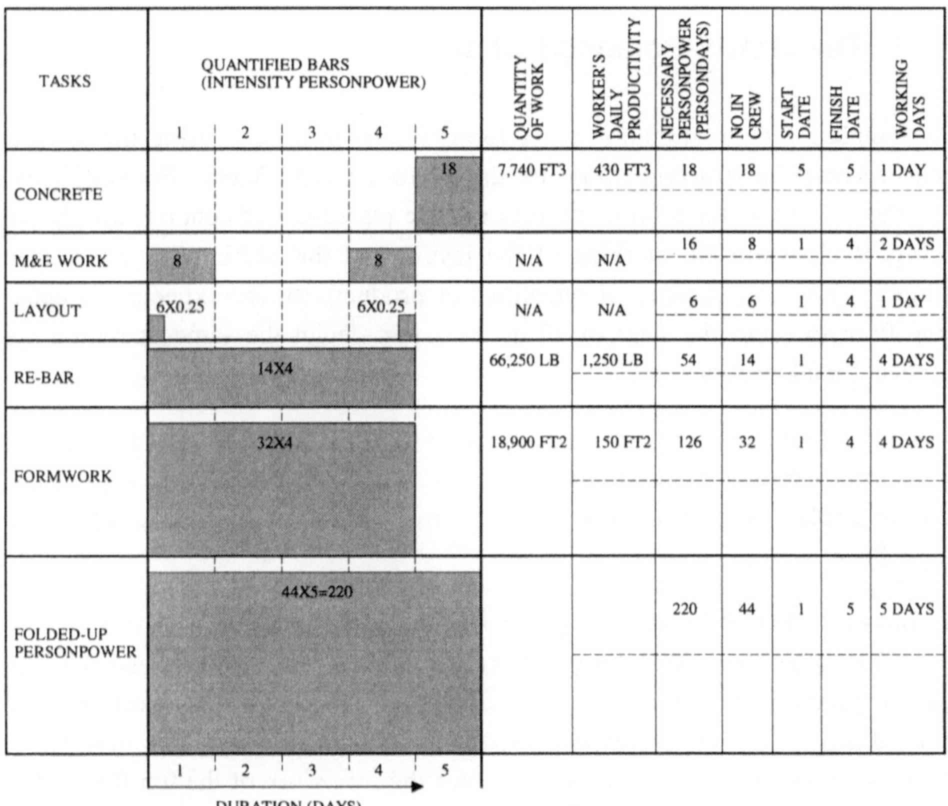

TASKS	QUANTIFIED BARS (INTENSITY PERSONPOWER)					QUANTITY OF WORK	WORKER'S DAILY PRODUCTIVITY	NECESSARY PERSONPOWER (PERSONDAYS)	NO.IN CREW	START DATE	FINISH DATE	WORKING DAYS
	1	2	3	4	5							
CONCRETE					18	7,740 FT3	430 FT3	18	18	5	5	1 DAY
M&E WORK	8			8		N/A	N/A	16	8	1	4	2 DAYS
LAYOUT	6X0.25			6X0.25		N/A	N/A	6	6	1	4	1 DAY
RE-BAR	14X4					66,250 LB	1,250 LB	54	14	1	4	4 DAYS
FORMWORK	32X4					18,900 FT2	150 FT2	126	32	1	4	4 DAYS
FOLDED-UP PERSONPOWER	44X5=220								220	44	1	5	5 DAYS

Fig. 9.11. The template for the construction of the structural elements of a typical floor .

9.3.2 The Template for Structural Work

Fig. 9.11 shows the template for the construction of the structural elements of a typical floor. The tasks of the microtemplate have been folded to produce rectangular bars and the placement of concrete has been added on the template. In addition, the alphanumeric part provides the cumulative information for the structural elements grouped together.

9.3.3 The Matrix-Balanced Chart

The template for the structural work forms the basis for preparing the matrix-balanced chart for structural work, for the 4th to the 22nd floors. For simplicity, only the formwork, the reinforcing bars and the placement of concrete are shown in Fig. 9.12, while the marking of the layout and the M&E work have been omitted. Since no changes of quantities or productivity are expected to occur from floor to floor, the sizes of all the bars that depict the same operation are identical for all locations.

In addition to the construction of the floors, Fig. 9.12 shows visually the moving of the formwork and the scaffolding. The matrix-balanced chart is the appropriate chart to display these operations, since they relate between two floors rather on a single floor.

According to Fig. 9.12, the formwork and the scaffolding of the 4th floor are scheduled to be dismantled during the construction of the 7th floor and they are used to produce the formwork of the 8th floor. Then, the formwork and the scaffolding of the 5th floor are scheduled to be dismantled during the construction of the 8th floor and they are used to produce the formwork of the 9th floor. The same procedure should be repeated for the following floors. According to this schedule, 4 sets of formwork are needed for the construction of the building, and, at any time, there are 3 floors supported on formwork and scaffolding. This schedule allows the top floor, below the floor being constructed, to have cured for 5 days, the lower supported floor to have cured for 10 days, and the higher unsupported floor to have cured for 15 days. In general, this is sufficient time to develop the required strength to hold the floors as they are constructed.

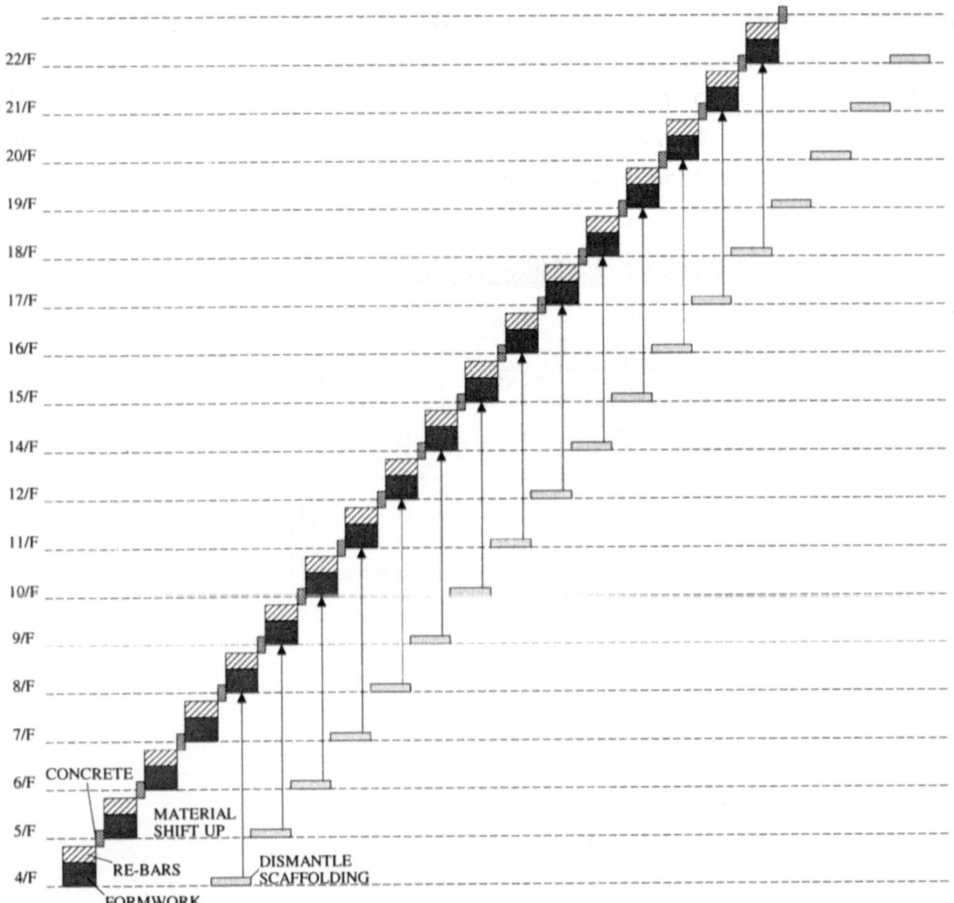

Fig. 9.12. Matrix-balanced chart for the construction of the structural frame, including the moving of the formwork and the scaffolding from floor to floor.

9.4 SCHEDULING THE FINISHING OF THE BUILDING

After the formwork and the scaffolding are removed, the floors are ready to start building the non-structural elements and proceed with the finishing. Among the guest rooms, the bathrooms and the common areas on each floor, the building of bathrooms constitutes the most time consuming task. Thus, the operations on the floors are scheduled around the building of the bathrooms.

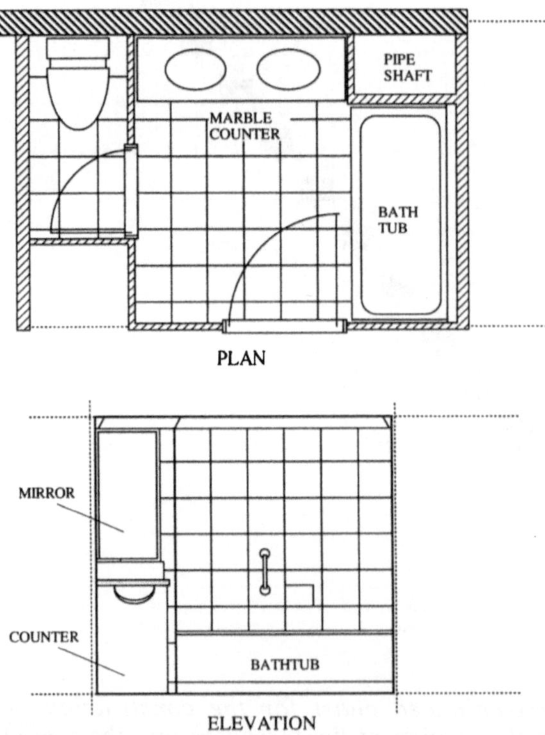

Fig. 9.13. Plan and elevation of a typical bathroom.

9.4.1 Finishing the Bathrooms

Fig. 9.13 shows the plan and elevation of the typical bathroom to be repeated in all the guest rooms of the 18 identical floors. Fig. 9.14 shows the template schedule for the 14 tasks that comprise the building and finishing of the twelve bathrooms of a typical floor. This template includes the quantities of work for each task, the daily productivity of the workers, the necessary personpower, the number of workers in each crew, and the duration of each task. The start and finish days have not been entered, since the exact scheduling should be determined in conjunction with the finishing of the guest rooms and the common areas, as well as in conjunction with finishing the other floors. However, it is shown that the finishing of the bathrooms of a single floor would require 13 weeks, if the individual tasks were scheduled sequentially with no float time.

Fig. 9.15 shows the matrix-balanced schedule for finishing the bathrooms for the 18 identical floors. This schedule assumes that the work on the bathrooms is independent of the work on the guest rooms and the common areas. The total required time is 36 weeks, and each task is scheduled so that there is a single crew of the same trade on the site at any given time. Notice that each week is depicted as having 6 working days, with no Sundays displayed on the chart.

Certain tasks, like *marble tiles, ceiling frame and board, millwork,* and *painting* define the most critical sequence of events. These tasks are executed sequentially from floor to floor with the same number of workers and each takes 8 days. Other tasks, however, continue with a variable intensity from floor to floor. Marking the layout of the bathroom is critical for the first 3 floors and 6 workers finish the task in 2 days. Then, for the next 6 floors, the number of workers is reduced to 4, so they need 3 days. Finally, for the rest of the floors, 2 workers need 6 days, but at that time the marking of the layout is not critical any more for the final completion of the project. Similarly, other tasks are executed with a variable intensity at different floors, including the concrete blocks, and M&E.

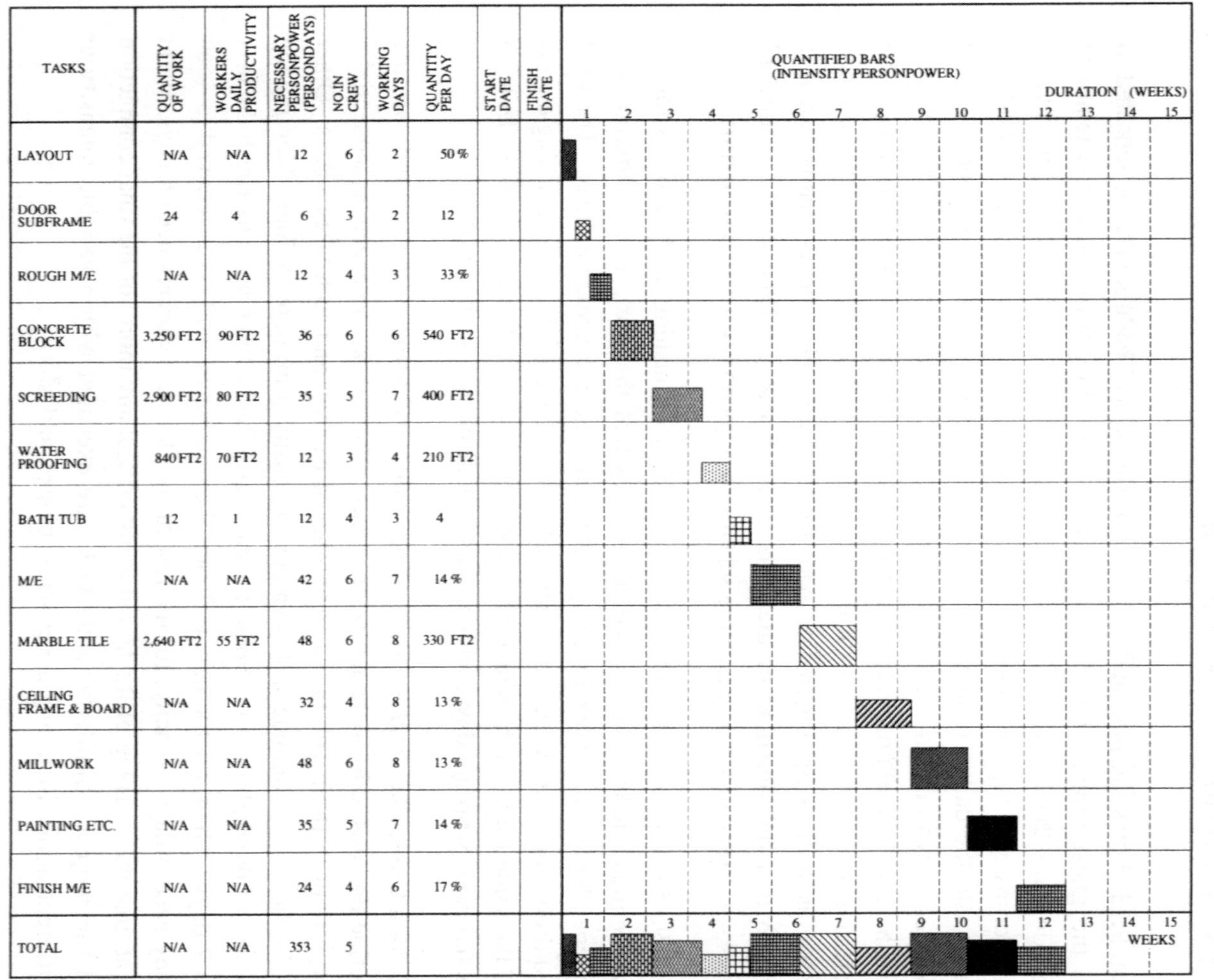

TASKS	QUANTITY OF WORK	WORKERS DAILY PRODUCTIVITY	NECESSARY PERSONPOWER (PERSONDAYS)	NO.IN CREW	WORKING DAYS	QUANTITY PER DAY	START DATE	FINISH DATE	QUANTIFIED BARS (INTENSITY PERSONPOWER) / DURATION (WEEKS)
LAYOUT	N/A	N/A	12	6	2	50 %			
DOOR SUBFRAME	24	4	6	3	2	12			
ROUGH M/E	N/A	N/A	12	4	3	33 %			
CONCRETE BLOCK	3,250 FT2	90 FT2	36	6	6	540 FT2			
SCREEDING	2,900 FT2	80 FT2	35	5	7	400 FT2			
WATER PROOFING	840 FT2	70 FT2	12	3	4	210 FT2			
BATH TUB	12	1	12	4	3	4			
M/E	N/A	N/A	42	6	7	14 %			
MARBLE TILE	2,640 FT2	55 FT2	48	6	8	330 FT2			
CEILING FRAME & BOARD	N/A	N/A	32	4	8	13 %			
MILLWORK	N/A	N/A	48	6	8	13 %			
PAINTING ETC.	N/A	N/A	35	5	7	14 %			
FINISH M/E	N/A	N/A	24	4	6	17 %			
TOTAL	N/A	N/A	353	5					

Fig. 9.14. *Template for the twelve bathrooms of a floor.*

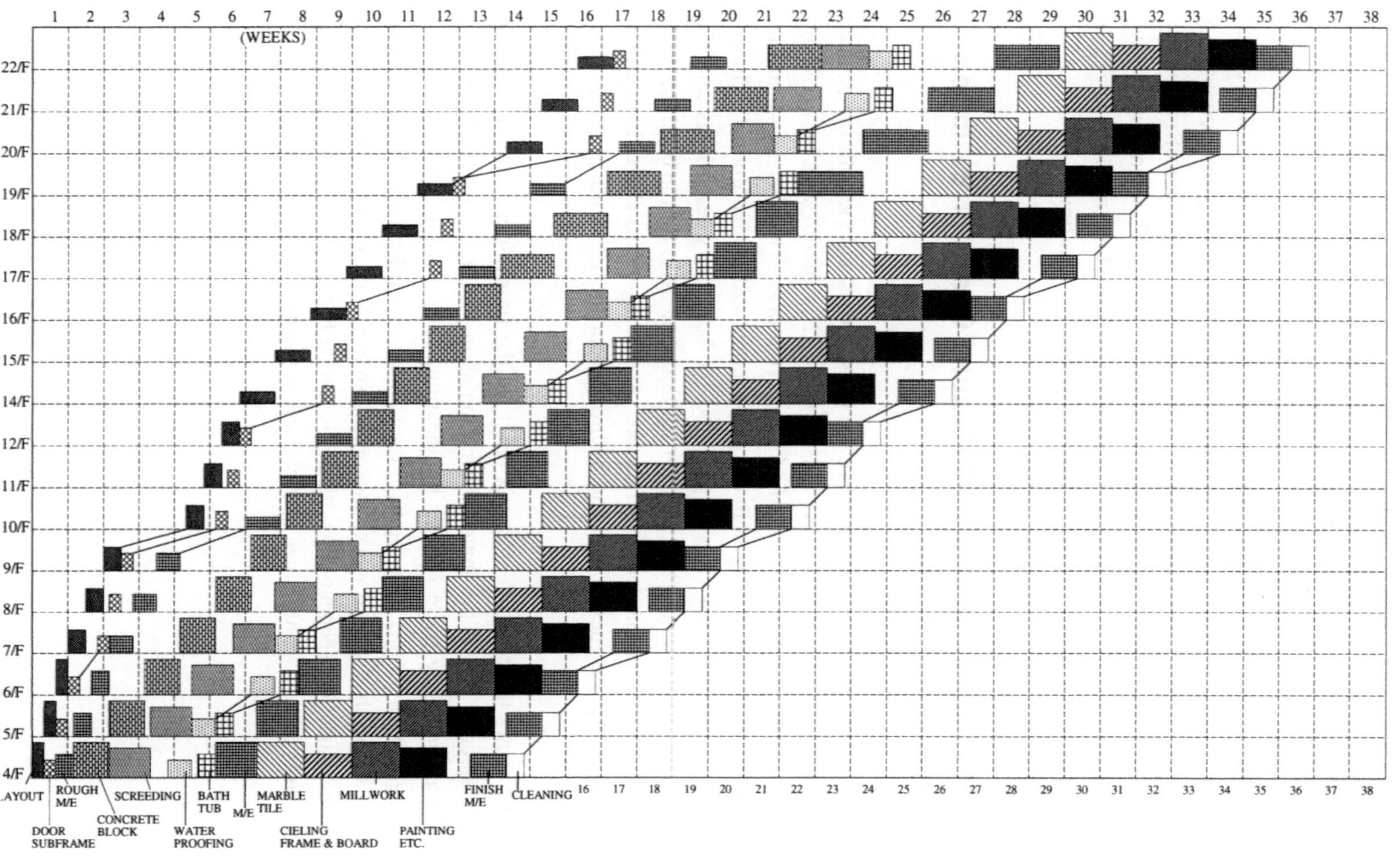

Fig. 9.15. Matrix-balanced chart for the twelve bathrooms of a floor.

9.4.2 Finishing the Guest Rooms

The finishing of the guest rooms follows the same approach as the finishing of the bathrooms. Fig. 9.16 shows the template schedule for all the guest rooms of a typical floor. The 17 tasks that comprise the finishing of the guest rooms are identified and presented with the associated information. This template shows that the finishing of the guest rooms of a single floor would require 11.5 weeks, if the individual tasks were scheduled sequentially with no float time.

9.4.3 The Combined Matrix-Balanced Chart for Bathrooms and Guest Rooms

There are several common tasks between the guest rooms and the bathrooms, such as *marking the layout, door sub frames, rough M&E, concrete block, screeding, M&E, millwork, painting, finish M&E,* and *cleaning.* These tasks should be executed by the same crews for both the guest rooms and the bathrooms. Thus, a combined matrix-balanced chart is prepared for both the guest rooms and the bathrooms, as shown in Fig. 9.17. On the 4th floor, the tasks for the bathrooms are outlined with a thicker line for identification. According to this chart, the required time for building the guest rooms and bathrooms for the 18 identical floors is 37 weeks.

Fig. 9.18 shows the constituent matrix chart for the finishing schedule for the 18 identical floors. This is the same information as in Fig. 9.17, but the tasks have been re-arranged by trade instead by location. Fig. 9.18 is quite useful for allocating work by trade, showing both the number of workers per day, as well as the floor where they should work. According to Fig. 9.18, the more intense tasks have been scheduled sequentially with no float time between floors, while the less intense tasks have discontinuities or a variable intensity as the work progresses.

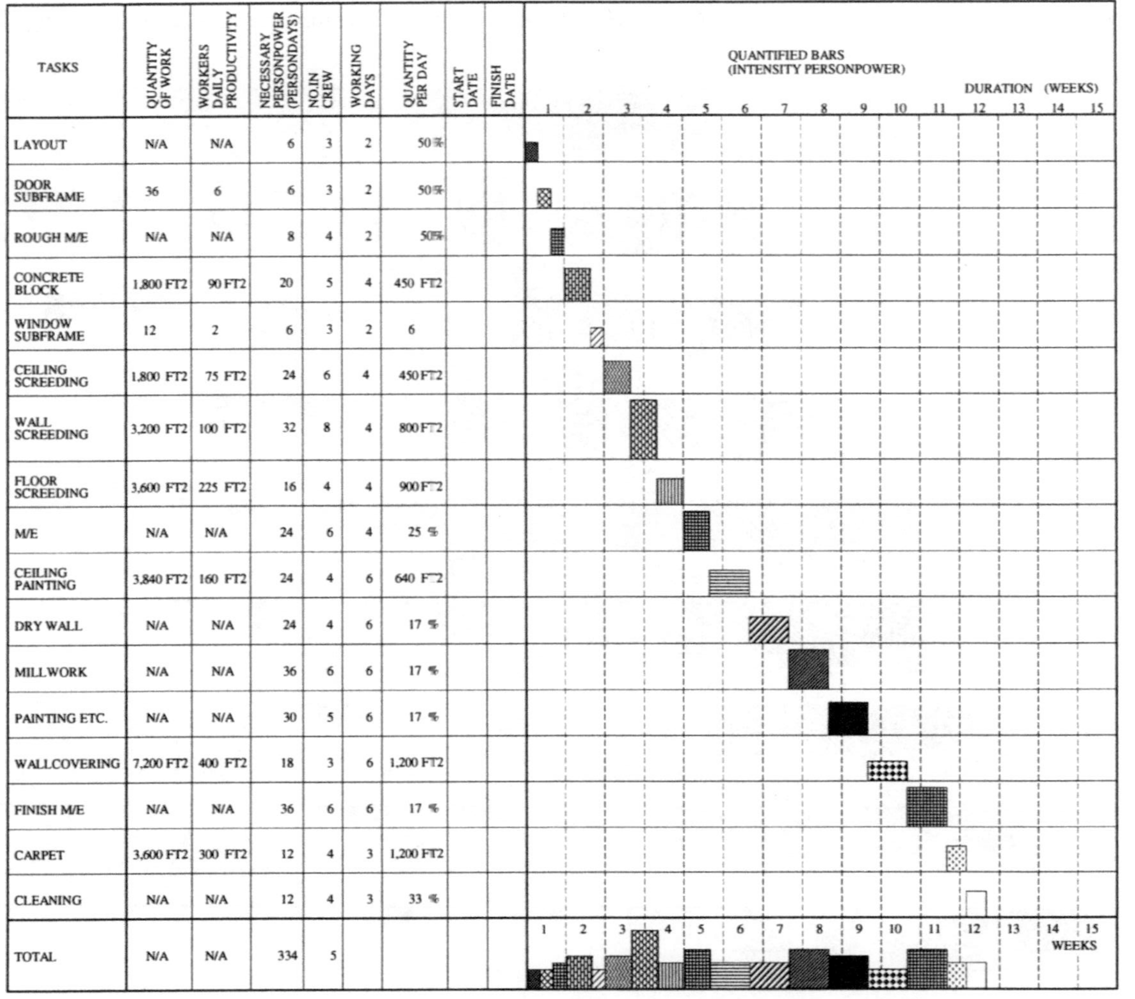

TASKS	QUANTITY OF WORK	WORKERS DAILY PRODUCTIVITY	NECESSARY PERSONPOWER (PERSONDAYS)	NO.IN CREW	WORKING DAYS	QUANTITY PER DAY	START DATE	FINISH DATE	QUANTIFIED BARS (INTENSITY PERSONPOWER) / DURATION (WEEKS)
LAYOUT	N/A	N/A	6	3	2	50 %			
DOOR SUBFRAME	36	6	6	3	2	50 %			
ROUGH M/E	N/A	N/A	8	4	2	50 %			
CONCRETE BLOCK	1,800 FT2	90 FT2	20	5	4	450 FT2			
WINDOW SUBFRAME	12	2	6	3	2	6			
CEILING SCREEDING	1,800 FT2	75 FT2	24	6	4	450 FT2			
WALL SCREEDING	3,200 FT2	100 FT2	32	8	4	800 FT2			
FLOOR SCREEDING	3,600 FT2	225 FT2	16	4	4	900 FT2			
M/E	N/A	N/A	24	6	4	25 %			
CEILING PAINTING	3,840 FT2	160 FT2	24	4	6	640 FT2			
DRY WALL	N/A	N/A	24	4	6	17 %			
MILLWORK	N/A	N/A	36	6	6	17 %			
PAINTING ETC.	N/A	N/A	30	5	6	17 %			
WALLCOVERING	7,200 FT2	400 FT2	18	3	6	1,200 FT2			
FINISH M/E	N/A	N/A	36	6	6	17 %			
CARPET	3,600 FT2	300 FT2	12	4	3	1,200 FT2			
CLEANING	N/A	N/A	12	4	3	33 %			
TOTAL	N/A	N/A	334	5					

Fig. 9.16. Template for the twelve guest rooms of a floor.

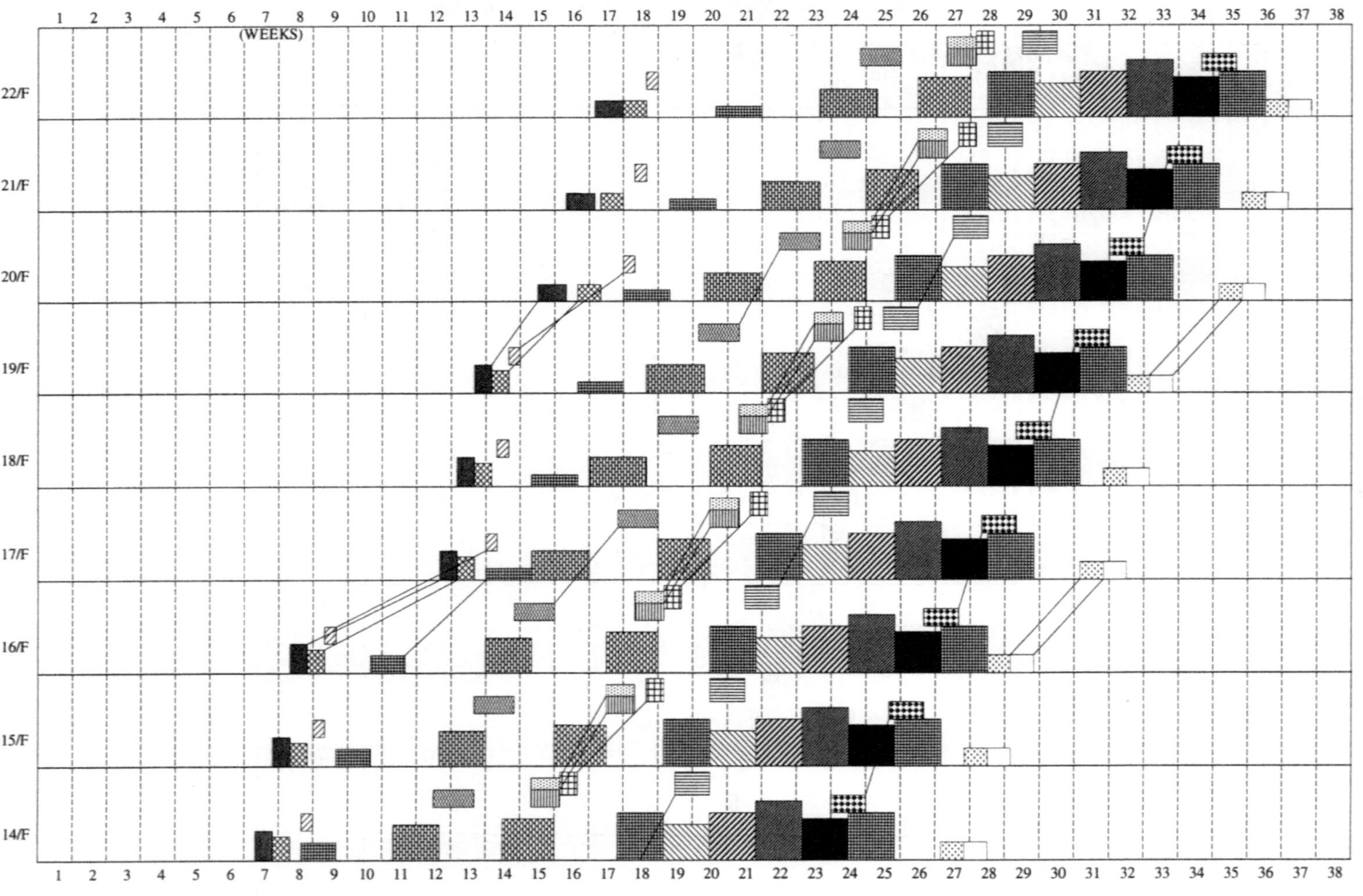

Fig. 9.17. Combined matrix-balanced chart for bathrooms and guest rooms.

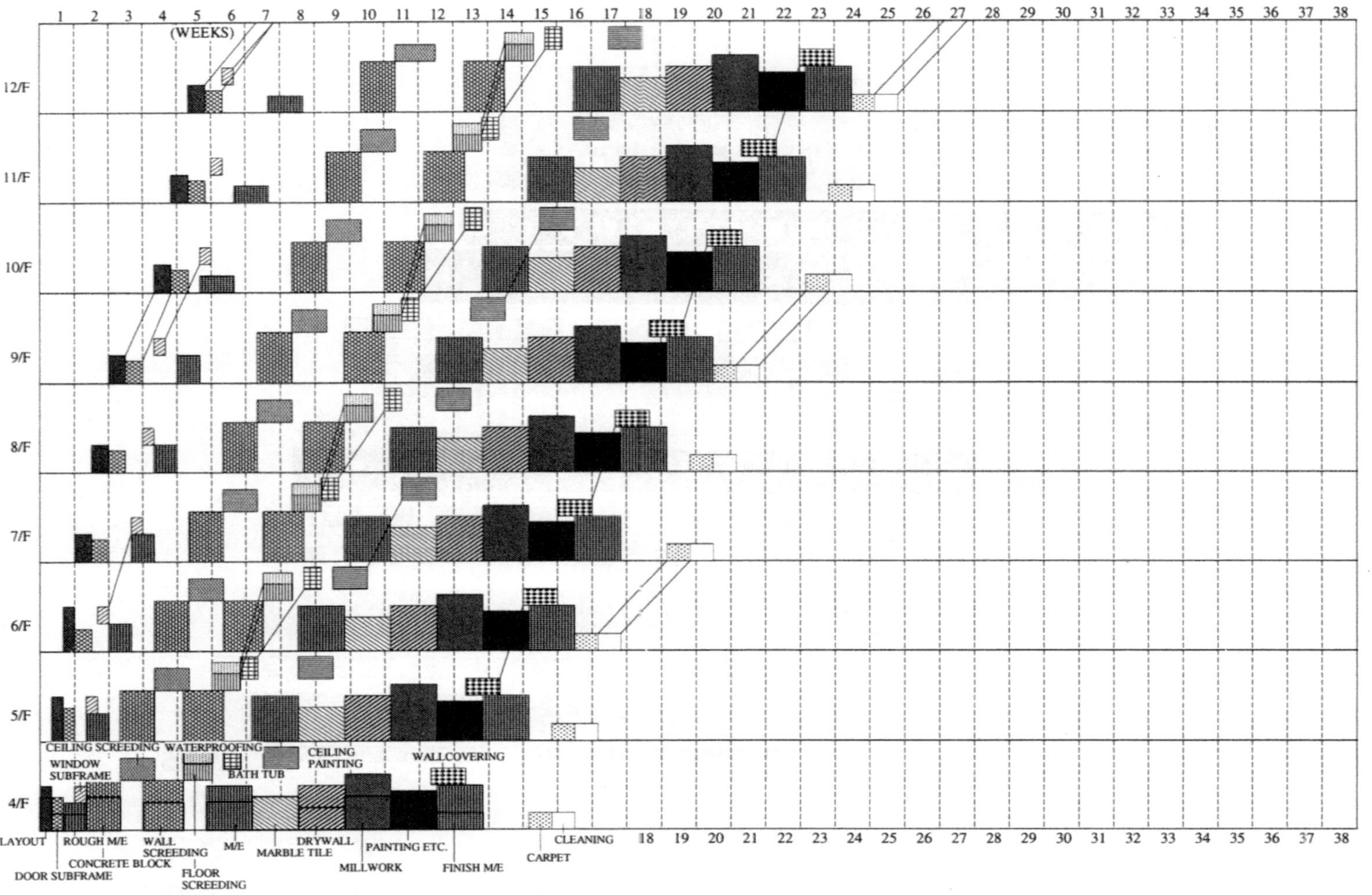

Fig. 9.17. Combined matrix-balanced chart for bathrooms and guest rooms (continued).

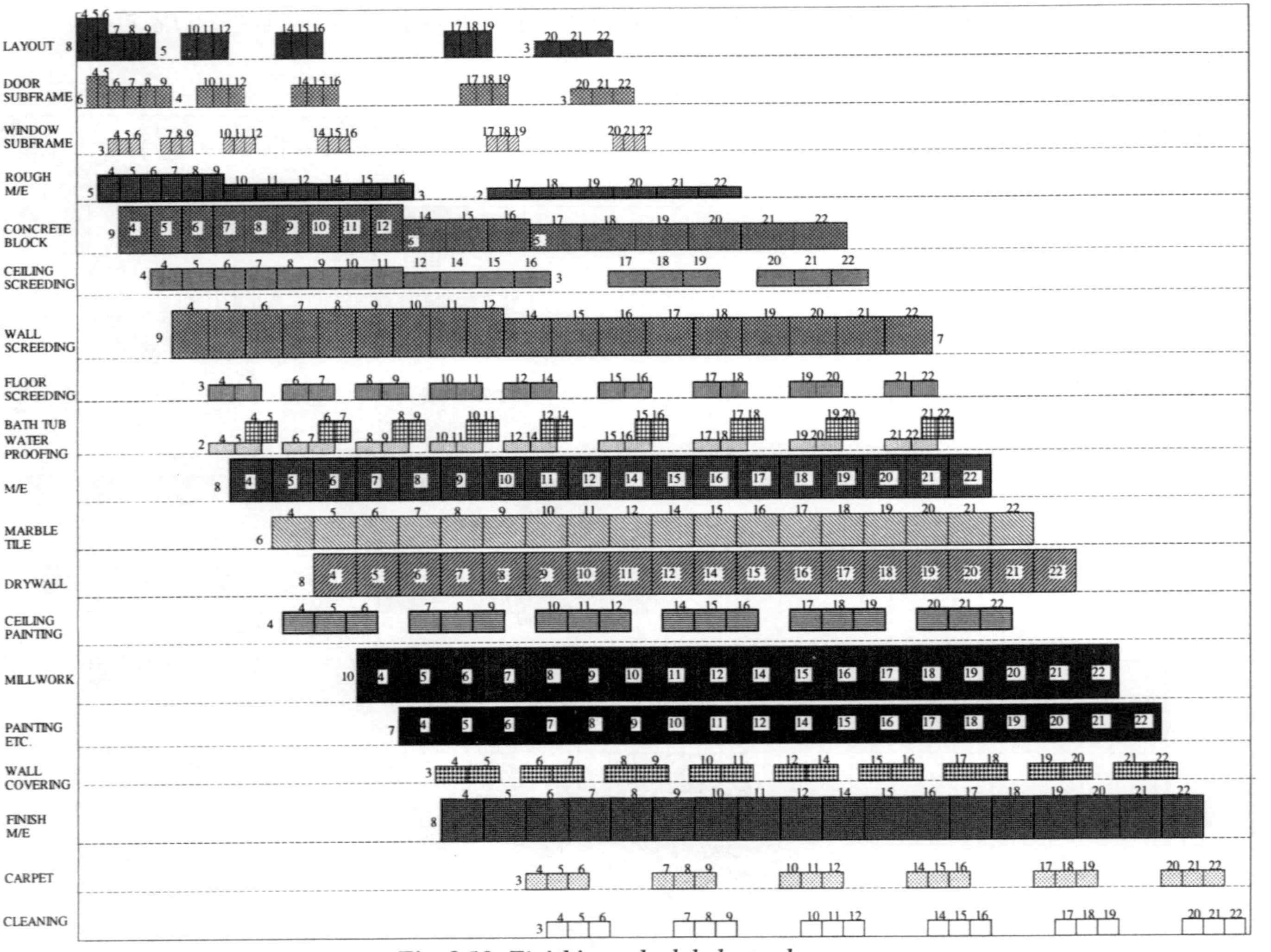

Fig. 9.18. Finishing schedule by trade.

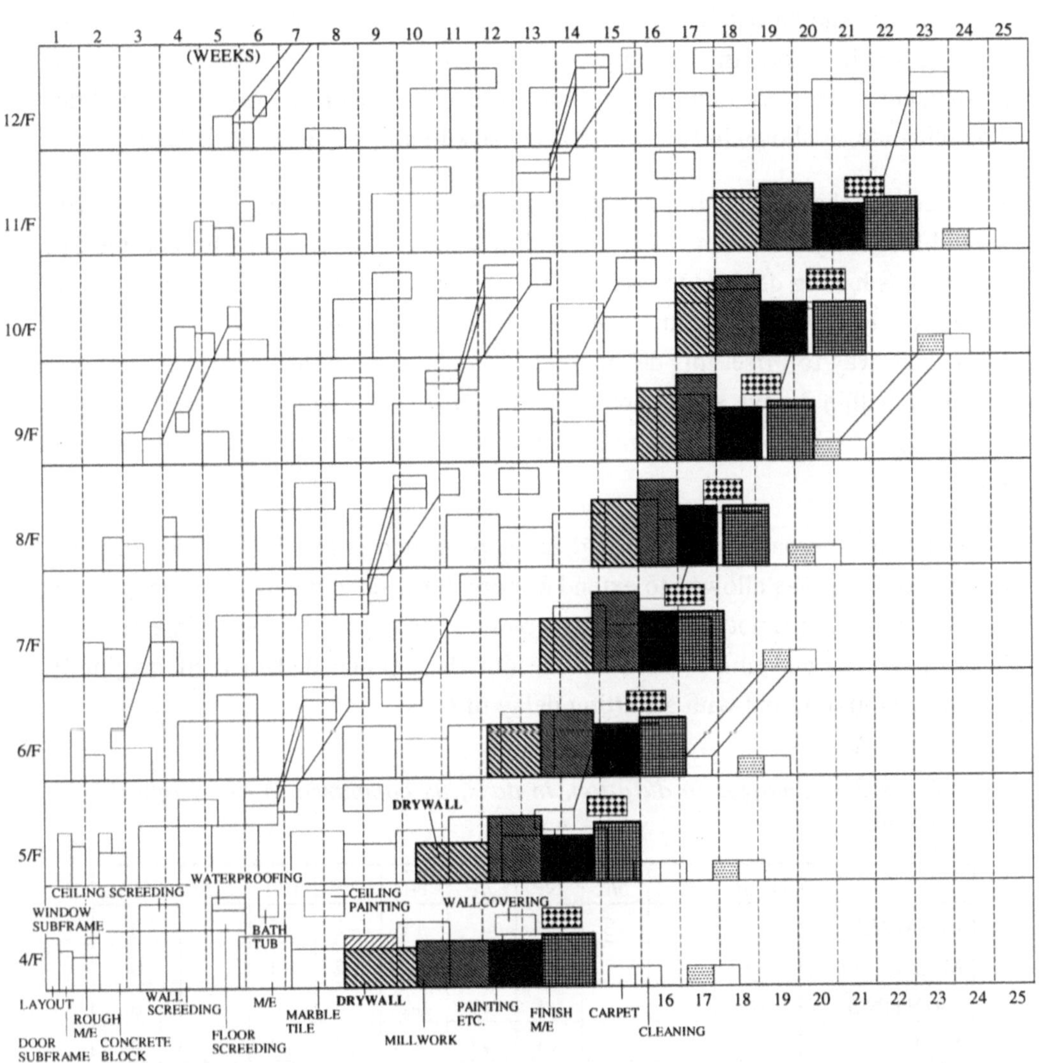

Fig. 9.19. Correction of schedule for compensating delays.

9.4.4 Recovering a Delay in Finishing

Fig. 9.19 presents a delay of the finishing schedule and a revised, accelerated schedule for the finishing of the other floors to recover the delay. The tasks, as scheduled in Fig. 9.17, are shown outlined. Only the tasks that deviate from the schedule are shown hatched. A single task, the building of *drywalls*, deviated unintentionally from the schedule on the 4th and the 5th floors, while the subsequent tasks were modified in order to catch up with the original schedule. The schedule, as shown in Fig. 9.19 comes back to normal on the 12th floor.

According to the information displayed on Fig. 9.17, the building of the *drywalls* should last 8 days for each floor. Instead, it lasted 11 days on the 4th and the 5th floors, thus having delayed the schedule at the 6th floor by 6 days. This delay, as shown on Fig. 9.19, was attributed to reduced personpower on the site[2]. An immediate way to offset this delay would have been to build the *drywalls* on the 6th floor within 2 days and to accelerate the *millwork, painting* and *finish M&E* accordingly. However, such radical increases in personpower would not be feasible.

A systematic approach to offset the delay is presented in Fig. 9.19. The *millwork* on the 4th floor was allowed to extend 3 more days, since the delay of *drywall* on the 5th floor would not allow the carpenters to proceed without an interruption. Then, *painting* and *finish M&E* on the 4th floor proceeded in their originally scheduled duration but with a starting delay of 6 days.

Table 9.3. *Changes in duration, in days, as compared to the original schedule.*

	START	4/F	5/F	6/F	7/F	8/F	9/F	10/F	11/F	FINAL
DRYWALL		-3	-3			+1	+2	+2	+1	0
MILLWORK	-3	-3			+1	+2	+2	+1		0
PAINTING	-6			+1	+2	+2	+1			0
M&E	-6		+1	+1	+1	+1	+1	+1		0

A coordinated accelerated schedule is adapted for the *drywall, millwork, painting, finish M&E,* and *wall covering* for the higher floors. Table 9.3 shows the difference, in days, between the original schedule and the modified schedule. A negative number indicates a delay, while a positive number indicates an

---

2   A similar delay could have resulted from reduced productivity.

acceleration. Despite the initial delay of 6 days, no task is accelerated by more than 2 days, which corresponds to 25% of its originally estimated duration. Thus, an acceleration by 2 working days implies a 25% increase in personpower, while an acceleration by 1 working day implies a 13% increase in personpower.

On the 5th floor, *millwork* returns to its originally planned duration of 8 days. Furthermore, *finish M&E* is executed 1 day faster than originally scheduled by allocating more personpower, a practice that continues until the 9th floor. Notice, that the need to start *finish M&E* at a certain date on the 10th floor dictates this acceleration by 1 day.

On the 6th floor, drywall returns to its originally planned duration of 8 days, and *painting* is accelerated by 1 day, while the other two tasks are executed similarly to the 5th floor. On the 7th floor, *millwork* is accelerated by 1 day, *painting* by 2 days and *finish M&E* by 1 day, as compared to their original schedules. On the 8th and the 9th floors, all 4 tasks are accelerated. On the 10th floor, *painting* returns to its original schedule of 8 days, while the other tasks are still accelerated. Finally, on the 11th floor, only *drywall* is accelerated by 1 day. The duration of the tasks returns to the original schedule at the 12th floor, where the delay has been eliminated.

The delay for *wall covering* was recovered by eliminating the originally scheduled float time between the 5th and 6th floors, and the 7th and 8th floors.

CHAPTER 10

THE RENOVATION OF A BUILDING INTERIOR

The proposed Visual Scheduling and Management System (VSMS) was employed to assist the project manager to schedule and effectively manage the renovation of the interior of a high-rise building.

A scheduling complexity of the project resulted from the required phased construction, so the client could continue to occupy most of the building during the renovation process. Thus, the scheduling should address both construction and moving of people and furniture, in a working environment that requires extensive wiring for communications. Section 10.1 outlines the project with its particularities and presents the initial planning for all floors, in a simplified connoting bar chart.

The construction scheduling of the renovation did not require the use of VSMS microtemplates. Instead a single template was sufficient to schedule each segment of the renovation. Section 10.2 presents the planning of the project and the initial scheduling template for the 26th floor, a typical self-contained segment of the project. This typical segment served as a pilot project to study the implied scheduling assumptions and derive the necessary conclusions in order to schedule the other parts of the building.

Despite its nature as a pilot project, the deadline for the completion of the typical segment was firmly set. Section 10.3 presents the execution of the renovation and the decisions that the project manager had to take in order to speed up the process and complete the project on time. Section 10.3 derives conclusions as well on how to proceed with the scheduling of the remaining part of the project. Section 10.4 shows the scheduling and control of the following two segments of the project, all on the same floor, in a matrix-balanced chart. Finally, Section 10.5 summarizes the experiences and presents the evaluation of the project management that employed the VSMS as the scheduling and control device for this project.

The remaining of the project constituted a repetitive process, as far as the employment of the proposed Visual Scheduling and Management System. So, this Chapter focuses only on the renovation of the typical segment and the schedule of the next construction segment. The rest of the renovation is not presented.

10.1 THE PROJECT[1]

This project refers to the renovation of the interior space of 9 floors, in a 45 story high-rise building located in downtown Boston. Except for the lobbies outside the elevators, the plan was to renovate entirely the floors from the 26th to the 34th, all occupied by a major financial services firm. The project included the demolition of all the existing interior construction until reaching the main structure of the building. Then, new interior partitions would be built, with all new wiring, new dropped ceilings and new carpeting. Furthermore, new kitchens and restrooms would be built, requiring new plumbing as well. Finally, all interior doors would be new and some of the furniture would be built-in to the new construction. Special emphasis was paid in the appropriate wiring of the renovated space for the necessary electronic communications.

---

[1]   Most of the data have been disguised.

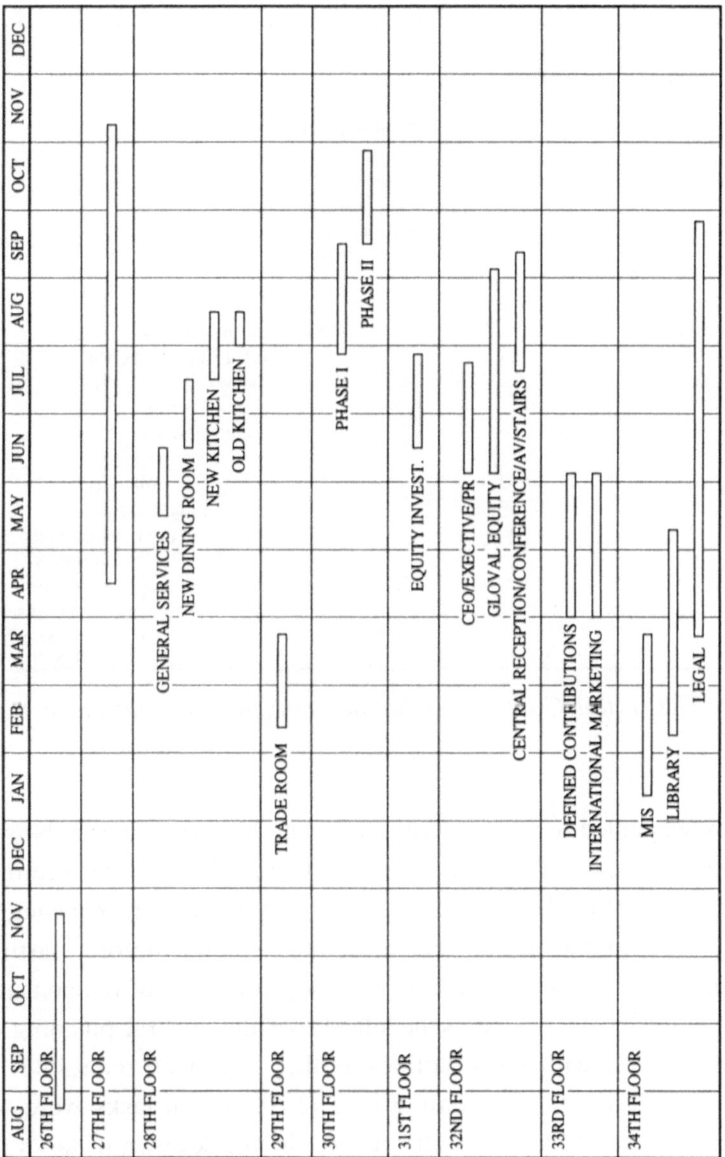

Fig. 10.1. The initial scheduling for the renovation of the nine floors.

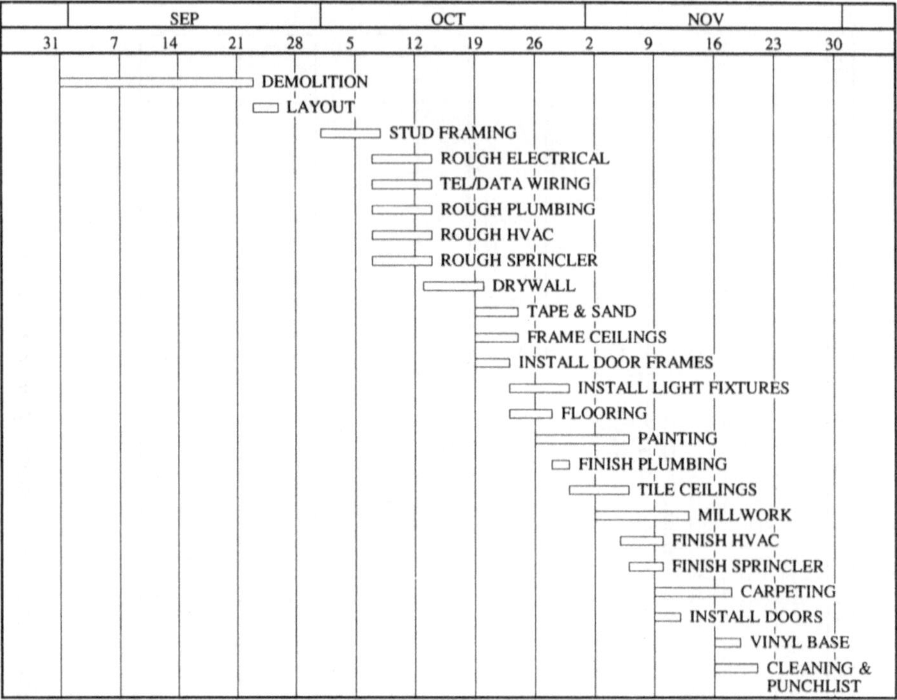

Fig. 10.2. *The initial Gantt chart for planning the renovation of the 26th floor.*

The project was scheduled to start on August 20 and be completed by November 11 of the following year. Fig. 10.1 shows a Gantt chart of the preliminary construction schedule floor by floor, as set by the construction manager. This schedule was based on the initial data available a month before starting the construction, and it had been derived based on the experience of the construction manager with similar projects. The schedule shows the general planning of the construction operations, with the deadlines as they had been requested by the client. In order to derive the scheduling of each floor, the tasks were broken down into a series of sub tasks. Fig. 10.2 shows the break down of tasks for the renovation of the 26th floor, in a Gantt chart.

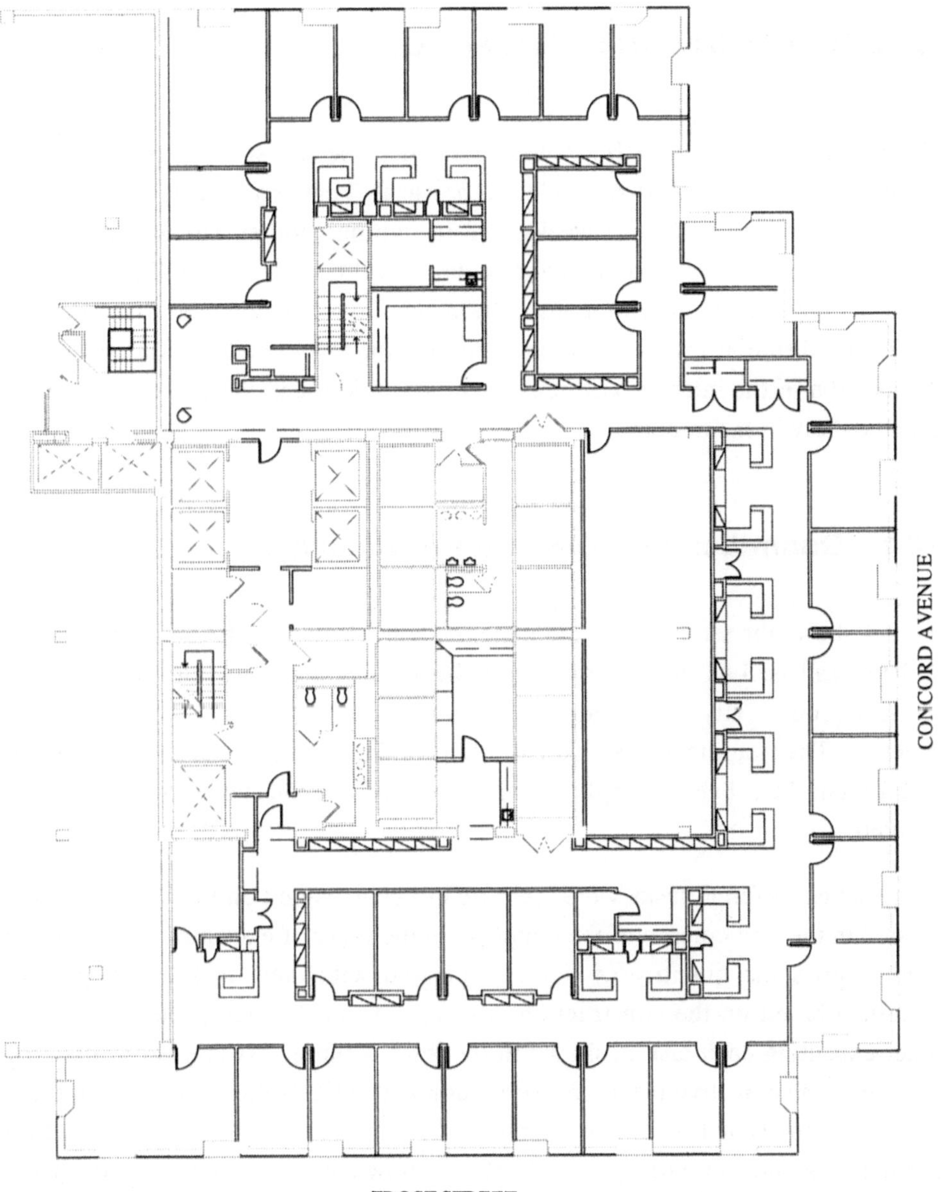

Fig. 10.3. *The architectural drawing of the renovation of the 26th floor.*

10.2 SCHEDULING THE 26TH FLOOR

The renovation of the 26th floor was selected to be the starting point for the construction. The floor was scheduled to be vacated entirely and its construction should be completed within 12 weeks, before starting another part of the project. The architectural plan of the renovation of the 26th floor is shown in Fig. 10.3. As mentioned before, all interior construction was new and the new design was significantly different from the old one. Among the most notable differences was the relocation of the interior partitions, so they would touch the exterior windows perpendicularly in the middle.

10.2.1 Quantities of Work and Productivity

Fig. 10.4 shows the template for planning the construction of the 26th floor. This template was based on the information on the architectural drawing shown in Fig. 10.3, and productivity data available to the construction manager from similar projects. The template was constructed in late August, after the design development had been completed and the design had been reviewed and approved.

Twenty-seven different tasks were identified to be executed on the floor and they are listed in the first column of the template, in the order of execution. The second column shows the quantity of work associated with each task, as they were determined based on the construction drawing. The estimated productivity of a worker executing each task is shown in the third column. At this early planning stage, this is a subjective piece of information that reflects the experience and the judgment of the scheduler. The number of workers-days is calculated based on the quantities and the daily productivity, as shown in the fourth column of the template. The number of workers-days is estimated and it is inserted directly in the fourth column of the template for those tasks that the quantity and the daily productivity cannot be measured, or are meaningless to measure.

10.2.2   Duration and Precedences of Tasks

By establishing the number of the available workers per day for each task, shown in the fifth column of the template of Fig. 10.4, the duration of each task is calculated and inserted in the sixth column of the template. To the extend that the calculated duration meets the overall scheduling plans, no further adjustments are needed at this level. However, if the duration of a task is unreasonably long, then an increase of the employed number of workers will result to a shorter duration. In any case, adjustments can occur later as well, when the project duration will be estimated.

The seventh column displays the quantity of the work of each task that should be completed in every working day. For those tasks that their quantity of work cannot be measured, the quantity of the work that should be completed every working day is given as a percentage of the total work of the task. The quantity of work to be completed each day is a very important piece of information for monitoring and control, and it will be compared later with the actual data from the construction site, both to be displayed in the control template.

Precedences among the different tasks are defined next, and the quantified bar chart shown in the right part of the template is constructed. The depicted intensity is personpower and the intensity and duration of each task corresponds to the data set on the alphanumeric part of the template. A vertical dotted line shows the ending of each week. Weekends are displayed on the quantified bar chart, although there is no work scheduled during Saturdays and Sundays. Waiting for the city permit, after the floor layout is completed and before the actual construction of the stud framing, is shown with a gap in the construction schedule and the appropriate notation.

TASKS	QUANTITY OF WORK	WORKER'S DAILY PRODUCTIVITY	NECESSARY PERSONPOWER (PERSONDAYS)	NO.IN CREW	WORKING DAYS	QUANTITY PER DAY	START DATE	FINISH DATE
DEMOLISHING	N/A	N/A	80	5	16	6 %	8/31	9/22
LAYOUT	N/A	N/A	6	2	3	33 %	9/23	9/25
STUD FRAMING	11,400 FT2	380 FT2	30	6	5	2,280 FT2	10/ 1	10/ 7
ROUGH PLUMBING	N/A	N/A	15	3	5	20 %	10/ 7	10/13
ROUGH ELECTRIC	N/A	N/A	15	3	5	20 %	10/ 7	10/13
TEL/DATA WIRING	N/A	N/A	10	2	5	20 %	10/ 7	10/13
ROUGH HVAC	N/A	N/A	15	3	5	20 %	10/ 7	10/13
ROUGH SPRINKLER	N/A	N/A	15	3	5	20 %	10/ 7	10/13
INSULATION	10,000 FT2	1,250FT2	8	2	4	2,500 FT2	10/13	10/16
GYPSUM BOARD	21,000 FT2	470 FT2	45	9	5	4,230 FT2	10/13	10/19
ALUMINIUM INSERT	330 FT	83 FT	4	2	2	166 FT	10/19	10/20
WOOD BASE	650 FT	54 FT	12	3	4	162 FT	10/19	10/22
TAPE & SAND	20,500 FT2	510 FT2	40	8	5	4,080 FT2	10/19	10/24
FRAME CEILING	9,600 FT2	480 FT2	20	4	5	1,920 FT2	10/19	10/23
DOOR FRAMES	42	3	16	4	4	12	10/19	10/22
LIGHT FIXTURES	N/A	N/A	15	3	5	20 %	10/23	10/29

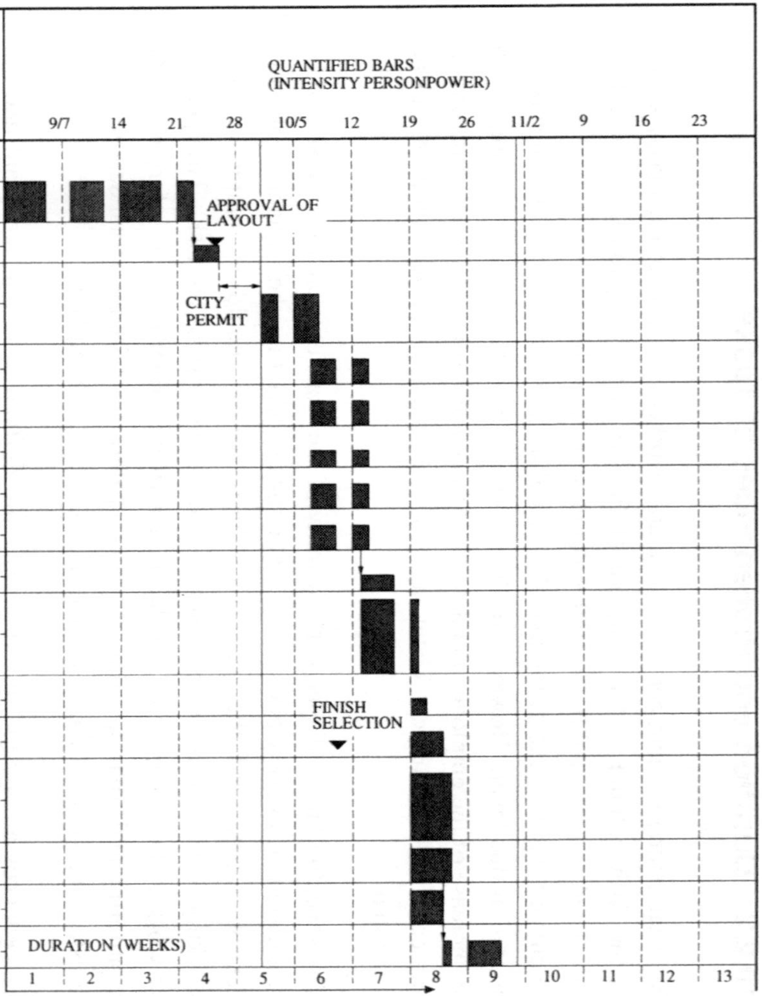

Fig. 10.4. The initial template for planning the renovation of the 26th floor.

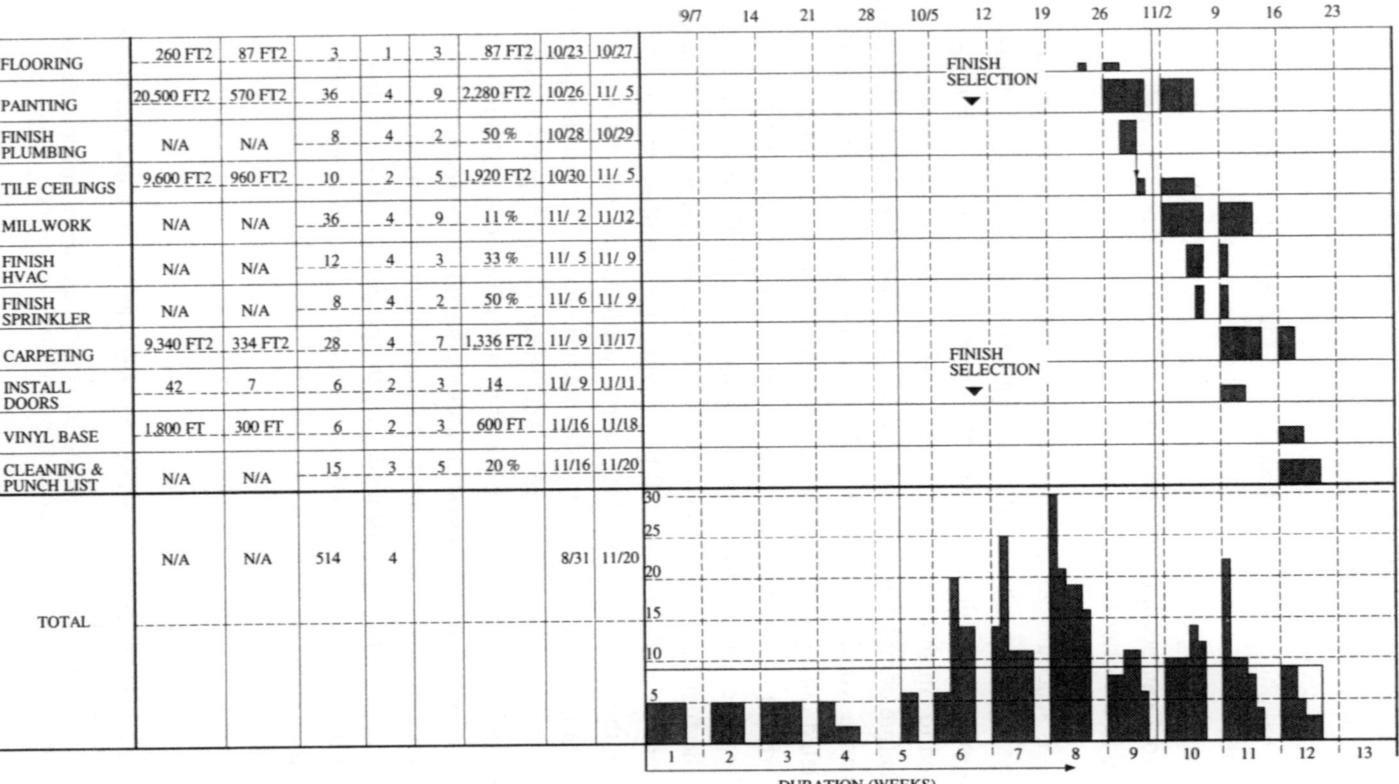

Fig. 10.4. The initial template for planning the renovation of the 26th floor (continued).

Precedences among the different tasks are indicated by the location of the corresponding quantified bars along the time axis. The nature of each task dictates a certain sequential, overlapping, or parallel execution with respect to the other tasks. Demolition is the first task to start, followed by marking the layout on the bare floor. Then, after the city permit has been obtained, the stud framing begins. Since the city permit is expected to be issued by October 1, the demolition and floor layout can occupy the whole month of September, although they could be completed in a shorter time period.

Stud framing is scheduled to start immediately after the permits are obtained and, a day before finishing the stud framing, rough plumbing, electric and communications wiring, ducts, and sprinkler work will start. All the rough works are scheduled to finish at the same time, and insulation and gypsum boards will start a day before completing all the rough works. The selection of the design and materials for the wood baseboard, the vinyl baseboard[2] and the paint should have been completed during the rough works and the aluminum detail insert[3] and the wood base will be executed during taping and sanding the gypsum partitions. At the same time, the ceiling frame will be suspended and the door frames will be installed. The first light fixtures will be installed after a large part of the ceiling frame is completed and the floor will be prepared for installing the carpet. At the beginning of the 9th week, painting starts, while at the same time the finish plumbing is completed and the ceiling tiles are installed. After half the painting job has been completed, millwork starts. According to the approved architectural drawings, the millwork included the secretary's workstations and built-in shelves. The finish heat and ventilation system and the sprinkler were completed during the installation of millwork and carpeting started in the sections that millwork had been completed. Doors were installed after the carpet was in place and the vinyl base was the last item to be installed. Inspection and cleaning were scheduled to be the last task to be performed.

---

2   Offices had a vinyl baseboard, while common areas with intense traffic had a stronger and protective wooden baseboard.
3   The aluminum insert is an architectural detail where an aluminum profile is designed to be inserted in a groove to decorate large areas of walls between doors.

Finally, the 8th and the 9th columns of the template are completed based on the relative position of the bars on the quantified bar chart. These columns contain the starting day and ending day of each task.[4]

The last row of the template of Fig. 10.4 shows the total scheduled person-time, the average number of workers per day, the average duration of the tasks and the average quantity completed each day. The bar on the right shows the cumulative personpower on the 26th floor on a daily basis, as well as the average personpower as a folded-up task.

10.2.3 Adjustments for Resource Leveling

Although this template was used for early planning, there is a major scheduling issue to observe. There is a high concentration of workers on the site in the middle and last thirds of the construction period. Furthermore, there are peaks on certain days, reaching a maximum of 30 workers on Monday, October 19. Such peaks result from the constrained schedule, both by the delay of the city permit and the deadline of November 23, for the completion of the construction.

A series of schedule changes, shown on Fig. 10.5 result to a more balanced work force on the site. The changes are displayed in gray, while the outlined tasks indicate the tasks as were scheduled in the template of Fig. 10.4. The effort in preparing the template shown in Fig. 10.5 focused on starting earlier as many tasks as possible, and on avoiding the parallel execution of many tasks.

---

[4] Alternatively, these columns could have been filled after establishing the precedent relationships, and the starting and ending dates and then executing a critical path algorithm. However, at this level of complexity, the graphic part of the template is easier to be constructed first, as a visual display of the scheduling process.

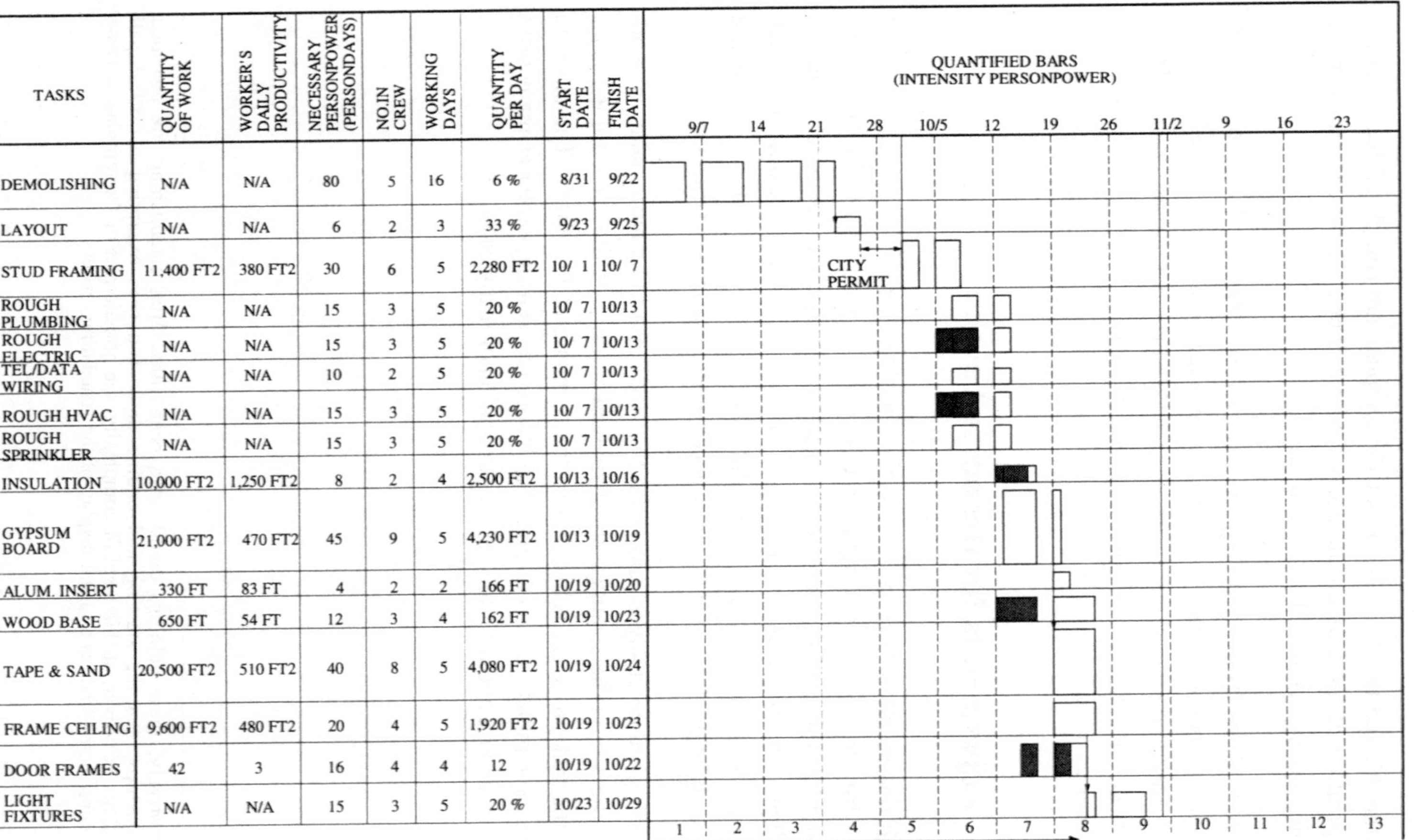

TASKS	QUANTITY OF WORK	WORKER'S DAILY PRODUCTIVITY	NECESSARY PERSONPOWER (PERSONDAYS)	NO. IN CREW	WORKING DAYS	QUANTITY PER DAY	START DATE	FINISH DATE
DEMOLISHING	N/A	N/A	80	5	16	6 %	8/31	9/22
LAYOUT	N/A	N/A	6	2	3	33 %	9/23	9/25
STUD FRAMING	11,400 FT2	380 FT2	30	6	5	2,280 FT2	10/ 1	10/ 7
ROUGH PLUMBING	N/A	N/A	15	3	5	20 %	10/ 7	10/13
ROUGH ELECTRIC	N/A	N/A	15	3	5	20 %	10/ 7	10/13
TEL/DATA WIRING	N/A	N/A	10	2	5	20 %	10/ 7	10/13
ROUGH HVAC	N/A	N/A	15	3	5	20 %	10/ 7	10/13
ROUGH SPRINKLER	N/A	N/A	15	3	5	20 %	10/ 7	10/13
INSULATION	10,000 FT2	1,250 FT2	8	2	4	2,500 FT2	10/13	10/16
GYPSUM BOARD	21,000 FT2	470 FT2	45	9	5	4,230 FT2	10/13	10/19
ALUM. INSERT	330 FT	83 FT	4	2	2	166 FT	10/19	10/20
WOOD BASE	650 FT	54 FT	12	3	4	162 FT	10/19	10/23
TAPE & SAND	20,500 FT2	510 FT2	40	8	5	4,080 FT2	10/19	10/24
FRAME CEILING	9,600 FT2	480 FT2	20	4	5	1,920 FT2	10/19	10/23
DOOR FRAMES	42	3	16	4	4	12	10/19	10/22
LIGHT FIXTURES	N/A	N/A	15	3	5	20 %	10/23	10/29

Fig. 10.5. A study to level the personpower on the 26th floor, keeping the same deadline.

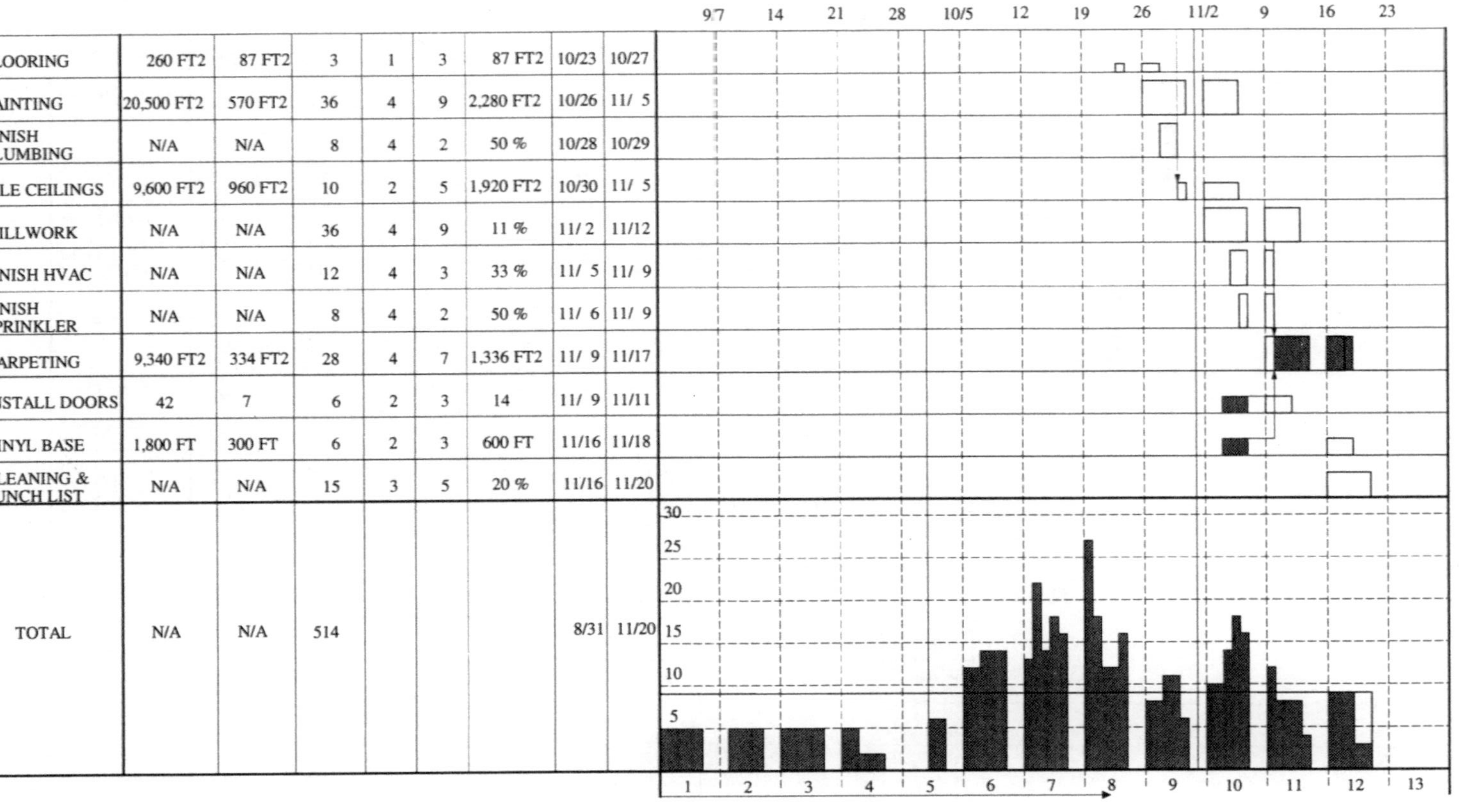

FLOORING	260 FT2	87 FT2	3	1	3	87 FT2	10/23	10/27
PAINTING	20,500 FT2	570 FT2	36	4	9	2,280 FT2	10/26	11/ 5
FINISH PLUMBING	N/A	N/A	8	4	2	50 %	10/28	10/29
TILE CEILINGS	9,600 FT2	960 FT2	10	2	5	1,920 FT2	10/30	11/ 5
MILLWORK	N/A	N/A	36	4	9	11 %	11/ 2	11/12
FINISH HVAC	N/A	N/A	12	4	3	33 %	11/ 5	11/ 9
FINISH SPRINKLER	N/A	N/A	8	4	2	50 %	11/ 6	11/ 9
CARPETING	9,340 FT2	334 FT2	28	4	7	1,336 FT2	11/ 9	11/17
INSTALL DOORS	42	7	6	2	3	14	11/ 9	11/11
VINYL BASE	1,800 FT	300 FT	6	2	3	600 FT	11/16	11/18
CLEANING & PUNCH LIST	N/A	N/A	15	3	5	20 %	11/16	11/20
TOTAL	N/A	N/A	514				8/31	11/20

Fig. 10.5. A study to level the personpower on the 26th floor, keeping the same deadline (continued).

TASKS	QUANTITY OF WORK	WORKER'S DAILY PRODUCTIVITY	NECESSARY PERSONPOWER (PERSONDAYS)	NO. IN CREW	WORKING DAYS	QUANTITY PER DAY	START DATE	FINISH DATE
DEMOLISHING	N/A	N/A	80	5	16	6 %	8/31	9/22
LAYOUT	N/A	N/A	6	2	3	33 %	9/23	9/25
STUD FRAMING	11,400 FT2	380 FT2	30	6	5	2,280 FT2	10/ 1	10/ 7
ROUGH PLUMBING	N/A	N/A	15	3	5	20 %	10/ 8	10/14
ROUGH ELECTRIC	N/A	N/A	15	3	5	20 %	10/ 7	10/13
TEL/DATA WIRING	N/A	N/A	10	3	4	25 %	10/ 1	10/ 6
ROUGH HVAC	N/A	N/A	15	3	5	20 %	10/ 7	10/13
ROUGH SPRINKLER	N/A	N/A	15	3	5	20 %	10/ 7	10/13
INSULATION	10,000 FT2	1,250 FT2	8	3	3	3,750 FT2	10/14	10/16
GYPSUM BOARD	21,000 FT2	470 FT2	45	9	5	4,230 FT2	10/14	10/20
ALUMINIUM INSERT	330 FT	83 FT	4	2	2	166 FT	10/19	10/20
WOOD BASE	650 FT	54 FT	12	3	4	162 FT	10/ 8	10/13
TAPE & SAND	20,500 FT2	510 FT2	40	8	5	4,080 FT2	10/21	10/27
FRAME CEILING	9,600 FT2	480 FT2	20	4	5	1,920 FT2	10/19	10/23
DOOR FRAMES	42	3	16	4	4	12	10/ 1	10/ 6
LIGHT FIXTURES	N/A	N/A	15	3	5	20 %	10/26	10/30

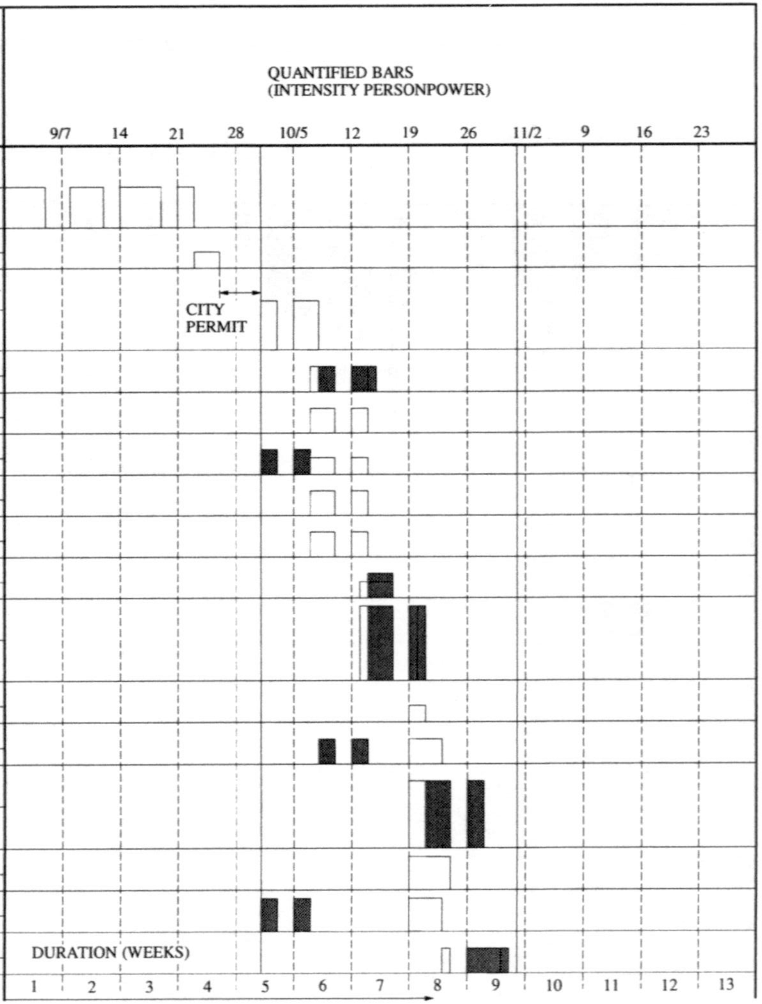

Fig. 10.6. A study to level the personpower on the 26th floor, extending the deadline by one week.

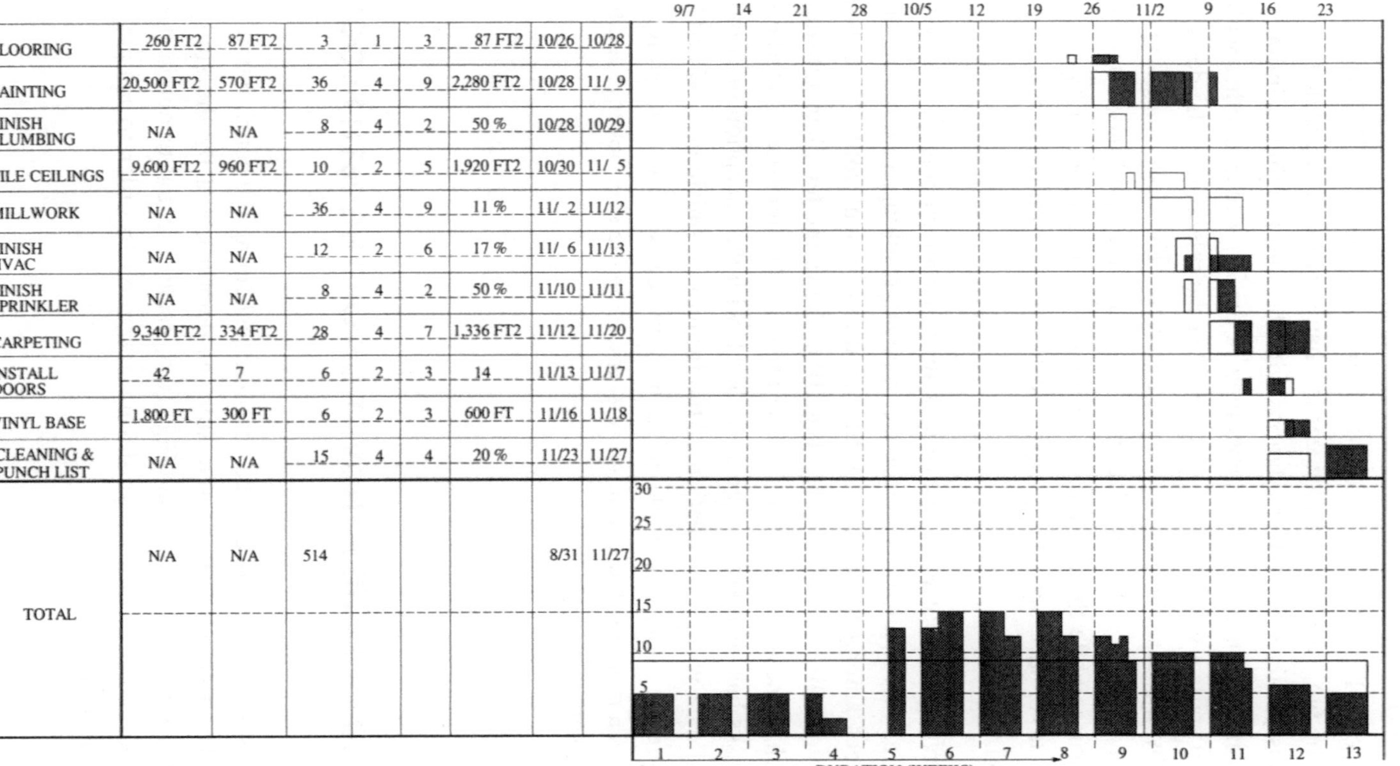

FLOORING	260 FT2	87 FT2	3	1	3	87 FT2	10/26	10/28
PAINTING	20,500 FT2	570 FT2	36	4	9	2,280 FT2	10/28	11/ 9
FINISH PLUMBING	N/A	N/A	8	4	2	50 %	10/28	10/29
TILE CEILINGS	9,600 FT2	960 FT2	10	2	5	1,920 FT2	10/30	11/ 5
MILLWORK	N/A	N/A	36	4	9	11 %	11/ 2	11/12
FINISH HVAC	N/A	N/A	12	2	6	17 %	11/ 6	11/13
FINISH SPRINKLER	N/A	N/A	8	4	2	50 %	11/10	11/11
CARPETING	9,340 FT2	334 FT2	28	4	7	1,336 FT2	11/12	11/20
INSTALL DOORS	42	7	6	2	3	14	11/13	11/17
VINYL BASE	1,800 FT	300 FT	6	2	3	600 FT	11/16	11/18
CLEANING & PUNCH LIST	N/A	N/A	15	4	4	20 %	11/23	11/27
TOTAL	N/A	N/A	514				8/31	11/27

Fig. 10.6. A study to level the personpower on the 25th floor, extending the deadline by one week (continued).

In the template of Fig. 10.5, both rough electric and rough HVAC start at the beginning of the 6th week, or two days earlier than previously scheduled. This is possible because of their precedent relations with the stud framing. Similarly the installation of insulation starts at the beginning of the 7th week, together with the wood base that starts a week earlier, assuming that the selection of the design and the material by the designer can be reached earlier. The door frames are also moved two days earlier. The installation of doors and the vinyl base can also be completed earlier, while the carpeting is proposed to be postponed by one day, after all other tasks have been completed, except for some millwork and the final inspection and cleaning.

The cumulative personpower at the site is more balanced than it was on the template of Fig. 10.4, while the changes are minimal, resulting from reconsidering the precedences among the tasks. A further improvement could be based on extending the deadline of the project. Fig. 10.6 shows the template scheduling, following such a one week extension of the project. The number of workers for most of the tasks has been kept at the same level, with the exception of crews for telephone and data wiring, installation of the insulation, finishing of HVAC and cleaning, where the number of workers has been increased. The extension of the deadline allows a more even distribution of workers on the site, never exceeding a total of 15 workers in a single day.

10.3 EXECUTING THE RENOVATION OF THE 26TH FLOOR

The template of Fig. 10.4 provided the basis for scheduling the construction of the 26th floor. The tightness of the schedule, as demonstrated by the studies of alternative schedules in Fig. 10.5 and Fig. 10.6, made essential to obtain the city permit on-time and to avoid delays during execution in order to maintain the deadline of November 23.

During construction, data were collected to monitor and control the execution of the project. The daily data included:

- the number of the workers on the site,
- the task that they were working, and
- the quantity of the completed work for each task, often expressed as a percentage of the work that had been completed until that day.

These daily reports were used to produce periodically a series of control templates during the execution of the construction. A control template, as presented in Chapter 4, monitors the executed work and forecasts the remaining tasks or parts of tasks to be executed.

10.3.1   Control Template In-Progress

The control template of Fig. 10.7 was prepared on October 23. The graphics part to the left of that date is shown in gray, denoting the part of the schedule that should have been completed. The tasks, as they were initially scheduled in the template of Fig. 10.4, are displayed with a thin outline while the executed tasks are displayed with a hatch pattern. Thick horizontal lines denote waiting for decisions external to the construction of the depicted tasks, and milestones on change orders and stop orders are also displayed on the template.

For the tasks that have been completed, the corresponding second row in the alphanumeric part of the template has been filled with the actual data on that task. That row is empty for those tasks that have been re-scheduled, except for the start and finish dates that portray the new schedule. The corresponding second row of the alphanumeric part of the template is not filled for those tasks that have not been either completed or re-scheduled.

As it is shown on this control template, many tasks had been delayed. The delays can be attributed to the change orders and stop orders that are displayed visually on this template. Until October 23, five change orders had been accepted by the client:

TASKS	QUANTITY OF WORK	WORKER'S DAILY PRODUCTIVITY	NECESSARY PERSONPOWER (PERSONDAYS)	NO.IN CREW	WORKING DAYS	QUANTITY PER DAY	START DATE	FINISH DATE
DEMOLISHING	N/A	N/A	80	5	16	6 %	8/31	9/22
			80	5	16	6 %	8/31	9/22
LAYOUT	N/A	N/A	6	2	3	33 %	9/23	9/25
			6	2	3	33 %	9/23	9/25
STUD FRAMING	11,400 FT2	380 FT2	30	6	5	2,280 FT2	10/ 1	10/ 7
							10/ 6	11/ 3
ROUGH PLUMBING	N/A	N/A	15	3	5	20 %	10/ 7	10/13
							10/13	10/19
ROUGH ELECTRIC	N/A	N/A	15	3	5	20 %	10/ 7	10/13
							10/ 7	11/ 5
TEL/DATA WIRING	N/A	N/A	10	2	5	20 %	10/ 7	10/13
			10	2	5	20 %	10/ 7	10/13
ROUGH HVAC	N/A	N/A	15	3	5	20 %	10/ 7	10/13
			27	3	11	9 %	10/ 7	10/21
ROUGH SPRINKLER	N/A	N/A	15	3	5	20 %	10/ 7	10/13
							10/13	11/ 5
INSULATION	10,000 FT2	1,250FT2	8	2	4	2,500 FT2	10/13	10/16
	10,000 FT2	1,250FT2	8	2	4	2,500 FT2	10/20	10/23
GYPSUM BOARD	21,000 FT2	470 FT2	45	9	5	4,230 FT2	10/13	10/19
							10/20	11/ 6
ALUMINIUM INSERT	330 FT	83 FT	4	2	2	166 FT	10/19	10/20
							10/26	10/27
WOOD BASE	650 FT	54 FT	12	3	4	162 FT	10/19	10/22
							10/27	10/30
TAPE & SAND	20,500 FT2	510 FT2	40	8	5	4,080 FT2	10/19	10/24
							10/26	11/10
FRAME CEILING	9,600 FT2	480 FT2	20	4	5	1,920 FT2	10/19	10/23
							10/28	11/ 3
DOOR FRAMES	42	3	16	4	4	12	10/19	10/22
	42	3	16	4	4	12	10/ 6	10/ 9
LIGHT FIXTURES	N/A	N/A	15	3	5	20 %	10/23	10/29
							10/28	11/ 3

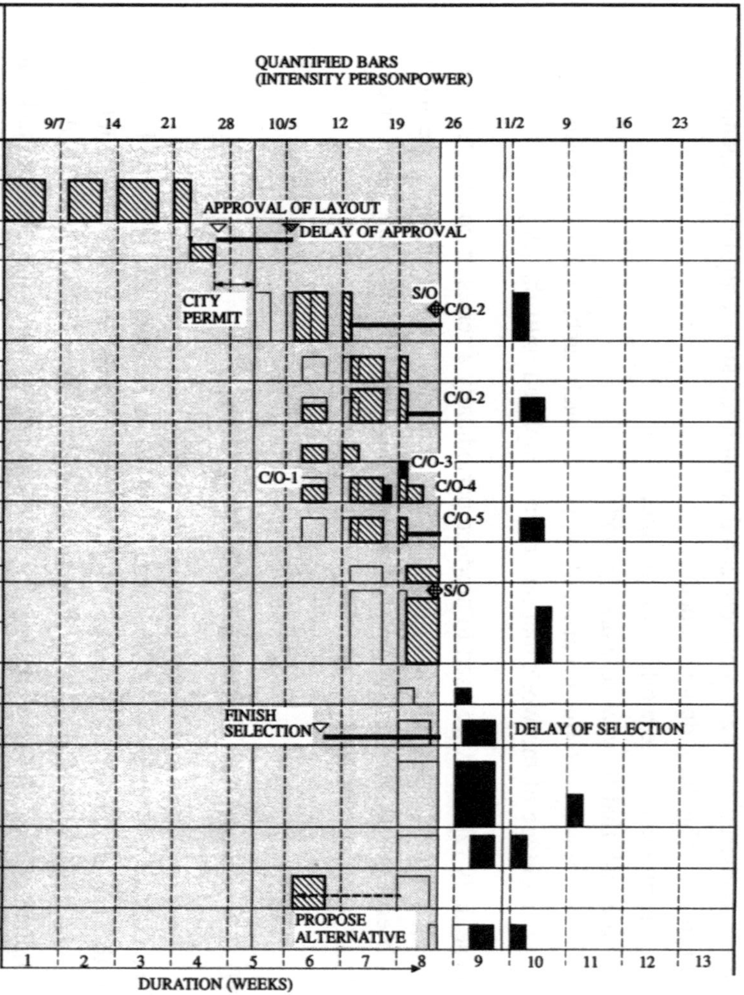

Fig. 10.7. *The control template of October 23 (in progress), for the renovation of the 26th floor.*

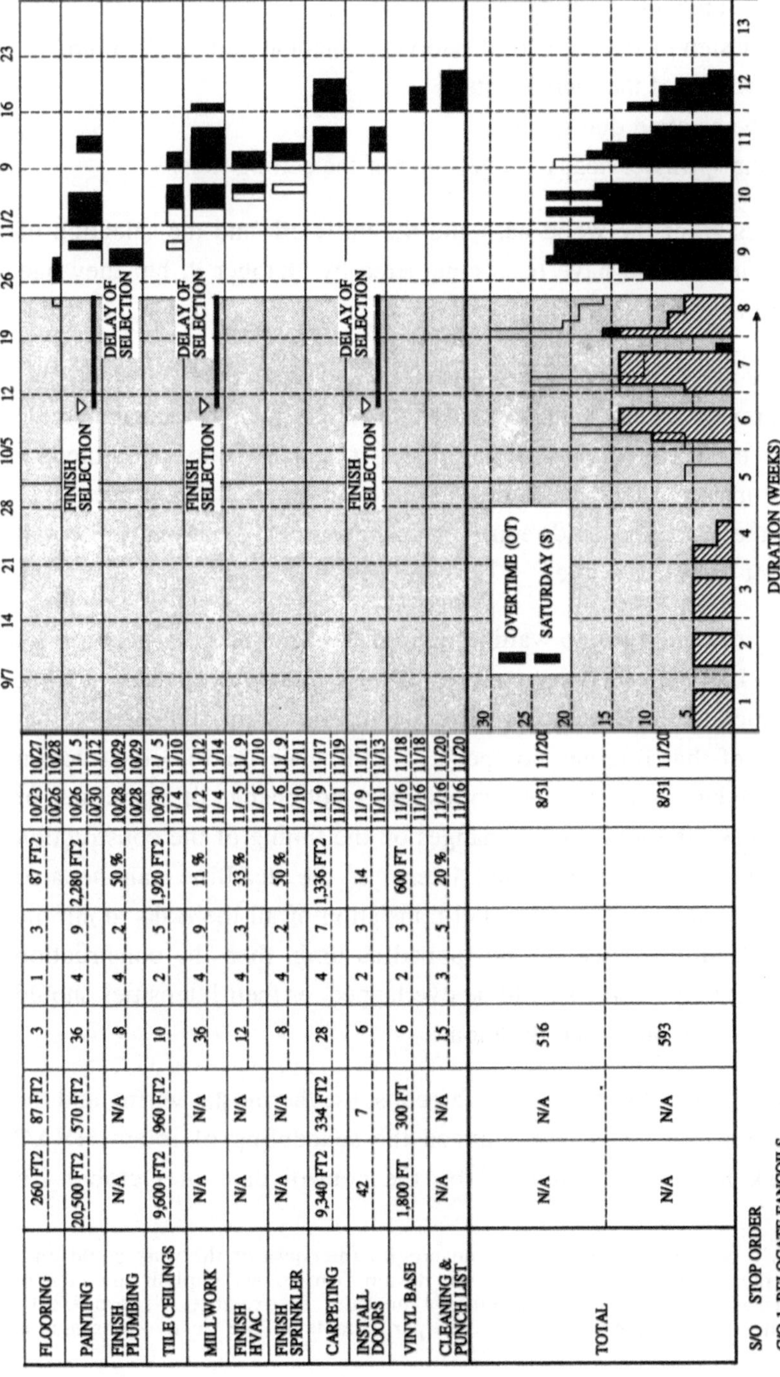

Fig. 10.7. The control template of October 23 (in progress), for the renovation of the 26th floor (cont.).

- relocation of the fan coils,
- change of the design of the secretarial stations to include built-in furniture,
- change of the wiring of the thermostats,
- insulation of the existing ducts, and
- relocation of the sprinkler heads to the center of the ceiling tiles.

Furthermore, the design of the wood base and the millwork and the selection of the doors and painting should have been completed by October 9, but they had not been completed as of October 23.

Change orders refer mostly to changes of quantities and locations. As such, they alter the initial estimate of the quantities and the estimate for the required crews and duration of the tasks. In a construction project, it is possible to accommodate small changes and maintain the schedule. On the other hand, change orders that alter the scope of the program could require major resource allocations and could have a direct impact on the schedule.

Delays in decision making result to waiting periods that can have a direct impact on the schedule. In Fig. 10.7, the waiting time is shown as a foreign task represented by a thick line. Since no construction resources are allocated on that task, the thickness of that line has no special significance for the construction manager.[1] The introduction of this foreign task does not change the quantities of the tasks but occupies time that causes changes on the timing of the construction tasks, which are forced to be executed later. If the deadline can be also postponed, these changes result to a parallel translation of all the tasks along the time axis. If the deadline cannot be postponed as long, then the construction tasks following the external delay should be overlapped, or their intensities should be increased, in order to reduce their duration.

The change orders on the relocation of the fan coils, the thermostat wiring and the insulation of the existing ducts had changed the scheduling of rough HVAC although that task had been completed by the control date of October 23.

---

[1] From the owner's perspective, however, a meaningful thickness of this line could and should signify the resources allocated by the design firm to accomplish the task of updating the drawings. That could provide a measure to expedite the process by establishing a measure of the effort from the participants in the design-construction process.

Similarly, the relocation of the sprinkler head to the tile centers had delayed the rough sprinkler task, which had been also completed by the control date.

The change order for the secretarial stations was a major change order that altered the scope of the program and as such affected the schedule heavily. Although the initially estimated quantity of work for the stud framing had been completed, more stud framing would be required for the built-in stations. By October 23, drawings were not available. However, the project manager guessed the quantity of work that needed be done, and he estimated that work to start a week later, on November 2, as shown on Fig. 10.7. Rough electric, gypsum board, tape and sand, painting, millwork, carpeting, and cleaning were all affected by this change order and had to be re-scheduled. Specifically on the gypsum board and insulation, a stop order was issued on October 23 to accommodate the changes to be introduced.

In addition, certain tasks that had been planned to start before October 23 had not started yet. These tasks, not directly related to change orders, were: aluminum insert, frame ceiling, light fixtures and flooring.

Finally, the wood base delay is attributed to the delay of selection of the wood base design as well as the change order on the secretarial stations.

Despite the delays of the renovation, the owner insisted in keeping the initial deadline of November 23. Since the duration of the tasks had to be expedited, overtime work and work on the weekends were considered. Given that the labor cost is significantly higher in the weekends, a graphic display of work executed after regular working hours has been introduced on the control template. Rough HVAC had included work on Saturday, October 17, and overtime on Monday, October 19, in order to cope with the changes.

TASKS	QUANTITY OF WORK	WORKER'S DAILY PRODUCTIVITY	NECESSARY PERSONPOWER (PERSONDAYS)	DETAILED ACTUAL PERSONPOWER	NO.IN CREW	WORKING DAYS	QUANTITY PER DAY	START DATE	FINISH DATE	DESIGN MILESTONES
DEMOLISHING	N/A	N/A	80		5	16	6 %	8/31	9/22	
			0		0	0				
			80		5	16	6 %	8/31	9/22	
LAYOUT	N/A	N/A	6		2	3	33 %	9/23	9/25	9/25
			0		0	0				
			6		2	3	33 %	9/23	9/25	10/ 5
STUD FRAMING	11,400 FT2	380 FT2	30		6	5	2,280 FT2	10/ 1	10/ 7	
	2,600 FT2	190 FT2	14	8+2S+14OT	2	5		10/ 3	10/ 7	
	14,000 FT2	320 FT2	44	38+2S+14OT	6	10	1,920 FT2	10/ 6	11/ 7	
ROUGH PLUMBING	N/A	N/A	15		3	5	20 %	10/ 7	10/13	
			0		0	0				
			15		3	5	20 %	10/13	10/19	
ROUGH ELECTRIC	N/A	N/A	25		5	5	20 %	10/ 7	10/13	
			27	15+6S+6SS	5	5		10/ 4	10/ 8	
			52	46+6S+6SS	5	13	8 %	10/ 7	11/ 8	
ROUGH HVAC	N/A	N/A	15		3	5	20 %	10/ 7	10/13	
			12	8+2S+2OT	2	6		10/ 7	10/21	
			27	23+2S+2OT	3	11	9 %	10/ 7	10/21	
ROUGH SPRINKLER	N/A	N/A	15		3	5	20 %	10/ 7	10/13	
			9	6+3S	3	3		11/ 5	11/ 7	
			24	21+3S	3	8	13 %	10/13	11/ 7	
GYPSUM BOARD	21,000 FT2	470 FT2	45		9	5	4,230 FT2	10/13	10/19	
	5,200 FT2	430 FT2	12	6+6S	6	2		11/ 5	11/ 9	
	26,200 FT2	470 FT2	56	50+6S	6	9	2,820 FT2	10/20	11/ 9	
ALUMINIUM INSERT	330 FT	83 FT	4		2	2	166 FT	10/19	10/20	
			0		0	0				
	330 FT	83 FT	4		2	2	166 FT	10/30	10/31	
WOOD BASE	650 FT	54 FT	12		3	4	162 FT	10/19	10/22	10/10
			0		0	0				
	650 FT	43 FT	15		3	5	129 FT	11/ 6	11/12	10/29
TAPE & SAND	20,500 FT2	510 FT2	40		8	5	4,080 FT2	10/19	10/24	
	3,000 FT2	500 FT2	6	4+2SS	2	3		11/11	11/13	
	23,500 FT2	460 FT2	51	49+2SS	5	12	2,300 FT2	10/26	11/13	
FRAME CEILING	9,600 FT2	480 FT2	20		4	5	1,920 FT2	10/19	10/23	
			0		0	0				
	9,600 FT2	533 FT2	18		3	6	1,599 FT2	11/ 2	11/ 7	
DOOR FRAMES	42	3	16		4	4	12	10/19	10/22	
			0		0	0				
	42	3	16		4	4	12	10/ 6	10/ 9	
LIGHT FIXTURES	N/A	N/A	25		5	5	20 %	10/26	11/ 5	
			0		0	0				
			45		3	15	7 %	10/29	11/14	

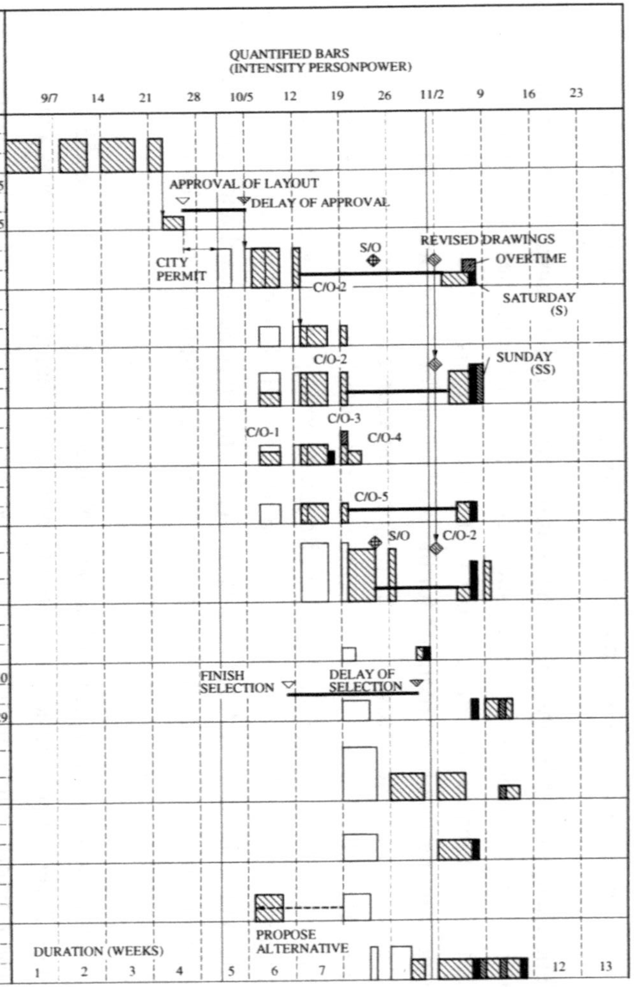

Fig. 10.8. The control template at the completion of the renovation of the 26th floor.

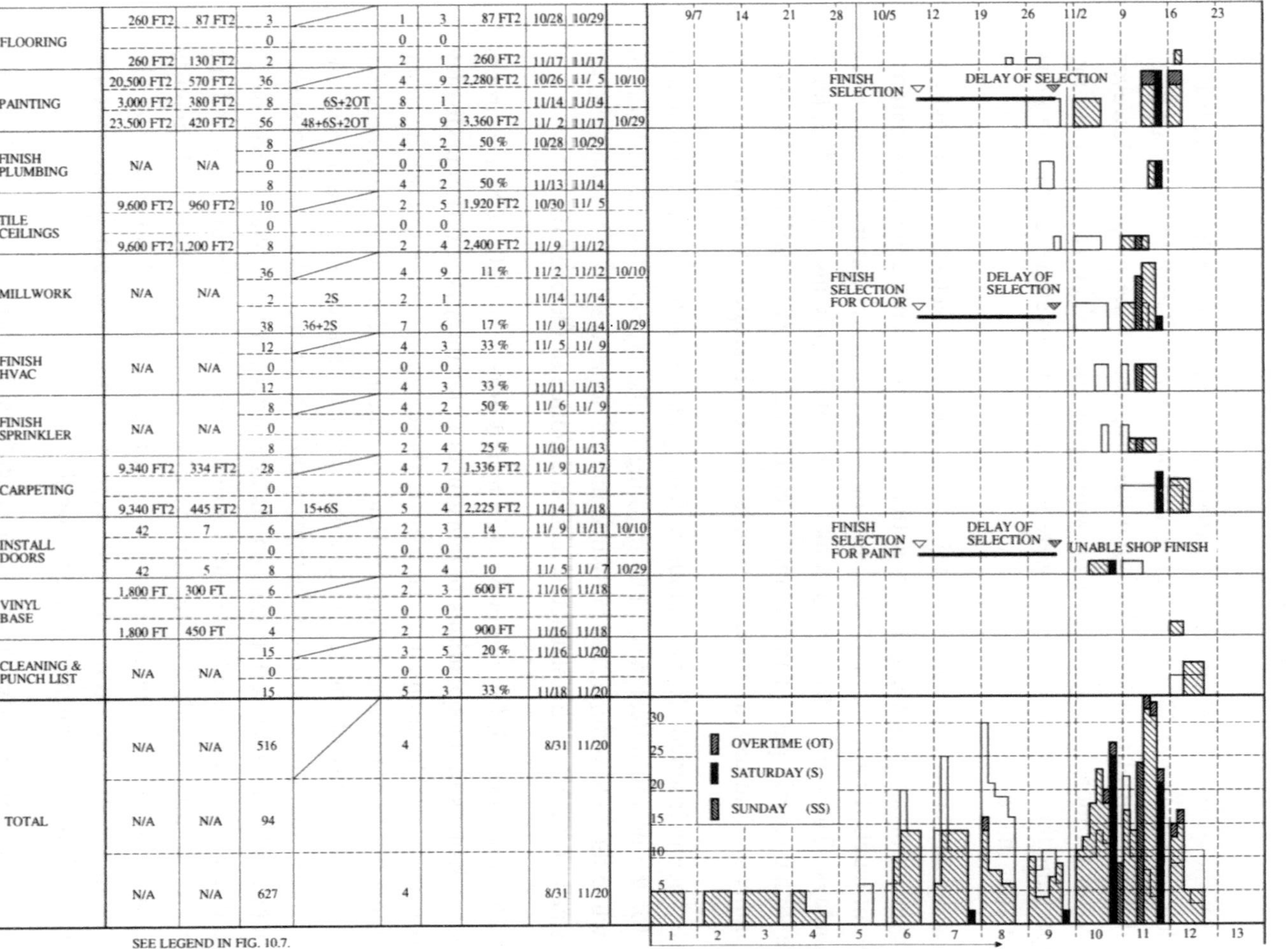

Task										
FLOORING	260 FT2	87 FT2	3		1	3	87 FT2	10/28	10/29	
			0		0	0				
	260 FT2	130 FT2	2		2	1	260 FT2	11/17	11/17	
PAINTING	20,500 FT2	570 FT2	36		4	9	2,280 FT2	10/26	11/ 5	10/10
	3,000 FT2	380 FT2	8	6S+2OT	8	1		11/14	11/14	
	23,500 FT2	420 FT2	56	48+6S+2OT	8	9	3,360 FT2	11/ 2	11/17	10/29
FINISH PLUMBING	N/A	N/A	8		4	2	50 %	10/28	10/29	
			0		0	0				
			8		4	2	50 %	11/13	11/14	
TILE CEILINGS	9,600 FT2	960 FT2	10		2	5	1,920 FT2	10/30	11/ 5	
			0		0	0				
	9,600 FT2	1,200 FT2	8		2	4	2,400 FT2	11/9	11/12	
MILLWORK	N/A	N/A	36		4	9	11 %	11/2	11/12	10/10
			2	2S	2	1		11/14	11/14	
			38	36+2S	7	6	17 %	11/ 9	11/14 · 10/29	
FINISH HVAC	N/A	N/A	12		4	3	33 %	11/ 5	11/ 9	
			0		0	0				
			12		4	3	33 %	11/11	11/13	
FINISH SPRINKLER	N/A	N/A	8		4	2	50 %	11/ 6	11/ 9	
			0		0	0				
			8		2	4	25 %	11/10	11/13	
CARPETING	9,340 FT2	334 FT2	28		4	7	1,336 FT2	11/ 9	11/17	
			0		0	0				
	9,340 FT2	445 FT2	21	15+6S	5	4	2,225 FT2	11/14	11/18	
INSTALL DOORS	42	7	6		2	3	14	11/ 9	11/11	10/10
			0		0	0				
	42	5	8		2	4	10	11/ 5	11/ 7	10/29
VINYL BASE	1,800 FT	300 FT	6		2	3	600 FT	11/16	11/18	
			0		0	0				
	1,800 FT	450 FT	4		2	2	900 FT	11/16	11/18	
CLEANING & PUNCH LIST	N/A	N/A	15		3	5	20 %	11/16	11/20	
			0		0	0				
			15		5	3	33 %	11/18	11/20	
TOTAL	N/A	N/A	516		4			8/31	11/20	
	N/A	N/A	94							
	N/A	N/A	627		4			8/31	11/20	

SEE LEGEND IN FIG. 10.7.

Fig. 10.8. *The control template at the completion of the renovation of the 26th floor (continued).*

10.3.2 Final Control Template

Fig. 10.8 shows the actual execution of the renovation of the 26th floor, as it was recorded by November 23. After the control template of October 23, there were several more control templates depicting the progress of the project. However, there were no more change orders or waiting periods. The revised drawings incorporating the secretarial stations were available on November 2, and the work started after that date.

Following the same notation as in Fig. 10.7, the initial scheduling of tasks is displayed with an outline, and the actual execution with a hatched pattern. Different hatched patterns indicate overtime work, work on Saturdays and work on Sundays. The same information is included in the newly inserted fifth column of the alphanumeric part of the template, entitled *detailed actual personpower*. An *S* indicates Saturday, *SS* indicates Sunday and *OT* indicates overtime.

The also newly inserted eleventh column displays the scheduled versus the actual dates for the design milestones. The marking of the layout was delayed for 10 days, while the light fixtures, the millwork and the doors were selected on October 29, instead of the originally planned selection deadline of October 10.

Fig. 10.8 shows more information on the change orders as well. Change orders introduce changes in the quantities of construction, resulting to a different display of those tasks on the template. However, these changes are important to be shown in a different manner on the template, so that a distinction is made between changes in the areas of the tasks resulting from an inaccurate estimate of the productivity[2] and changes resulting from additional work. The template shows the changes of quantities resulting from change orders in the alphanumeric part,[3] An additional row is inserted between the initial estimate of the quantity and the constructed quantity to display this information. Thus, the constructed quantity should be equal to the summation of the initially estimated quantity and the quantity in the change order. If that were not true, it would imply that the quantities of work had been estimated wrongly.

---

2   When the intensity is personpower or cost. A different productivity does not change the area of a task if the quantity of work is displayed.

3   It could be also shown on the graphics part by a different hatching or color.

Table 10.1. Productivity by task: estimated and actual.

TASK		PLAN	ACTUAL	±%	CAUSE
STUD FRAMING	Quantity (ft²)	11,400	14,000	23%	(1)
	Quantity per personday	380	320	-16%	(2)
GYPSUM BOARD	Quantity (ft²)	21,000	26,200	25%	(1)
	Quantity per personday	470	470		(3)
WOOD BASE	Quantity (ft)	650	650		
	Quantity per personday	54	43	-20%	(4)
TAPE & SAND	Quantity (ft²)	20,500	23,500	15%	(1)
	Quantity per personday	510	460	-10%	(2)
FRAME CEILING	Quantity (ft²)	9,600	9,600		
	Quantity per personday	480	530	10%	(6)
FLOORING	Quantity (ft²)	260	260		
	Quantity per personday	90	130	44%	(6)
PAINTING	Quantity (ft²)	20,500	23,500	15%	(1)
	Quantity per personday	570	420	-26%	(4), (5)
TILE CEILING	Quantity (ft²)	9,600	9,600		
	Quantity per personday	960	1200	25%	(6)
CARPETING	Quantity (ft²)	9,340	9,340		
	Quantity per personday	330	450	36%	(6)
INSTALL DOORS	Quantity	42	42		
	Quantity per personday	7	5	-29%	(4)
VINYL BASE	Quantity (ft)	1,800	1,800		
	Quantity per personday	300	450	50%	(6)

(1)   Change order for the secretarial stations.
(2)   Stop and change orders.
(3)   The additional partitions for the secretarial stations were low rise and easier to build.
(4)   Delay of design selection.
(5)   Less prefabrication, more overtime.
(6)   Increased efficiency because of built-in contingencies in the original schedule, a tighter actual schedule, and intense supervision.

In the third column, the workers' daily productivity is presented separately for the initially planned quantity as opposed to the quantity resulted from the change order. It is expected that the productivity on the change order is lower, implying less programming and a lower efficiency.

Table 10.1 was assembled after the completion of the 26th floor. In addition to quantities of work, it contains the initially estimated productivity for each task, as opposed to the actual productivity. This information was used to plan the renovation of the rest of the floors, and it is particularly useful to plan future construction projects.

10.4 PLANNING THE REST OF THE PROJECT

The scheduling of the rest of the project was based on the data from the construction of the 26th floor. At the completion of the 26th floor, the architectural decisions had been almost completed, since all floors should share the same identity. Furthermore, specific information on both quantities and the productivity of each trade was available. According to the initial schedule, shown in Fig. 10.1, the 34th floor was next in line to be renovated. However, the entire floor was not available at the same time. The 34th floor, shown in the architectural drawing in Fig. 10.9, was separated in three main sections: the Management Information Systems (MIS) section, the Library section, and the Legal section. Thus, these three sections should be scheduled as three different entities.

The construction of the MIS should last up to 7 weeks and the construction of the Legal section should start after the completion of the MIS section. The Library section was available to start construction together with the MIS section and should be completed not later than the Legal section. Following these requirements, the renovations of the MIS and the Legal sections were two independent projects to be executed the one after the other, but the renovation of the Library section could be combined to be executed in parallel with either project.

The quantities of the identified 24 tasks, the workers' productivity, the necessary personpower, *etc.*, were calculated in a similar manner as for the planning template of the 26th floor. At this point, the validity of the available data had been tested and there was more confidence in the implied assumptions.

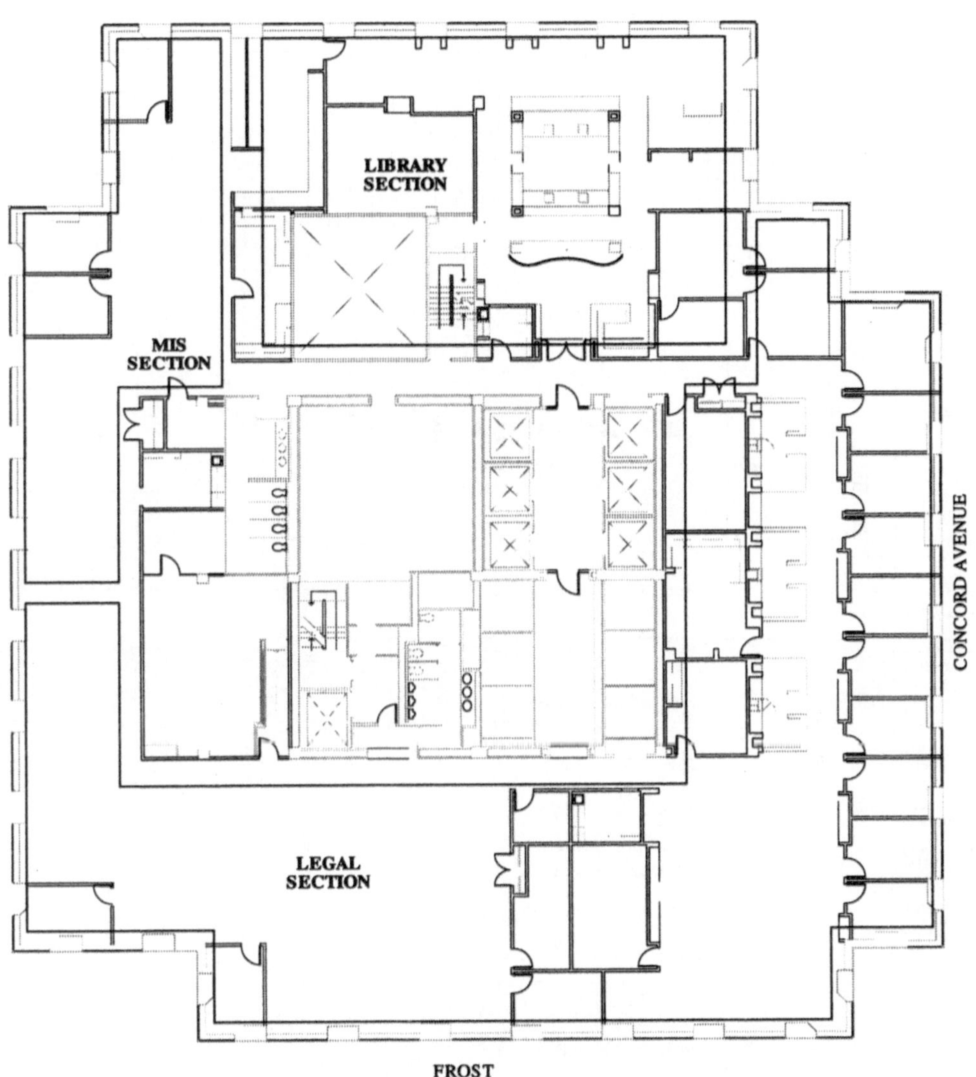

Fig. 10.9. *The architectural drawing of the renovation of the 34th floor.*

TASKS	QUANTITY OF WORK	WORKER'S DAILY PRODUCTIVITY	NECESSARY PERSONPOWER (PERSONDAYS)	DETAILED ACTUAL PERSONPOWER	NO. IN CREW	WORKING DAYS	QUANTITY PER DAY	START DATE	FINISH DATE
DEMOLISHING	N/A	N/A	20		4	5	20 %	12/14	12/18
	N/A	N/A	28		4	7	14 %	12/21	12/30
LAYOUT	N/A	N/A	4		2	2	50 %	12/28	12/29
	N/A	N/A	4		2	2	50 %	12/30	12/31
STUD FRAMING	1,440 FT2	360 FT2	4		2	2	50 %	12/30	12/31
	520 FT2	260 FT2	2		2	1	100 %	1/ 4	1/ 4
ROUGH PLUMBING	N/A	N/A	4		2	2	50 %	12/31	1/ 4
	N/A	N/A	4		2	2	50 %	1/ 5	1/ 6
ROUGH ELECTRIC	N/A	N/A	4		2	2	50 %	12/31	1/ 4
	N/A	N/A	4		2	2	50 %	1/ 5	1/ 6
ROUGH HVAC	N/A	N/A	4		2	2	50 %	12/30	12/31
	N/A	N/A	4		2	2	50 %	1/ 4	1/ 5
ROUGH SPRINKLER	N/A	N/A	4		2	2	50 %	12/31	1/ 4
	N/A	N/A	4		2	2	50 %	1/ 5	1/ 6
GYPSUM BOARD	2,300 FT2	380 FT2	6		2	3	720 FT2	1/ 4	1/ 6
	1,040 FT2	350 FT2	3		2	2	700 FT2	1/ 7	1/ 8
ALUMINIUM INSERT	40 FT	40 FT	1		1	1	40 FT	1/ 6	1/ 6
	40 FT	40 FT	1		1	1	40 FT	1/ 7	1/ 7
WOOD BASE	110 FT	55 FT	2		2	1	55 FT	1/ 6	1/ 6
	110 FT	55 FT	2		2	1	55 FT	1/ 7	1/ 7
TAPE & SAND	2,200 FT2	370 FT2	6		3	2	1,100 FT2	1/ 6	1/ 7
	990 FT2	330 FT2	3		1	3	330 FT2	1/ 8	1/12
FRAME CEILING	2,800 FT2	470 FT2	6		2	3	940 FT2	1/13	1/15
	3,260 FT2	470 FT2	7		2	4	940 FT2	1/19	1/22
DOOR FRAMES	4	2	2		2	1	4	12/31	12/31
	4	2	2		2	1	4	1/ 4	1/ 4
LIGHT FIXTURES	N/A	N/A	6		2	3	33 %	1/19	1/21
	N/A	N/A	6		2	3	33 %	1/22	1/26

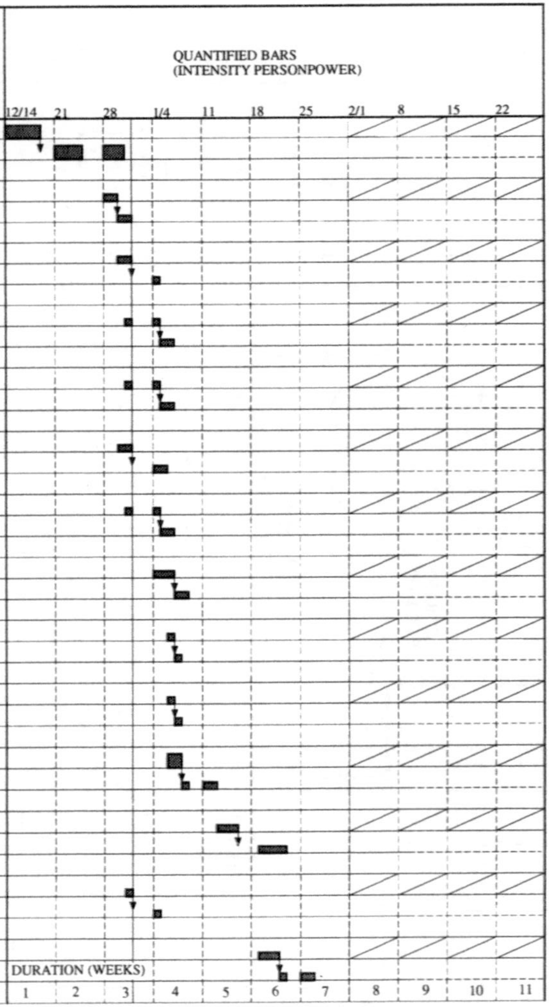

DESIGN MILESTONES | QUANTIFIED BARS (INTENSITY PERSONPOWER)

DURATION (WEEKS): 1 2 3 4 5 6 7 8 9 10 11

Fig. 10.10. The combined template for planning the renovation of the 34th floor, MIS & Library.

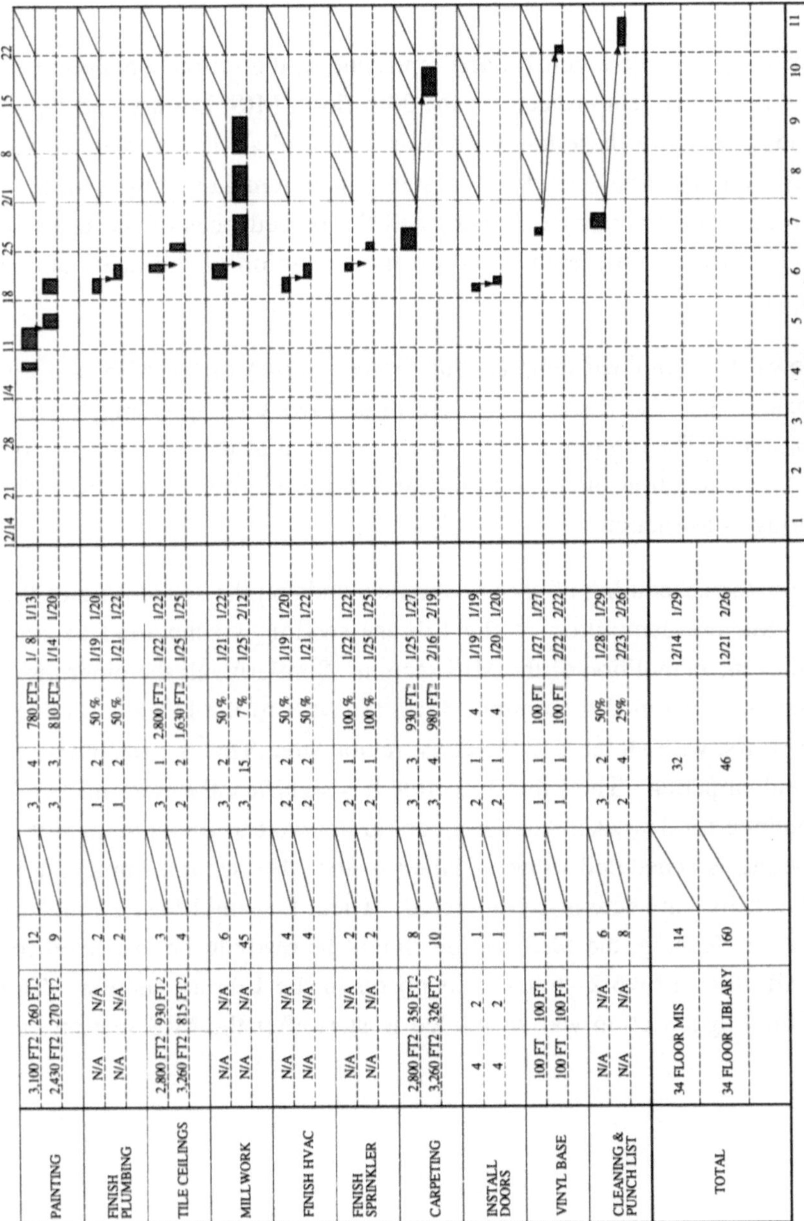

Fig. 10.10. The combined template for planning the renovation of the 34th floor, MIS & Library (continued).

10.4.1   Combined Templates

Three different templates were constructed representing the initial scheduling of the tasks on the three different projects on the 34th floor: MIS, Library and Legal sections. Although each of these templates was as useful as the template of the 26th floor, they should not be considered as stand-alone templates. Instead, they should be seen as complementary templates and the precedences of the tasks in each template should be considered based on the execution of the tasks of the other two templates.

Fig. 10.10 shows the combined template for the renovation of the MIS and the Library sections of the 34th floor. There are three rows corresponding to each task on this template. The top row refers to the renovation of the MIS, the second row refers to the renovation of the Library, and the third row[4] is reserved for actual data during construction.

On this template, the scheduling of each section depends on the scheduling of the other section. So, the demolition of the Library section is scheduled to start immediately after the demolition of the MIS section. Similarly, all the other tasks on the template are scheduled to continue from the MIS to the Library sections with the same crews, without leaving the construction site. This is possible up to the millwork and carpeting. The Library section has significantly more millwork that should continue for 3 weeks. Carpeting could not wait to accommodate that delay, so carpeting is scheduled to be installed in the MIS section immediately after the millwork in that section is completed. Then, the vinyl base should be installed and, after cleaning, the MIS section should be ready to be inspected for occupancy, while the millwork should still go on in the Library section. The renovation of the Legal section was scheduled to start after the MIS section had finished.

---

[4] More rows can be inserted during construction to display useful information, such as work from change orders, *etc.*

10.4.2   Matrix-Balanced Chart

The simultaneous presentation and the coordinated scheduling of two locations, along with tasks and timing, derives from the notion of the matrix-balanced chart. Omitting the alphanumeric data related to the planning of each task, the matrix-balanced chart for the MIS and the Library sections is obtained, as shown in Fig. 10.11. In this chart, each quantified bar is imported from the template shown in Fig. 10.10, maintaining its location on the time axis and its precedences with the other tasks. However, the vertical axis has been compressed, and the new axis represents location rather than task.

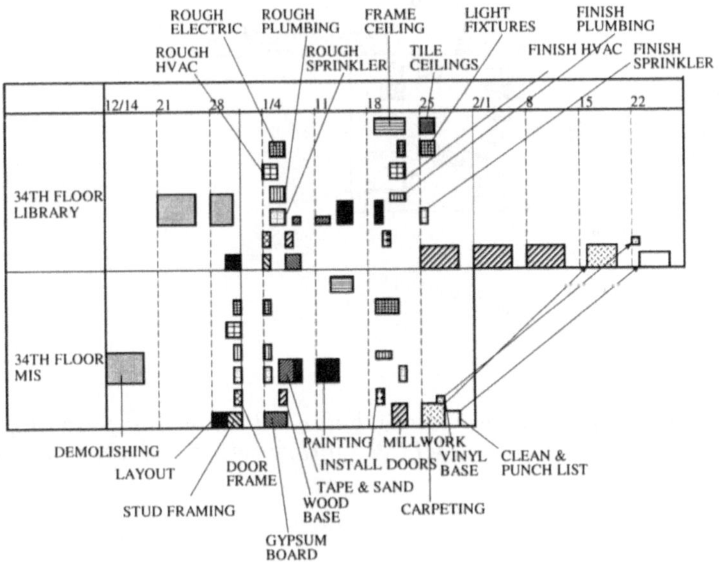

Fig. 10.11. The matrix-balanced chart for planning the renovation of the 34th floor, MIS & Library (week-end displayed).

In Fig. 10.12, the tasks are shown continuous over the weekend. An omission of the display of the week-ends makes a chart easier to read, and it has been the preferred representation in all the bar charts until this chapter. However, the display of the week-ends is more realistic and allows the planner to schedule overtime work to speed up the construction or catch up prior delays, if necessary.

In addition, Fig. 10.12 shows changes in the schedule, based on different assumptions[5] than the schedule shown in Fig. 10.10 or Fig. 10.11. Demolishing is completed in 2 weeks, there is more rough electric work to be done, and the millwork is expected to last longer than the schedule shown in the previous figures.

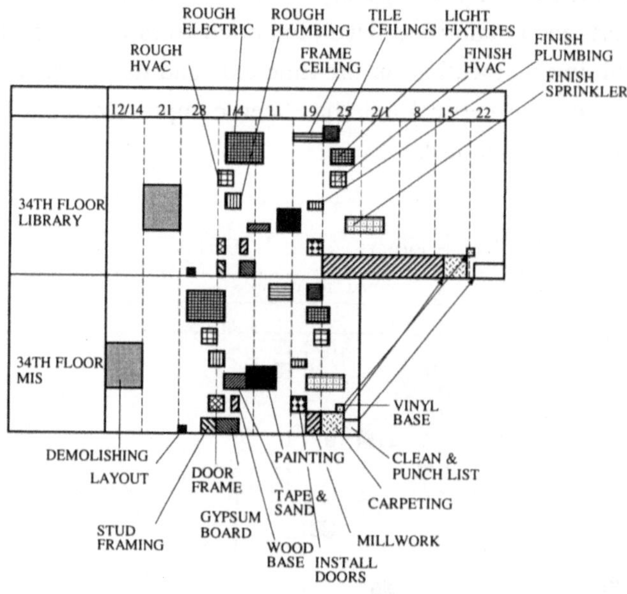

Fig. 10.12. An alternative matrix-balanced chart for planning the renovation of the 34th floor, MIS & Library (week-end not displayed).

---

5 These different assumptions were considered during planning and they are presented in the context of providing alternative visual displays for variations of the project.

10.5 VSMS IN THE CONSTRUCTION PROCESS[6]

The employment of the Visual Scheduling and Management System contributed to an efficient construction process in threefold: it provided a powerful analytical tool for the project manager, it improved the communication of quantitative information, and it became a recording device for documenting the construction.

10.5.1 VSMS as an Analytical Tool

The construction of the 26th floor was a pilot segment of the whole project, intended to provide the construction manager with the insight information on how to schedule and control the renovation of an occupied building in a busy downtown area. At the beginning of the project, several issues needed to be worked further, including the relationships with the other design participants, the identification and sequencing of the operations, and the meeting of the deadlines and the budget. As such, the representation of the project, with emphasis on cost and time was crucial for the project manager. Not only he had to digest what was happening on the job, but he had to analyze the available data, predict the future course of action and control it effectively. The visual aspects of the VSMS allowed him to depict the development of the project in a comprehensive way and manipulate the objects/tasks to study alternative courses of action. The emphasis on those analyses was on predicting the actual labor cost, especially when over-time, and work on the week-ends was a necessity in order to meet the client's deadline.

The structuring of the VSMS around productivity and the immediate relationship between the quantity of work, the productivity and the duration of the task, also guided the project manager to think in a certain way that kept close to the actual development of the project. Such a focus on productivity had an immediate impact on the thinking and data collection for the project. The updated

---

6   This Section is based on an interview with Dr. Henry Irwig and Mr. David Shershenian of Beacon Construction, construction manager for this project.

productivity shown in Table 10.1 is a result of such an analysis with an immediate value for scheduling the rest of the floors and allowing the project manager to build the necessary contingencies in the schedule and budgets to follow.

10.5.2   VSMS as a Communication Device

The third meaningful dimension introduced in the quantified bar charts was of the high interest of the project manager, the superintendent and the subcontractors, and improved the communication among these parties. The superintendent was more involved in collecting data on the workers' presence on the site, the task that they were working and the amount of completed work on a daily basis, knowing that these data would translate immediately to a visual representation of the project. Furthermore, the visual representation gave him a greater control on the job site and a graphics way to communicate with the subcontractors. Training of a junior superintendent was also facilitated with the employment of the VSMS, both for visualizing the data and for collecting the data.

In this specific project, however, communication with either the client or the other design participants was not a target for VSMS. The employed labor, the size of the project, and the profile of the client influenced that decision. VSMS displays resources associated with each task. When resources are scarce, or an increment of resources is disproportional and costly, then an optimal resource allocation on each task and the associated task duration should be considered and brought to the client's attention. In this project, more labor could be solicited, and the space was sufficient for many workers without reliance on heavy equipment or space constraints. At the same time, the construction process did not involve tasks on a critical path that could have created bottlenecks and lengthy delays. Furthermore, the size of the project was relatively small and the client was quite clear on his objectives, but unfamiliar with construction. That resulted to specific demands on the final product, the deadlines and the allocated budget, without any particular interest in knowing and getting involved on how the operations were either scheduled or executed. Similarly, the designer was interested in high design quality and innovative design solutions produced from a smooth and flawless operation but without a specific interest on how many people were on the site or on how they were scheduled. Finally, regulatory agencies or the surrounding community were nor involved in this project, thus there was no need for using the VSMS as a communication device to display the taken course of action and the imbedded effort on sets of tasks.

On the other hand, typical VSMS templates could have been used by the project manager for presentations before the project was awarded. Such presentations could demonstrate a certain sophistication on scheduling and controlling construction operations on complicated sites in occupied buildings.

10.5.3 VSMS as a Recording Device

As the VSMS was employed to collect the appropriate data from the site and provide the analytical functionality to the project manager, the operations were recorded in detail, regarding quantities or work, productivity and the execution of the tasks. The value of these data is significant both for the continuation of this project and for future projects. However, in addition to collecting raw data to be used for the analysis and design for this or future projects, the execution of the completed parts of the project was meticulously documented. Such a documentation shows the experienced delays and their causes, the concentration of personpower, the work executed overtime and on weekends, and the overall flow of the project. The control template should be seen as a photographic and objective image of the execution of the project. So, the documentary character of the VSMS can substantiate specific arguments in the construction process and can minimize the risks in future operations.

BIBLIOGRAPHY

[1]   Adams, J. R., and N. S. Kirchof, editors. 1981. *A Decade of project management: selected readings from the Project management quarterly*, 1970 through 1980. Drexel Hill, Pa.: Project Management Institute.

[2]   Adams, J. R., S. E. Barndt and M. D. Martin. 1979. *Managing by project management*. Dayton, Ohio: Universal Technology Corporation.

[3]   Adrian, J. J. 1981. *The construction management process*. Reston Pub. Co., Reston, VA.

[4]   Ahuja, H. N. 1984. *Construction management: techniques in planning and controlling construction projects*. Wiley, New York.

[5]   Antill, J. M., and R. W. Woodhead. 1985. *Critical path methods in construction practice*. New York, Wiley.

[6]   Archibald, R. D. 1992. *Managing high-technology programs and projects*. 2nd ed. New York, Wiley.

[7]   Augustine, N. R., preface. 1989. *Managing projects and programs*. Boston, Mass.: Harvard Business School Press. The Harvard business review book series.

[8]   Awani, A. O. 1983. *Project management techniques*. New York: PBI.

[9]   Baker, K. R. 1974. *Introduction to sequencing and scheduling*. New York, Wiley.

[10] Baudin, M. 1990. *Manufacturing systems analysis: with application to production scheduling*. Englewood Cliffs, N.J.: Prentice-Hall, Yourdon press computing series.

[11] Bell, P. C. 1985. Visual Interactive Modeling as an Operations Research Technique. *Interfaces* 15, 26-33.

[12] Bent, J. A., and A. Thumann. 1989. *Project management for engineering and construction*. Prentice Hall, New York.

[13] Bergen, S. A. 1986. *Project management: an introduction to issues in industrial research and development.* Oxford, OK, UK; New York, NY, USA: B. Blackwell.

[14] Bernad, J., and M. Paker. 1985. *Les Plannings.* Les éditions d'organisation, Paris.

[15] Bisschop, J. and A. Meeraus. 1982. On the Development of a General Algebraic Modeling System in a Strategic Planning Environment. *Math. Prog. Study* 20, 1-29.

[16] Burbridge, R.N.G., editor. 1988. *Perspectives on project management.* London: Peregrinus on behalf of the Institution of Electrical Engineers. IEE management of technology series; 7.

[17] Burnstein, D., and F. Stasiowski. 1982. *Project Management for the Design Professional.* Whitney Library for Design, New York.

[18] Cherneff, J., R. Logcher and D. Sriram. 1989. Automatic construction scheduling from drawings. *Proceedings of Construction Congress I, Excellence in the Construction Project,* San Francisco, CA, May 5-8; ASCE, New York, p. 210-216.

[19] Clark, W. 1957. *The Gantt Chart,* ed. 3. Sir Isaac Pitman & Sons, London.

[20] Cleland, D. I. 1990. *Project management: strategic design and implementation.* 1st ed. Blue. Ridge Summit, PA: TAB Professional and Reference Books.

[21] Cleland, D. I. and W. R. King. 1983. *Systems analysis and project management.* 3rd ed. New York: McGraw-Hill, McGraw-Hill series in management.

[22] Cleland, D.I., and W. R. King, editors.1988. *Project management handbook.* 2nd ed. New York: Van Nostrand Reinhold.

[23] Clough, R. H., and G. A. Sears. 1991. *Construction project management.* 3rd ed. New York: Wiley.

[24] Conway, R. W., W. L. Maxwell and L. W. Miller. 1967. *Theory of Scheduling.* Addison-Wesley, Reading, Mass.

[25] Davies, C., A. Demb and R. Espejo. 1979. *Organization for program management.* Chichester; New York: Wiley.

[26] Davis, E. W., editor. 1983. *Project management: techniques, applications, and managerial issues* 2nd ed. Norcross, GA: Industrial Engineering & Management Press, Institute of Industrial Engineers.

[27] Dean, B. V., editor. 1985. *Project management: methods and studies.* Amsterdam; New York: North-Holland; New York, N.Y.: Sole distributors

for the U.S.A. and Canada, Elsevier Science Pub. Co., 1985. Studies in management science and systems; v. 11.

[28] DeGoff, R. A. 1985. *Construction management: basic principles for architects, engineers, and owners.* Wiley, New York.

[29] DeSanctis, G., 1984. Computer Graphics as Decision Aids: Directions for Research. *Decision Sci.* 15, 463-487.

[30] Dyer, L., and G. D. Paulson. 1976. *Project management: an annotated bibliography.* Ithaca: New York State School of Industrial and Labor Relations, Cornell University. Cornell industrial and labor relations bibliography series; no. 13.

[31] Echeverry, D., C. W. Ibbs and S. Kim. 1989. Construction schedule generation using AI tools. *6th Conference on Computing in Civil Engineering*, Atlanta, GA, Sept. 11-13; ASCE, New York, p. 44-51.

[32] Fisher, M. L. 1986. Interactive Optimization. *Ann. Opns. Res.* 5, 541-556.

[33] Foley, J. D., and A. Van Dam. 1982. *Fundamentals of Interactive Computer Graphics.* Addison-Wesley, Reading, Mass.

[34] Fox, J. R. 1984. *Evaluating management of large, complex projects: a framework for analysis.* Division of Research, Graduate School of Business Administration, Harvard University; 1-784-058.

[35] Fox, J. R. 1986. *Comparing the management of large, complex projects with the management of routine industrial activities.* Division of Research, Harvard Business School; 1-786-030.

[36] Fox, M. 1987. *Constraint-directed search: a case study of job-shop scheduling.* London: Pitman; Los Altos, Calif.: Morgan Kaufmann Publishers. Research notes in artificial intelligence.

[37] Frame, J. D. 1987. *Managing projects in organizations: how to make the best use of time, techniques, and people.* 1st ed. San Francisco: Jossey-Bass. The Jossey-Bass management series.

[38] French, S. 1982. *Sequencing and scheduling: an introduction to the mathematics of the job-shop.* Chichester, West Sussex: E. Horwood; New York: Wiley. Ellis Horwood series in mathematics and its applications.

[39] Gantt, H. L. 1919. *Organizing for Work.* Harcourt, Brace & Howe, New York.

[40] Geoffrion, A. M. 1987 Introduction to Structured Modeling. *Mgmt. Sci.* 33, 547-588.

[41] Goldhaber, S., C. K. Jha and M. C. Macedo Jr. 1977. *Construction management: principles and practices*. Wiley, New York.

[42] Goodman, L. J., and R. N. Love, editors. 1980. *Project planning and management: an integrated approach*. New York: Published in cooperation with the East-West Center, Hawaii. Pergamon Press. Pergamon policy studies on socio-economic development.

[43] Goodman, R. A. 1981. *Temporary systems: professional development, manpower utilization, task effectiveness, and innovation*. New York, N.Y.: Praeger. Praeger special studies. Praeger scientific.

[44] Graham, R. J. 1985. *Project management: combining technical and behavioral approaches for effective implementation*. New York: Van Nostrand Reinhold.

[45] Gray, C. F. 1981. *Essentials of project management*. Princeton, N.J.: PBI.

[46] Grool, M. C., et al, editors. 1986. *Project management in progress: tools and strategies for the 90s: international resource on the applications of ideas, knowledge, and experiences concerning projects and project management*. Amsterdam; New York: North-Holland; New York, N.Y., U.S.A.: Sole distributors for the U.S.A. and Canada, Elsevier Science Pub. Co., 1986.

[47] Hajek, V. G. 1984. *Management of engineering projects*. 3rd ed. New York: McGraw-Hill.

[48] Halpin D. W., and L. S. Riggs. 1992. *Planning and analysis of construction operations*. New York: Wiley.

[49] Harrison, F. L. 1985. *Advanced project management*. 2nd ed. Aldershot: Gower.

[50] Haviland, D. S. 1984. *Managing architectural projects: the project management manual*. AIA, Washington DC.

[51] Jacobs, F. R., and V. A. Mabert, editors. 1986. *Production planning, scheduling, and inventory control: concepts, techniques, and systems*. 3rd ed. Norcross, Ga.: Industrial Engineering and Management Press, Institute of Industrial Engineers.

[52] Jones, C. V. 1988. The Three-Dimensional Gantt Chart. *Operations Research* 36, 6 891-903.

[53] Jones, C. V., and W. L. Maxwell. 1986. A System for Scheduling with Interactive Computer Graphics. *IIE Trans.* 18, 298-303.

[54] Kavanagh, T. C., F. Muller, J. J. O'Brien. 1978. *Construction management: a professional approach*. McGraw-Hill, New York.

[55] Keen, P. G. W., and M. S. Scott Morton. 1978. *Decision Support Systems: An Organizational Perspective*. Addison-Wesley, Reading, Mass.

[56] Kelley, A. J., editor. 1982. *New dimensions of project management*. Lexington, Mass.: Lexington Books.

[57] Kelley, J. 1961. Critical path planning and scheduling: mathematical basis. Operations Research, vol. 9, no. 3, p. 296-321.

[58] Kerzner, H. 1982. *Project management for executives*. New York: Van Nostrand Reinhold.

[59] Kerzner, H. 1989. *Project management: a systems approach to planning, scheduling, and controlling*. 3rd ed. New York: Van Nostrand Reinhold.

[60] Kerzner, H., and H. J. Thamhain. 1984. *Project management for small and medium size businesses*. New York: Van Nostrand Reinhold.

[61] Knutson, J., and I. Bitz 1991. *Project management: how to plan and manage successful projects*. AMACOM, New York.

[62] Lemberski, M. R., and U. H. Chi. 1984. Decision Simulators Speed Implementation and Improve Operations. *Interfaces* 14, 4 1-15.

[63] Levy, S. M. 1987. *Project management in construction*. New York: McGraw-Hill.

[64] Lewis, J. P. 1991. *Project planning, scheduling & control: a hands-on guide to bringing projects in on time and on budget*. Chicago, Ill.: Probus.

[65] Litke, H. D. 1991. *Projektmanagement: Methoden, Techniken, Verhaltensweisen*. Munchen: C. Hanser.

[66] Lock, D. 1988. *Project management*. 4th ed. Aldershot, Hants., England; Brookfield, Vt., U.S.A.: Gower.

[67] Lock, D., editor. 1987. *Project management handbook*. Aldershot, Hants, England: Gower Technical Press.

[68] Lumsden, P. 1968. *The line of balance method*. London, Pergamon Press.

[69] Maister, D. H. 1982. *Scheduling the professional service firm*. Division of Research, Graduate School of Business Administration, Harvard University; HBS 82-71.

[70] Malcolm, D. G., J. H. Roseboom, C. E. Clark and W. Fazar. 1959. Application of a technique for R and D program evaluation (PERT). Operations Research, vol. 7, no. 5, p. 646-669.

[71]   Martin, C. C. 1976. *Project management: how to make it work*. New York: Amacom.

[72]   Maurel, E., D. Roux and D. Dupont. 1977. *Techniques opérationelles d'ordennancement, fondées sur la méthode PERT "potentiels-tâches."* Eyrolles, Paris.

[73]   Miller, J. G. 1979. *Hedging the master schedule*. Division of Research, Graduate School of Business Administration, Harvard University; HBS 79-12.

[74]   Moder, J. J., C. R. Phillips and E. W. Davis. 1983. *Project management with CPM, PERT, and precedence diagramming*. 3rd ed. New York: Van Nostrand Reinhold.

[75]   Morad, A. A., and Y. Belivean. 1989. Visual scheduling. *Proceedings of Construction Congress I, Excellence in the Construction Project*, San Francisco, CA, May 5-8; ASCE, New York, p. 391-397.

[76]   Mulvey, J. M. 1978. *Strategies in modeling: a personnel scheduling example*. Division of Research, Graduate School of Business Administration, Harvard University; HBS 78-11.

[77]   Newman, W. M., and R. F. Sproull. 1979. *Principles of Interactive Computer Graphics*, ed. 2. McGraw-Hill, New York.

[78]   Nunnaly, S. W. 1987. *Construction methods and management*. Englewood Cliffs, Prentice-Hall.

[79]   Pollalis, S.N. 1992. *A Visual Representation System for the Scheduling and Management of Projects*. Architectural Knowledge Systems, Delft, Holland.

[80]   Pollalis, S.N., and Y. Ueda. 1988. *A Visual scheduling and management system*, Laboratory of Construction Technology No. LCT-88-2, Graduate School of Design, Harvard University.

[81]   Pollalis, S.N., and Y. Ueda. 1991. *Task management*, US Patent 5,016,170, U.S. Patent Office, Washington DC..

[82]   Rabelo, L.C. 1989. Using hybrid neural networks/expert systems for intelligent scheduling in flexible manufacturing systems. *International Joint Conference on Neural Networks*, Washington DC, June 18-22.

[83]   Roberts, J. M. 1980. *Construction management: an effective approach*. Reston Pub. Co., Reston, VA.

[84]   Rogers, R.V. 1989. Interactive graphic-aided scheduling system, *Comp. Ind. Eng.*, vol. 17 no. 1-4.

[85]   Roman, D. D. 1986. *Managing projects: a systems approach*. New York: Elsevier.

[86]   Rosenau, M. D. 1981. *Successful project management: a step-by-step approach with practical examples*. Belmont, Calif.: Lifetime Learning Publications.

[87]   Rougvie, A. 1987. *Project evaluation and development*. London: Mitchell, in association with the Chartered Institute of Building, 1987. Aspects of construction.

[88]   Samaras, T. T., and K. Yensuang. 1979. *Computerized project management techniques for manufacturing and construction industries*. Englewood Cliffs, N.J.: Prentice-Hall.

[89]   Shaheen, S. K. 1987. *Practical project management*. New York: Wiley.

[90]   Silverman, M. 1987. *The art of managing technical projects*. Englewood Cliffs, N.J.: Prentice-Hall.

[91]   Spinner, M. 1992. *Elements of project management: plan, schedule, and control*. 2nd ed. Englewood Cliffs, N.J.: Prentice-Hall.

[92]   Sprague, R. H., and E. D. Carlson. 1982. *Building Effective Decision Support Systems*. Prentice Hall, Englewood Cliffs, N.J.

[93]   Stephanou, S. E., and M. M. Obradovitch. 1985. *Project management, systems development and productivity*. Malibu, Calif.: D. Spencer Publishers.

[94]   Stuckenbruck, L. C. 1981. *The Implementation of project management: the professional's handbook*. Drexel Hill, PA: Project Management Institute; Reading, Mass.: Addison-Wesley Pub. Co.

[95]   Turban, E. 1968. "The Line of balance: a management by exception tool." *The Journal of Industrial Engineering*, vol. 19, no. 9, p. 440-448.

[96]   Visualization in Scientific Computing — A Synopsis. 1987. *IEEE Comput. Graph. Appl.* 7, 62-70.

[97]   Walker, A. 1984. *Project management in construction*. London; New York: Granada.

[98]   Wangh, L. M. 1989. Knowledge-based construction scheduling. *6th Conference on Computing in Civil Engineering*, Atlanta, GA, Sept. 11-13; ASCE, New York, p. 84-91.

[99]   Willis, E. M. 1986. *Scheduling construction projects*. New York: Wiley.

CREDITS

Most of the concepts of the proposed Visual Scheduling and Management System have been patented to Professor Spiro N. Pollalis and Mr. Yasuo Ueda with the U.S. Patent No. 5,016,170 of May 14, 1991.

Fig. 2.1, 2.8, 3.3, 3.4, 3.5, 3.7, 3.10, 3.16, 3.17, 3.18, 3.19, 3.20, 3.21, 4.1, 4.2, 4.7, 5.5, 5.6, 5.7, 5.8, 5.10, 6.2, 6.3, and 6.7; and Tables 4.1, 6.1, 6.2, and 6.3 appear in the U.S. Patent No. 5,016,170 of May 14, 1991.

Fig 2.9, 2.10, 2.11, 5.3, 5.4, 6.1, 6.8, 8.1, 8.5 were developed by Mr. Yasuo Ueda, special student at the Graduate School of Design, Harvard University, 1987-88, under the supervision of Prof. S.N. Pollalis.

Fig 2.7, 4.5 and 4.6 were developed by Mr. Masaji Kominato, special student at the Graduate School of Design, Harvard University, 1989-90, under the supervision of Prof. S.N. Pollalis.

Fig. 9.1, 9.2, 9.3, 9.4, 9.5, 9.6, 9.7, 9.8, 9.9, 9.10, 9.11, 9.12, 9.13, 9.14, 9.15, 9.16, 9.17, 9.18, 9.19, 10.4, 10.5, 10.6, 10.7, 10.8, 10.10, 10.11, and 10.12; and Table 10.1 were developed by Mr. Hiroshi Mimura, special student at the Graduate School of Design, Harvard University, 1992-93, under the supervision of Prof. S.N. Pollalis.

Fig. 10.1 and 10.2 were developed by Mr. David Shrestinian, of Beacon Construction Co.